Praise for *Learning Primary Geography*

'*Learning Primary Geography: Ideas and inspiration from classrooms* is enticing, informative and full of ideas, topics and approaches that provide active and stimulating geography teaching and learning. Well illustrated by a very wide range of classroom case studies, it shows how geography engages and motivates children. Geographical enquiry is well explained and fully underpins the book's thesis and structure. Susan Pike demonstrates how enquiry approaches deepen and extend children's knowledge and understanding of the local and wider world and of geography. This is a book that every primary teacher should read, be excited by and draw on constantly to create vigorous and invigorating geography teaching and learning for their children.'
—*Professor Simon Catling, Professor Emeritus of Primary Education,*
Oxford Brookes University, UK

'In *Learning Primary Geography: Ideas and inspiration from classrooms* Susan Pike has created a must-have resource for primary teachers, whether geography subject leaders or general practitioners. The chapters take us through a carefully structured approach to under-standing the changing nature of primary geography, to pedagogical approaches that are grounded in the subject and also in understandings of how children learn, to insightful sections on the value of children's own knowledges of the places and spaces they are familiar with, and finally, sections which connect to the content of geography. The book provides many real-world, practical examples of how to put ideas into practice, based on research with teachers conducted over a number of years. I can see that this is going to become a core text for the PGCE Primary Humanities specialist course that I lead.'
—*Dr Fran Martin, Senior Lecturer in Education, University of Exeter, UK*

'This book is an asset. The title of the book illustrates exactly what the book does: it connects theory and practice and it gives (student) teachers ideas and inspiration to make their pupils wonder and learn about the world around them.'
—*Marian Blankman, Senior Lecturer in Geography, Department of Education, Inholland*
University of Applied Sciences, Haarlem, Netherlands

'*Learning Primary Geography* links up theories and practices in primary geography very effectively. It provides a strong framework for teaching geography through enquiry for all children. The numerous illustrated examples from classrooms will inspire many teachers of geography.'
—*Professor Daniela Schmeinck, Professor of Science Education and*
Social Sciences, University of Cologne, Germany

'This book is a practical and progressive aid to both student and practising teachers, providing a framework for delivering Primary Geography curricular in a creative and engaging manner.'
—*Joe Usher, Lecturer in Education, St Patrick's College,*
Dublin, Ireland

'This book acts as both an inspirational and teacher-friendly resource. It offers a comprehensive overview of the pedagogy of discovery in relation to geography and, crucially, provides teachers with the instruction necessary to adopt such an approach. Children's position at the core of the learning experience is highlighted from the outset and throughout. With Susan's book at their disposal, teachers can banish dull and tedious geography from their classrooms for good!'

—*Amy Kelly, St Brigid's Infant School, Dublin, Ireland*

'A thoroughly enjoyable and knowledgeable book surrounding learning experiences in geography. Concisely and clearly expressed, and very rich in concepts and ideas. I believe this one of the best books to support teachers in their teaching and in children's learning of geography.'

—*Caoimhe McCarrick, St Agnes National School, Dublin, Ireland*

'A collection that makes geography fun, worthwhile and doable! A gem of a resource for any teacher, well researched and filled to the brim with inspiring and engaging ideas! This book encapsulates the essence of geographical enquiry and shows how children's own geographies can create rewarding and meaningful exercises in citizenship. This is now my "go to" book for geography.'

—*Caitríona Ní Cassaithe, St Joseph's Co-Educational School,*
Dublin, Ireland

'*Learning Primary Geography* is an invaluable resource for any practitioner. It provides a rich array of theory, case studies and photos to help in the planning and implementation of interesting and exciting lessons whilst ensuring geographical learning is at the centre of all activities.'

—*AnneMarie Lynchehan, St Canice's Boys' National School, Finglas, Dublin*

Learning Primary Geography

Learning Primary Geography: Ideas and inspiration from classrooms celebrates children's learning in primary geography. It is a book for all student and practising teachers who would like children to learn about their world in an enjoyable and stimulating way. Every page presents inspiring examples of children's learning, and explains how and why creative approaches such as enquiry learning, learning outside the classroom and using imaginative resources work so well in primary geography. Using illustrated case studies from a range of schools and classrooms, each chapter showcases the fantastic work all children can do in primary geography.

The book explores a wide variety of geographical learning, with chapters focusing on key aspects of the subject, including:

- primary geography in the school grounds
- topical geography through issues and events
- learning about places in primary geography
- children's agency and action through primary geography.

Throughout the chapters, the role of primary geography in helping children develop all types of literacies, including spatial, critical and digital literacies, is explored.

Written by a highly experienced teacher and lecturer in education, *Learning Primary Geography* is underpinned and illustrated by examples from a wide range of primary classrooms. It will be a source of support, guidance and inspiration for all those teaching geography in the primary school.

Susan Pike is Lecturer in Geography Education at St Patrick's College, a college of Dublin City University, Ireland.

Learning Primary Geography

Ideas and inspiration from classrooms

Susan Pike

Routledge
Taylor & Francis Group

LONDON AND NEW YORK

First published 2016
by Routledge
2 Park Square, Milton Park, Abingdon, Oxon OX14 4RN

and by Routledge
711 Third Avenue, New York, NY 10017

Routledge is an imprint of the Taylor & Francis Group, an informa business

British Library Cataloguing in Publication Data
A catalogue record for this book is available from the British Library

Library of Congress Cataloging in Publication Data
Pike, Susan, author.
   Learning primary geography: ideas and inspiration for the classroom/Susan Pike.
   pages cm
   Includes bibliographical references and index.
   1. Geography – Study and teaching (Primary) I. Title.
   G73.P57 2016
   372.89′1–dc23
   2015025823

ISBN: 978-1-138–92295-2 (hbk)
ISBN: 978-1-138–92297-6 (pbk)
ISBN: 978-1-315-68422-2 (ebk)

Typeset in Bembo
by Florence Production Ltd, Stoodleigh, Devon
Printed in Great Britain by Ashford Colour Press Ltd.

Credits and copyright

Thank you to the following people for permission to use their photographs and diagrams:

Figure 2.2 Margaret Roberts of the Geographical Association
Figure 2.4 Carol C. Kuhlthau, Leslie K. Maniotes and Ann K. Caspari
Figure 3.1 Tide: Global Learning
Figure 3.3b Tom O'Reilly, 4th Class, St Joseph's Boys National School
Figure 3.6 Paula Owens, Geographical Association
Figure 4.2 Rebecca Kitchen, Aylesbury High School, Buckinghamshire
Figure 7.1b, 7.1d Railway Procurement Agency
Figure 8.4a, 8.4b, 8.4c, 8.4d Strebe, Creative Commons via Wikipedia
Figure 9.1 Simon Catling, Oxford Brookes University

Contents

Case studies

Illustrations

Figures

Tables

Acknowledgements

First, thank you to the children who took part in the learning activities described in the case studies and photographs throughout this book. Your enthusiasm and willingness to share your questions, learning and reflections inspired this book and made it a pleasure to write. Thank you to the teachers of the classes described in the case studies: Orla Bannon, Caitriona Bryne, Kim Cartwright, Clíona Collins, Fiona Connelly, Collette Dunne, Anne Heneberry, Mary Foskin, Beryl Healy, Micheal Kilcrann, Áine Mitchell, Julie Montgomery, Gráinne Noone, Martina Sexton and Joanne Toal. Thank you also to principals and teachers who provided photographs and other information: Jane Brady, Ciara Brennan, Sandra Cammish, Fiona Collins, Fiona Connelly, Clare de Sausmarez, Peter Long, Iseult Managan, Fintan McCutcheon and Maeve Saunderson. Also, thank you to the parents and carers who agreed permissions for use of the children's work and photographs.

Second, enormous thanks to my colleagues at St Patrick's College for their support throughout the process of writing this book. Thank you to Professor Fionnuala Waldron, my Head of Faculty and colleague, for your support, guidance and extensive comments on the final draft of the book. I am also grateful to my colleagues who provided support and comments throughout the process of writing: Dr Sandra Austin, Maria Barry, Dr Bernie Collins, Dr Elizabeth Mathews and Joe Usher. Thank you also to the colleagues who shared their expertise: Dr Therese Dooley, Dr Penny Humby, Dr Eithne Kennedy and Dr Therese McPhillips.

Thank you also to all current student teachers and those who are now teachers and principals that I have taught at St Patrick's College, Drumcondra. Thank you especially to those of you, who provided reflections, comments, photographs and agreed to have your work or photographs in the book. It is your enthusiasm for geography with all your questions, lessons and reflections that inspired me to even consider this book!

Finally, thank you to my family, Daragh, Theo and Aoibhinn, for your endless patience and love!

In memory of Jodie Gilbert, 2007–2015. Always a ray of sunshine.

A world of geography – past, present and future of geography education

> My opinion about geography is fun! I love geography because it is fun learning about things about the world and things I did not know about the world. I love geography it's really interesting to learn about. I love to learn about the world and Brazil and other countries . . . That is the end of my opinion about geography.
>
> Fifth class pupil, aged 11

The wonder of geography

Geography is a very popular subject. This is evident through displays and activities in classrooms, corridors and grounds of our primary schools. It is a subject that is liked by children, teachers and parents. Geography makes significant contributions to children's learning in many dimensions. This book will support and challenge you in your professional role as teachers of geography in primary schools. It is hoped by embracing this book you will be inspired by the theories, ideas and examples found throughout the following chapters.

The book is designed to help you act on the following pillar questions:

- What do we know about children's learning in primary geography?
- What can children do in primary geography?
- How can we make these experiences interesting and challenging for children?
- How can we provide guidance for children learning geography?

This book is not designed as a set programme, such as a geography textbook or workbook; neither does it provide a 'solution' to what geography should be. It is designed to help you to enable engaging learning in geography, shaped by your professional expertise. This book draws from diverse principles in teaching and learning geography that I have learned over the years through research, teaching and collaboration with many primary teachers and classes in their classrooms.

Teachers facilitate children's learning

Teachers are very important people as you are the people who inspire children through teaching! Qualifications, specifically knowledge and skills, matter more for children's learning than any other single factor in a school or classroom (Darling-Hammond, 2006, 2010; Cochran-Smith, 2003; Hinde *et al.*, 2007; Haycock and Crawford, 2008). Teachers also need to know about the nature of geography and geography education in order to teach it effectively (Webster *et al.*, 1996; Firth, 2007).

Children can participate in decisions about how and what they learn

Children are also equally important as they have so much to contribute in geography! They are natural geographers and have very important questions and ideas about how they can learn geography (Catling, 2003; Martin, 2005; Roberts, 2010; 2013a; Pike 2011b). Children are amazingly motivated to learn, when they have a role in the teaching and learning process.

Geography provides children with quality learning experiences

Learning in geography is an important and meaningful experience for children! A primary geography education provides opportunities for children to experience:

*   Working through a 'geographic lens', to 'acquire and use spatial and ecological perspectives to develop an informed worldview' (Heffron and Downs, 2012).
*   Enjoyable and challenging learning experiences in schools (Catling, 2003; Pike, 2013; Kitchen 2013), through enquiry-based learning about the locality and the wider world.
*   Preparation for life in their future, as members of communities (Bednar, 2010), providing children with the essential 'geographic advantage' (Hanson, 2004; GA, 2009).

This book is about making geography interesting and engaging for children, teachers and parents, as will be shown in the case studies and photographs throughout. It is not about 'surface' learning or about doing 'something different' as a treat after learning in a 'proper' lesson from a textbook; the experiences outlined in the book are the learning! Little of the learning in this book involves expensive resources; it relies on what is already in schools: the school, the local environment, digital technologies, atlases and globes, as can be seen in Figure 1.1. However, there are fantastic resources for primary geography, such as photograph packs, constructions toys, mascots, maps and the locality, that can be bought instead of, or as well as, textbooks and workbooks. This may take planning and effort but it is easily achieved over time, as outlined in Chapter 10.

Learning in primary geography

The practices of geography education in different countries are fascinating, and there are many views about how and what should be taught in schools in geography. This argument was very apparent in the curriculum changes in England and continues to be debated in the United States, as well as other countries. In Ireland, the debate over a subject or skills-based curriculum is very current. Basically, the perspectives are about the two main dimensions of learning in geography, content and approaches:

Figure 1.1
Activity in geography lessons
(a) making maps, and (b) using a
range of books

Perspective A: Teachers should lead learning; they know best what children should learn. Children need a broad base of knowledge in geography.

Perspective B: Children should lead learning, with the support of the teacher. Children should learn a smaller range of topics, but have the opportunity to learn at a deeper level.

A model that captures these two arguments is outlined in Figure 1.2, showing pupil-led activity on the right and teacher-led activity on the left. This model evolved from the 14–19 Schools Geography Project in the 1980s in England, which aimed to make geography more engaging for young people. However, its origins can be traced back to ideas from Dewey about traditional vs progressive education (1938/2007). Naish's model shows how a range of learning activities can take place in geography lessons, led by teachers and/or children. Within this book, there is more emphasis on activity to the left of the model, that is argument B above, as this provides more meaningful, interesting and challenging opportunities. So, we can use activity from across this continuum. For example, there are times when we simply tell children new ideas and concepts. However, learning of such new ideas and concepts works best when it emerges from learning activities.

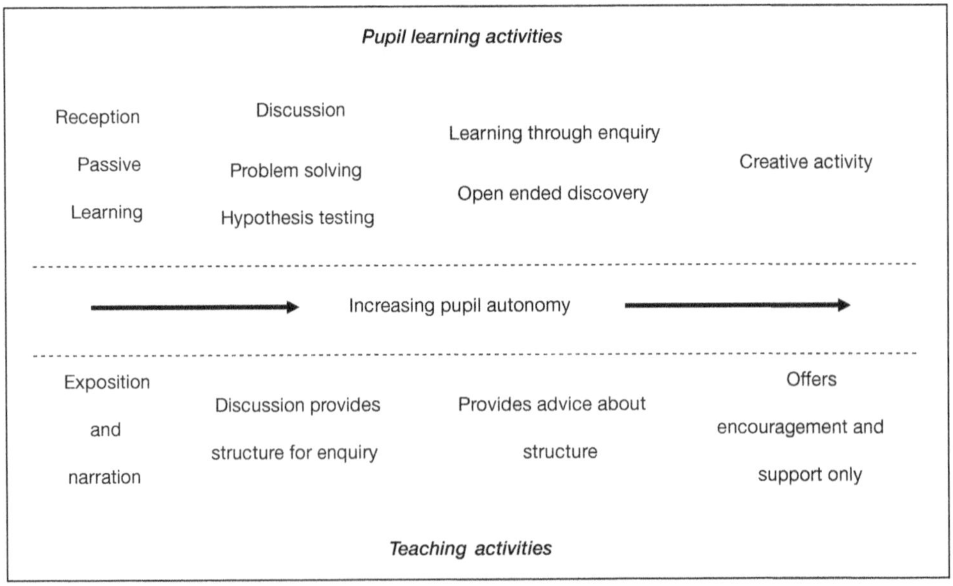

Pupil learning activities

Reception
Discussion
Learning through enquiry
Passive
Problem solving
Creative activity
Open ended discovery
Learning
Hypothesis testing

Increasing pupil autonomy

Exposition
Offers
and
Discussion provides
Provides advice about
encouragement and
structure for enquiry
structure
narration
support only

Teaching activities

Figure 1.2 A model for teaching and learning activity in primary geography (Naish et al., 1987)

Scanning down the list in Case Study 1.1, it is evident that those at the top are to the left of the model in Figure 1.2, while those at the bottom are to the right. Most of the activity that takes place in the schools featured in this book is to the bottom of the list and to the right of the model. In fact, when thinking about what children learn in geography, it is useful to think of geography as neither argument A nor B, but as a series of big ideas that can be taught through enquiry negotiated between children and teachers. Examples of big ideas are shown in Table 1.1, as a series of ideas that no matter what age a learner is, they will understand through good geographical experiences.

CASE STUDY 1.1 Learning through geography: all classes, St James' National School

The children in St James' are keen geographers; both teachers in this 2-teacher, 32 pupil school view geography as an important subject for children. The children had a range of experiences in geography, such as:

- Listening to their teachers talk about places.
- Answering questions from textbooks.
- Completing worksheets on geography topics.
- Using the internet to research about places.
- Investigating stories in the news and summarising what they found out.
- Using maps and globes to investigate places.
- Researching topics as homework, using books and the internet.
- Working in groups independently on geography topics, with the support of the teacher.
- Devising questions on topics they were about to do.

Table 1.1 Key concepts or 'big ideas' in geography

Leat, UK (1998)	Geography Advisors' and Inspectors' Network, UK (2002)	Holloway et al., UK (2003)	Leaving Certificate Geography, RoI (2006)
Cause and effect	Bias	Space	Location
Classification	Causation	Time	Spatial distribution
Decision-making	Change	Place	Area association
Development	Conflict	Scale	Inter-relationship
Inequality	Development	Social formations	Spatial interaction
Location	Distribution	Physical systems	Density
Planning	Futures	Landscape and environment	Pattern
Systems	Inequality		Region
	Interdependence	Change over time	

As can be seen from the example in Case Study 1.2, 'big ideas' or 'key concepts' are significant in geography, especially in any context where there is a tradition of content leading learning in geography. In Ireland, in the past, there has been a tendency for primary teachers to get children to 'learn off' place names in geography (Pike, 2006; Waldron et al., 2009). This is dull for children and wastes time that could be spent thinking and being a geographer! This is not to say location knowledge is not important, and the examples above and throughout this book show how children can learn about places names and locations in the context of the topics they are learning about. These ideas are explored explicitly in Chapters 3 (on literacies) and 8 (on places). Big ideas help us to conceptualise geography and to think about how we are enabling children to make sense of the world, not to learn every fact about it.

CASE STUDY 1.2 Learning through 'big ideas': 8–10 year olds, Australia, St Joseph's Boys' National School

Boys in St Joseph's Boys' National School feature a number of times in this book, as the school works on developing children's understanding and skills in geography across the classes. There are many reasons for this, but one is the interest of the boys; they really like learning geography, as they discover so much about the world. The boys in the fourth and fifth classes studied in Australia with an enquiring approach, but also through thinking about big ideas (Pike and Ryan, 2012). To begin the topic, the boys created concept maps of Australia. The lessons then focused on the use of key skills in order to develop their knowledge and understanding centred on the big ideas in geography:

- **What is Australia like? Looking at patterns**: Initially, pupils looked at the maps and satellite images, generating a great amount of discussion about what the pupils noticed, and it was interesting for us to see what their attention was drawn to.

- **What is life like in Australia? People and places**: The map activities acted as a stimulus for the pupils to generate questions on aspects of Australia they would like to know more about, including:
  - People's lives: what do people do? What is school like?
  - Plants and animals: what animals live there?
  - The weather: is it hot? Does it rain?

- **How does Australia compare to here? Investigating similarities and differences**: To establish that differences exist within our own communities, we asked pupils to look at how their own lives differed from each other. We then investigated the differences and similarities between Ireland and Australia. The pupils were given time to look at the resources then asked to complete a writing frame using questions from the previous activities. Finally, pupils used the information they had gathered to plan a trip to a location of their choice in Australia.

- **What is Australia really like? Diversity, finding out more**: An Australian friend of the teacher visited the class and was questioned at great length about the diversity of life in Australia. She was impressed with the work the pupils had carried out and what they could tell her about her home country, but through the discussions, she also challenged some of their ideas and helped them realise the complexities of Australia's geography. This type of learning in geography is outlined in more detail in Chapter 8.

To finish, the boys revisited their concept maps, and it was evident they had a lot to add! They finished by evaluating the topic, one pupil wrote:

> I thought that all of the stuff that I learned about Australia was very interesting because I did not know that lots of people lived in Australia. My favourite bit was when we had to pretend we were going to Australia. The part I did not like was the mind map. I also liked it when Julie came in and she answered all of our questions.

www.stjosephsprimary.ie

CASE STUDY 1.3 Our locality: making maps of activity in our area: 7–8 year olds, St Peter's Primary School

Children in second class decided to find out answers to enquiry questions about their locality, as shown in Figure 1.3. These questions were:

*   What makes Bray a good place for children?
*   How do people travel around in Bray?
*   Where can you find water in Bray?

Over a number of lessons, the children completed group projects, featuring their own 2D picture maps designed to answer their questions. They also created 3D maps, which were based on their original maps. Needless to say, the models were quite different than the maps. Both activities were creative, as the children worked together in making maps and models. The children's everyday experiences and imaginations were very evident in the work. An example of this was how the children had included the teacher in their map – with her magic umbrella for travelling around Bray! Another example was the out of proportion part of the map given over the boxing arena, not surprising as Ireland's world champion boxer, Katie Taylor is from Bray. However, with the scaffolding of their learning from their teachers, they also included information they would not have thought of in each of the maps and models.

www.stpetersbray.ie – www.stpetersbrayblog.com

The changing nature of primary geography

As can be seen from the examples above, geography can be an engaging subject, but this has not always been the case. Such as elsewhere in the world, up to the 1900s, despite the enlightened views of many philosophers and educationalists, learning by rote was the experience of most children in schools. In fact, the debates about how and what should be taught in geography have been played out internationally and over time. In the 1870s, the Elementary Education Acts in England and Wales (1870), the Scottish Education Act (1872) and the Powys Commission in Ireland (1870) investigated activity in schools and made recommendations. In Ireland, the recommendations were precise requirements for each subject at each level from infants to sixth class. The obligatory subjects were reading, writing, spelling and arithmetic for all classes with geography included from age 9 upwards. Pupils were examined in the subjects, and schools were financed according to the results gained. It is important to note that both standards and attendance improved during the time of these systems, but they did result in more rote learning than in previous systems.

Since 1900, there have been various influences, curricula and practices in primary geography. In Ireland, geography was valued so little that in 1900 it was merged with history, although local studies featured extensively. This change was short lived as in 1903 geography was re-instated, and featured again in the 1921 curriculum, and from 1926 was taught as a separate subject (Walsh, 2012). As the Republic of Ireland was a

Figure 1.3 Children constructing their knowledge in geography through engaging activity, St Peter's National School (a) making 3D maps, (b, c) presenting findings and (d) working geographically

new state, learning geography was nationalistic in nature. In fact, up to the 1960s, experiences for many children in primary geography in countries such as Ireland, England and the United States were predominantly the transmission type of learning (CACE, 1967), to the left in Figure 1.2. In the United States, geography education at this time had a 'litany of problems . . . dull textbooks, inadequately trained teachers, simple factual content . . . training in history not geography, lack of emphasis on geography in schools of education . . .' (Helburn, 1998, p. 212). During the 1960s, in response to dramatic changing social and economic conditions, curricular and classroom experiences began to change. In America, the High School Geography Project (1963–1971) aimed to create a 'dynamic, participatory learning environment in which students observed that geography is a conceptually rich and useful subject for daily life in their communities and the larger world'. This project with learner centred pedagogies was to the right of Figure 1.2. At a similar time in England, the Plowden Report, was published, with principles, pedagogies and content clearly influencing practice in England and Ireland, as well as other countries. The pedagogies of primary geography in the Irish 1971 curriculum were radically innovative, with learning through 'discovery methods' evident throughout the documents, especially the requirements for geography. Although the content was somewhat narrow, compared to later curricula, and focused on the locality and Ireland, with some reference to the wider world (DES, 1971).

Today the aims of the Irish geography curriculum remain ambitious and wide ranging, and relates to knowledge, understanding and appreciation of local, national and global environments and the development of geographical skills, including those of enquiry (DES/NCCA, 1999b). The primary curriculum recognises that children themselves must be actively engaged in making sense of the world; they need to be able to connect new knowledge to what they already know and construct their own meanings, as shown in Figure 1.3 (DES/NCCA, 1999a; 1999b). This has resulted in the emphasis on learning through enquiry in geography reflecting the power of children's role in their own learning (Catling, 2003; Roberts, 2003; 2013a). The curriculum is progressive and recognises, for example, the capacity of children to develop empathy with others, and to develop senses of space and place and action within their locality. This type of curriculum is not unique to Ireland; there are strong parallels between the current Irish curriculum and the primary geography curriculum in Australia and Wales. In other countries, such as Belgium and Northern Ireland, geography, history and science have been combined into one primary school subject and is recognised by teachers as a subject contributing to children's learning.

However, as Catling states, teaching and learning in primary geography is not just a product of the curriculum, but also of interpretation (2003, p169). In Ireland, research evidence showed a divergence between the 1971 and 1999 curricula requirements and classroom practices (Gash, 1985; INTO, 1995; Pike, 2006; 2011b). It is generally agreed that there were 'fundamental changes in ideology and methodologies with the curriculum involving a 'radical shift of ideological position and methodological approach' (Gash 1985 p. 85). With the introduction of the Primary School Curriculum (DES/NCCA, 1999a), there was evidence that children's experiences were shaped more by the structure and content of textbooks rather than curriculum requirements relating to reduced content and enquiry approaches (Devine, 2003; Waldron, 2003; Pike, 2006; 2012). In England, where change is more rapid, the 2000 curriculum was hardly implemented before the standard schemes of work produced by the Qualifications and Curriculum Authority (QCA) effectively 'became' the curriculum in many schools. Although these did provide for enquiry approaches and reduced content, they were considered to be prescriptive by teachers.

Overall, across different primary geography settings, there is evidence that the support and resources to enhance more pupil-centred enquiry or discovery methods can be lacking in many classrooms; it is always the teacher that decides what and how geography is taught (Catling, 2003; Alexander, 2010). Although, there is also evidence that in schools many teachers do facilitate children to work in more depth on fewer topics, using child-led enquiry approaches. This change is evident in relation to the study of distant places, where the tendency is now to study fewer distant places over a longer time to help children develop more understanding of the less familiar areas. There is strong evidence that children enjoy and learn from these experiences (Pike, 2011b; Smyth, 2010; McNally, 2012; Noronha, 2012). Research in primary geography in Ireland shows varied practices in schools; this book showcases just a few of the innovative classrooms in primary geography across Ireland. It aims to support teachers in Ireland primary geography, and to help and inspire them in their planning. Due to common ground between the Irish curricula and those in other countries, as well as consensus in what is good learning in geography, it is hoped this book will be helpful for any primary teacher, in any setting.

How will this book help me teach geography?

There are many decisions to be made about what geography will be learned and taught and how it will be taught. The way geography is experienced by children has a profound impact on their views of the subject (Naish *et al.*, 1987; Waldron *et al.*, 2009; Dolan *et al.*, 2014; Pike, 2012). How geography is taught is a result of a teacher's 'behaviour' and the 'strategies' they choose to use (Lambert and Balderstone, 2009). The Alexander Report (2010), an independent enquiry into teaching, found that good teaching:

- is well organised, planned and reflective;
- is based on sound subject knowledge;
- depends on effective classroom management;
- requires an understanding of children's developmental needs;
- uses exciting and varied approaches;
- inspires;
- encourages children to become autonomous learners;
- facilitates children's learning; and
- stimulates children's creativity and imagination.

A Rubik's cube can be used as an analogy to describe geography as it is multifaceted and includes a range of aspects such as skills, concepts, dispositions, place, space and themes, as shown in Figure 1.4. Imagine that each face of the Rubik's cube represented a different aspect of the subject. A good lesson or series of lessons will not be confined to one face of the cube but will twist the cube to mix the colours and include several aspects of geography in the one lesson. All lessons will have different aspects of each of these, but will have a focus on one or two sides of the cube. For example, when focusing on places, lessons will include spatial information and may use online or atlas-based maps; as teaching 'maps' or 'aerial images' without a context is poor practice, geography lessons

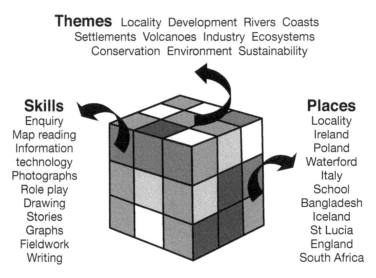

Themes Locality Development Rivers Coasts
Settlements Volcanoes Industry Ecosystems
Conservation Environment Sustainability

Skills
Enquiry
Map reading
Information
technology
Photographs
Role play
Drawing
Stories
Graphs
Fieldwork
Writing

Places
Locality
Ireland
Poland
Waterford
Italy
School
Bangladesh
Iceland
St Lucia
England
South Africa

Figure 1.4 Geography consists of interlinked themes, places and skills

Table 1.2 Possible activities in geography lessons

Geographical activities	Geography 'plus' activities
Out geographical enquiries	Working through enquiry frameworks
Photographs: using/interpreting aerial photographs, photographs	Working in groups or pairs
	Problem solving
Fieldwork: taking part in the many different types of fieldwork	Pattern finding and explaining
Exploring causes, effects and responses to local, national and global events	Reading and writing for different audiences/genres of writing
Exploring local, national and international issues	Thinking skills type activities
	Investigating events, places and people in the news
Mapping: making maps and models, using maps and models	Staying safe, avoiding danger, interacting with people
Exploring the features, patterns and changes in localities	Decision-making activities: using statistical data
Exploring people's lives in different places	Collection and use of numerical data

will probably have a 'place' and a 'theme' and will draw on other aspects of geography also. Geography lessons are multidimensional, rather than focusing on a single skill or concept. So geography lessons will probably have a 'place' or 'theme' focus, but will draw on the other aspects of geography too. There are also many cross-curricular activities that are particularly relevant to geography, such as using picture books or investigating current issues through the media. Some of these are exemplified in Table 1.2 and are explored elsewhere in the book. When planning to use different teaching strategies, it is important to consider the range of approaches used across the school, and across the term, as well as planning for variety within each lesson, Chapter 10 contains guidance for this.

Learning Primary Geography: Ideas and Inspiration for the Classroom aims to inspire you by showcasing great examples of children's learning in geography. The book shows how and why approaches such as enquiry learning, learning outside the classroom and using imaginative resources work so well with children. It outlines some of the theories and ideas behind such practices, but does not aim to outline every theory, idea and argument about education, rather it focuses on what children can do in geography. It is about how geography can be made both challenging and fun by involving children in making decisions about their learning. The book includes the learning experiences of many different classes, including children's activity, work and opinions. The book illustrates what can be done in schools and classrooms with children. It is not about labelling children as 'good' at geography or otherwise. In fact, such thinking about ability encourages and legitimates a narrow view of learning and achievement (Alexander, 2000; 2010). Within all the lessons in the case studies, differentiation of learning was occurring through the interactions between the teachers and children, rather than through having fixed expectations of children from the outset. Children with exceptional abilities in geography, and those who found the subject a challenge, all achieved success in learning. The voices of the children included in each chapter demonstrate their motivation and enthusiasm for the geographical enquiries they undertook.

This book focuses on children, but recognises the importance of teachers' roles in enabling quality learning. Allowing children to share the decision-making around their learning can also mean that our lives as teachers can become more balanced, as Kidd (2014, online) states: 'as a profession we need to learn to be kinder to ourselves and to each other. We need to recognise that the demands being placed on us in terms of marking loads and expectations are inhumane.'

Through reading and using this book, it is hoped you will perhaps plan effectively for geography, set fewer 'tasks' in geography and go with the children's thoughts and ideas as the driver of learning experiences.

The schools involved in this book varied in size from just 30 children in 2-teacher schools to those with over 400 children, with multiple teachers; they included rural, suburban and urban schools. Some schools were mixed; others were either girls or boys schools. The class sizes varied from just 10 children to over 30. Half of the schools were 'DEIS' (Delivering Equality in Schools) designated and others had mixed catchment areas. A number of the teachers involved had a particular expertise in geography, most did not. Some teachers were very new to the profession; others had been working as teachers for longer than they would tell me!

Learning Primary Geography: Ideas and Inspiration for the Classroom is based on geographical activities carried out in the following schools and classes:

- **Scoil Fhursa, Kilmore West, Coolock, Dublin**
  Middle Class, 9–10 year olds: Brazil, our changing locality – Coolock.

- **St James' National School, Stradbally, Waterford**
  Senior Room, 8–12 year olds: What work do people do in our area? How can we make our lane safer? Rocks in our locality.
  Junior Room, 4–8 year olds: Our school – past, present and future – What is life like in India? The world on our beach!

- **St Joseph's Boys' National School, Donavan, Co. Waterford**
  Middle Class, 9–10 year olds: Our school grounds, Australia, CraftEd Project – Pattern in the Locality, Young Geographer Competition.

- **Knockmahon National School, Bunmahon, Co. Waterford**
  Junior Class, 5–8 year olds: Connecting the world: food and global citizenship, Kenya.

- **St Patrick's Boys' National School, Drumcondra, Dublin**
  Older Class, 10–11 year olds: Does Dublin need a new Metro?
  Small Group, 12 year olds: The news – the full story, Issues in the news, Green Flag.

- **Newtown National School, Newtown, Waterford**
  Senior Class, 10–13 year olds: Why do we need rocks? Using ICT to enhance learning.

- **St Vincent de Paul Girls' National School, Dublin 9**
  Senior Class, 11–12 year olds: Australia, India, Classroom displays.

- **Canal Way Educate Together National School, Dublin 8**
  Junior Class, 4–5 year olds: Amazing geographies in the school grounds.

- **Drumcondra National School, Dublin 9**
  All Classes, 4–12 year olds: Puskin Project on Landscape.
  Senior Class, 8–12 year olds: Earth in Space.

- **St Peter's National School, Bray, Wicklow**
  Middle Class, 7–8 year olds: Our local area: Water, play and people.

- **Our Lady of Victories Infant National School, Ballymun**
  Senior Infants, 5–6 year olds: Polar environments, Signs of spring.

- **Warrenmount Girls' National School, Warrenmount, Dublin 8**
  Middle Class, 9–10 year olds: Our local area.

The following schools in England and Ireland also allowed me to take photographs in their classrooms and grounds:

- **Belle Vue Infants School, Aldershot, Hampshire**
- **Cloghans Hill National School, Cloghans Hill, Tuam, Co. Galway**
- **Portobello Educate Together National School, Dublin 8**
- **St Declan's Boys' National School, Waterford, Ireland**
- **St Francis CBS Boys' National School, Francis Street, Dublin 8**
- **Wallisdean Infant School, Fareham, Hampshire**
- **St Colmcille's National School, Gainstown, Co. Weatmeath**

Also thank you to the following schools for providing other material:

- **Balbriggan Educate Together National School, Balbriggan, Co. Dublin**
- **Scoil Íde, Corbally, Limerick**

Of the schools above, Balbriggan Educate Together National School, Knock-mahon National School, Our Lady of Victories Infants National School, Scoil Fhursa Boys' National School, St Francis CBS Boys' National School, St Joseph's Boys' National School, St Peter's National School and Warrenmount National School are DEIS designated schools, and Belle Vue is categorised in a similar way. The DEIS programme, managed by the Department of Education and Skills, Ireland is the policy instrument to address educational disadvantage. The DEIS action plan focuses on addressing and prioritising the educational needs of children and young people from disadvantaged communities (DES, 2015).

There are broad themes that feature in every chapter of this book, such as:

- children's experiences and views of learning;
- learning through enquiry in primary classrooms;
- learning new knowledge in primary geography;
- using and making spatial information – maps, globes, technology;
- using the school and its locality as a resource;
- developing children's literacies in all areas, including language and mathematics.

Theories, frameworks and examples of children's geographical learning are included in each chapter – these aspects of the chapters focus fully on children's experiences in learning. This book contains ten chapters on different aspects of teaching and learning geography, with the above themes cutting across these chapters.

Chapter 1: A world of geography – past, present and future of geography education

Chapter 1 has introduced you to what is great about geography and geography education. The chapter has also explored how geography can be conceptualised and how ideas about geography have changed over time.

Chapter 2: Learning through enquiry – the pedagogies of teaching and learning in geography

Many teachers who know, use and value the pedagogies of enquiry in planning for children's learning can still be wary of allowing children to be active decison-makers in the learning process, the pedagogies of enquiry in children's learning. However, as teachers we can also be confused or unwilling to take the steps towards allowing children to be part of the process of learning. This chapter shows each of the stages of enquiry, with varied examples from classrooms.

Chapter 3: Learning through experience – the literacies of geography

This chapter explores how the content of geography can be investigated through enquiry approaches that help children to develop the many literacies needed to understand the world. Some of these are very geographical, such as spatial literacies and critical literacies; others can be developed through geography, such as language and numerical literacies.

Chapter 4: Fabulous geography – avoiding dull learning in geography

Even though we try our best, all teachers can struggle when it comes to making certain topics in geography interesting. This chapter opens by outlining some of the fascinating research on children's experiences of and views of geography. It goes on to explore how potentially boring topics can be made exciting and challenging through practical, enquiry-based lessons.

Chapter 5: Our school, our world – primary geography through the school grounds

The school and its grounds are key resources for primary school geography. Through investigating their school grounds, children can begin to understand important concepts in geography such as location, change or development.

Chapter 6: Our geographical locality – primary geography through the locality

The locality of the school also contains a wealth of people and places to help children learn about their local area and the wider world. Through using their locality they can come to understand physical and human processes, as well as developing their personal geographies.

Chapter 7: Real geography – topical geography through issues and events

Geography is a dynamic subject, which is constantly in the news. Local and global news stories provide opportunities for children to ask questions and to find out why events are happening. There is also much to argue about in geography lessons! This chapter explores how schools use local, national and international issues and events in teaching geography.

Chapter 8: Connecting geography – learning about places

Place is a central idea in geography. This chapter complements the chapters on the school grounds and the locality by showing how children can look at places in their own country, continent and beyond. Research into children's ideas about place and examples of activities for developing children's sense of place are explored.

Chapter 9: Go geography – children's agency and action through geography

This chapter incorporates important areas to which geography makes a crucial contribution, such as development education, education for sustainable development and future studies. The chapter explores the importance of these areas for children's learning. The chapter encourages us to help answer children's difficult questions about globalisation, power and inequality.

Chapter 10: Making geography work – planning for learning in geography

This chapter consolidates much of the work covered in the other chapters, and helps us plan for primary geography. This chapter is not about targets, over-elaborate planning or accounting for everything that happens in a primary classroom! It is a chapter to help us think about how we can plan, with children, for interesting lessons. Creative ways to resource geography will be considered and exemplified.

Why should I read this book?

Learning Primary Geography: Ideas and Inspiration for the Classroom is a book that focuses on the role of the child in learning primary geography and how we can facilitate that learning process. It recognises the agency of children in curriculum making, enquiry learning and developing understanding in geography. The way children can work together, with the support of teachers, to help their understanding of their locality and the wider world features in every chapter. Each chapter uses examples of children's geographical learning and their views on their learning experiences. The book can never capture all the learning that occurred in each classroom, but by carrying out similar activities in classrooms, it is hoped readers will see the contributions geography can make to children's experiences in school and communities.

Table 1.3 Grouping of children in different settings

Age of children by end of school year	Class level in different countries					
	Republic of Ireland	Scotland Northern Ireland	England Wales Australia	Canada Netherlands	Poland	Class levels for this book
5	Junior Infants	Primary 1	Reception/ Foundation	1		Infants
6	Senior Infants	Primary 2	1	2	0th	
7	1st	Primary 3	2	3	1st	Younger classes
8	2nd	Primary 4	3	4	2nd	
9	3rd	Primary 5	4	5	3rd	Middle classes
10	4th	Primary 6	5	6	4th	
11	5th	Primary 7	6	7	5th	Older classes
12	6th	Secondary School			6th	

For the purpose of this book, children's ages are grouped according to their stage in primary school, as shown in Table 1.3. Children in Ireland can start school after they are 4 but before they are 6. In reality, most children start school between the ages of 4½ and 5½.

Reflection and action

- What were your experiences of learning geography at school?
- What type of geography teacher would you like to be?
- What do you think are the most important 'big ideas' for children in primary school to learn about?
- How should geography be taught in schools?
- What do you see as the barriers for you teaching geography in an interesting and engaging way?
- What support will you need to be a great geography teacher?

Further resources

Books on teaching primary geography

Catling, S. and Willy, T. (2008) *Achieving QTS Teaching Primary Geography*. Exeter: Learning Matters.

Roberts, M. (2003) *Learning Through Enquiry: Making Sense of Geography in the Key Stage 3 classroom*. Sheffield: Geographical Association.

Roberts, M. (2013) *Geography Through Enquiry: Approaches to Teaching and Learning in the Secondary School*. Sheffield: Geographical Association.

Scoffham, S. (2010) *Handbook of Primary Geography*. Sheffield: Geographical Association.
Tanner, J. and Whittle, J. (2013) *The Everyday Guide to Primary Geography*: Story. Sheffield: Geographical Association.

Online support: Geographical Association (GA)

The GA supports teachers at all levels of education in planning and resourcing geography: www.geography.org.uk

Professional media: Geography Champions

The Champions site is a professional networking site for primary teachers of geography. Join the site and then join up on your local group: http://geographychampions.ning.com

Social media: Facebook – Primary Geography Ireland

The Facebook page has over 3,000 members, who post and comment on all sorts of interesting links and resources for primary geography. Interesting events are also posted on the page. The visual nature of Facebook works very well as a source of geographical inspiration! www.facebook.com/primarygeographyireland

Social media: Twitter

Twitter has become a source of support for teachers. There are a large number of accounts (handles) and themes (hashtags) worth following on Twitter, including:

#geography teacher – ideas and inspiration for geography lessons
#edb – enquiry-based learning
#spdsese – sharing learning in SESE (Geography, History and Science Education in localities)

Chapter 2

Learning through enquiry – the pedagogies of teaching and learning in geography

Enquiry develops a 'need to know' which motivates children and helps them draw connections between subjects and between prior and new knowledge/skills. Through the enquiry approach, children can simultaneously develop understanding and skills.

Teacher, 10 years' experience, Ireland

Learning through enquiry is engaging and motivating for children. It helps them to learn and remember more than other activities. Enabling children to learn through enquiry also works well in classrooms, but it can be difficult to envisage and enable what we have not experienced or witnessed ourselves.

The chapter is based on the following key ideas:

- Geographical enquiry is one of the most motivating approaches to learning that can take place in a classroom.
- Children ask questions and we should use these questions in geography lessons.
- Teachers need to support and scaffold children's learning through enquiry in geography.
- Teachers need to have a good knowledge of the nature and content of geography to guide children in their enquiries.

The chapter outlines:

- theories of learning and how they inform practices in classrooms;
- models of learning through enquiry;
- examples from classrooms of every stage of enquiry learning;
- children's views of and ideas about learning through enquiry;
- ways to overcome barriers to the implementation of learning through enquiry in classrooms.

Each of these examples is described in full in subsequent chapters. For example, boys in Scoil Fhursa found out 'Why is Batman in Rio?', but fuller descriptions of their work on Brazil can be found in Chapters 6 and 9.

Definitions and origins of learning through enquiry

There are various definitions of learning through enquiry or enquiry-based learning (EBL), including:

> Enquiry Based Learning describes an environment in which learning is driven by a process of enquiry owned by the student.
>
> Centre for Excellence in Enquiry Based Learning,
> University of Manchester (2015)

> Enquiry-based learning starts by posing questions, problems or scenarios—rather than simply presenting established facts or portraying a smooth path to knowledge.
>
> Wikipedia (2015)

> Enquiry learning is a learner-centred approach that emphasises higher order thinking skills. It may take several forms, including analysis, problem solving, discovery and creative activities, both in the classroom and the community.
>
> UNESCO (2015)

The definitions above show that while definitions vary learning through enquiry is a process where learners have responsibility for the learning process, through thinking about their learning, asking questions and setting about collecting a range of information to help them answer their questions. As Roberts describes (2013b, p. 6):

• Enquiry is question driven and encourages a questioning attitude towards knowledge.
• Students study geographical data and sources of information as evidence.
• Students make sense of information for themselves in order to develop understanding.
• Students reflect on their learning.

In classrooms, learning through enquiry (LTE) or enquiry-based learning (EBL) is a way of working that enables more participation in the learning process by learners, as outlined in Table 2.1. Examples of children taking part in all these types of activities are shown in Figures 2.1, 2.3, 2.5 and 2.6, and throughout this book.

As outlined in Table 2.1, negotiated learning encompasses learning through enquiry as children have a role in decisions that are made about their learning. As discussed below, the interactions between teachers and children are essential in learning through enquiry. This can involve a 'shift' in how we think about learning. These ideas about teaching and learning have their roots in the writings of a number of key thinkers in education over a long period of time.

John Dewey

The value of experience and curiosity and of teaching and learning through enquiry can be attributed to the work of John Dewey. He saw education as a force for change in people's lives. His ideas were radical at the time he wrote his views on education. His areas of interest were amazingly broad, including pupils' learning spaces, their experience within schools and the organisation of schools themselves in terms of democracy and

Table 2.1 The participation dimension to learning

	Closed	Framed	Negotiated
Key idea	'Authority' of teacher.	'Access' to process and skills.	'Relevance' depending on children's priorities.
Teacher's role	Authority and source of knowledge.	Directing content, expectations and systems for activity.	Supporting, negotiating, scaffolding.
Children's role	Acceptance, routine performance, diligence.	Work within teacher's framework. Set some questions.	Discuss goals and methods critically, share responsibility. Devise criteria.
Focus	Knowledge and skills.	Knowledge, understanding and skills.	Child led learning, understanding and questioning.
Methods	Exposition, workbooks and sheets, exercises. Evaluated by teacher.	Exposition, discussion for children's ideas, tasks given.	Children plan and carry out work initiated by the group.
Content	Controlled by teacher often only as laid out in textbook.	Teacher controlled topics and tasks. Explicit criteria.	Discussed and decided on by all involved.

Source: Barnes *et al.*, 1987; Roberts, 2003; 2013a.

power. Despite his range of thoughts and ideas, Dewey's thinking on learning can be reduced to five key ideas:

- Learning is an active process.
- Tasks should be real-life and challenging.
- Children learn through experience and interactions.
- When the curriculum is appropriate, learning and growth are enhanced.

Central to John Dewey's many ideas was the belief that children and their interests should be the starting point for learning. As he stated, 'the child is the starting point, the centre, and the end. His [sic] development, his growth, is the ideal . . . the child's own instincts and powers furnish the material and give the starting point for all education' (Dewey, 1902, p. 276). He did not use the term 'enquiry', but it is clearly evident in his work. Dewey suggested as learners we should start with a 'problem or obstacle to our development; we analyse the situation; we identify possible solutions; we compare the implications of the different solutions and select the best course of action; we implement this in practice' (Dewey quoted in Boydston, 1976). Dewey's work is evident in many curricula; this is especially so in Ireland, where the curriculum places equal emphasis on how pupils learn and what they learn (DES/NCCA, 1999).

This focus on the process of learning was also characteristic of the English curriculum; however, there is now a shift in emphasis towards content rather than approaches (DfE, 2014). While core geographical knowledge is always important in the curriculum, Dewey's work illustrated the importance of both process and context in the learning process. His writing reminds us that, as teachers, crafting a meaningful, rigorous and relevant curriculum for children involves taking account of the content to be 'delivered', the process used to deliver that content and the context in which it is delivered.

Paulo Freire

Freire was an educator born to a middle class family in Brazil, but between the 1930s depression and the death of his father, his fortune changed. These events were highly influential in his thinking, and he dedicated his adult life to the role of education in the lives of poor people. He highly valued the process of learning, believing that (Freire, 2004, p. 15):

> Education makes sense because women and men learn that through learning they can make and remake themselves, because women and men are able to take responsibility for themselves as beings capable of knowing, of knowing that they know and knowing that they don't.

He was highly critical of the national system of education as well as practices in classrooms where teachers acted as 'depositors' and students as 'depositories', passively receiving, memorising and repeating content; this dynamic is represented by the activity to the left in Figure 1.2. Freire was highly critical of the role of power relationships in education and argued that knowledge was considered a gift bestowed on the more ignorant by the knowledgeable (1970). He felt that this meant students were simply

Figure 2.1 Generating ideas for geographical enquiry can involve many different experiences: (a) using non-fiction texts, (b) fieldwork in the locality, (c) talking about photographs and (d) using maps

forced to accept whatever programmes were delivered to them. Freire argued that people should work together towards informed action or 'praxis' through dialogue, with subsequent positions based on argument not power. Freire believed that learners and teachers should make decisions about how to co-construct knowledge, and the parallels with learning and acting through enquiry are apparent in his work. Freire believed that such learning activity would create respect, enhance communities, build social capital and lead to actions for justice and human flourishing (1994). Freire's focus was on learning enabling action, towards a 'pedagogy of the oppressed' or 'of hope', as he said, 'one of the tasks of the progressive educator . . . is to unveil opportunities for hope, no matter what the obstacles might be'. Freire's work was far reaching and his insights are highly relevant to classroom teaching in general and, in particular, to primary geography, which encourages children to ask questions, especially 'difficult' questions that challenge how we see the world!

Jerome Bruner

Bruner argued that children benefit from being more involved in the process of learning than they have in the past and emphasised the role of the teacher in providing guidance to accelerate children's thinking through enquiry. The approach he advocated was a practical one where children should learn through discovery and enquiry (1966):

> to instruct someone . . . is not a matter of getting him to commit results to mind. Rather, it is to teach him to participate in the process that makes possible the establishment of knowledge. We teach a subject not to produce little living libraries on that subject, but rather to get a student to think mathematically for himself, to consider matters as an historian does, to take part in the process of knowledge-getting. Knowing is a process not a product.

Bruner argued that it was also essential to transfer thinking processes from one context to another, and that teachers needed to help this 'process of manipulating knowledge to make it fit new tasks' (1977, p. 47). Therefore, he felt children needed to learn the fundamental principles of subjects rather than just master facts; in other words, children should work as geographers not simply learn geography in lessons. Bruner also recognised the power of education to influence children's thinking at all ages, as he stated: 'We begin with the hypothesis that any subject can be taught effectively in some intellectually honest form to any child at any stage of development' (1957, p. 234). Spiral curricula, such as those in Ireland and in Australia, are influenced by Bruner's ideas, that as children experience the curriculum, it should revisit 'basic ideas repeatedly, building upon them until the student has grasped the full formal apparatus that goes with them' (ibid., p. 13).

Research in classrooms and with both teachers and children reveal that the needs and wishes of the children are the most important aspect of planning in schools. The Cambridge Primary Review (Alexander et al., 2010) was a fully independent enquiry into the condition and future of primary education in England. It reviewed the research and collated new data, and found (2010, p. 290):

Pupil consultation benefits children by enhancing engagement with learning, their sense of agency and themselves as learners. It benefits teachers by deepening their insights into children's abilities and learning preferences, leading to more responsive teaching and willingness to give pupils more responsibility.

This type of action is described in different ways including the use of 'enquiry' and the term 'curriculum-making', which is described in the Geographical Association's 'Manifesto' (GA, 2009) and was encouraged through its Action Plan for Geography (GA, 2011).

Learning through enquiry in geography lessons

Although enquiry is all about children's learning, we must remember that the most important person in the room (or outside) when it comes to enabling learning through enquiry is the teacher. As Webster *et al.* (1996) noted, 'the most powerful determinant of children's learning, the difference that makes the difference was how teachers scaffolded the learning process' (p. 151). Through interacting with children, teachers shape children's learning to ensure they:

* ask questions, and know what to do with the questions next;
* source and analyse geographical data, including considering different views;
* develop, with the aid of their teacher, geographical frameworks to help them make sense of the world;
* gain new knowledge and understanding about the world;
* develop attitudes and values beyond their immediate experiences, and become able to critically view information they use; and
* apply their learning to new learning.

Due to the complexities of these processes, teachers need to be experts in the 'precise knowledge of the characteristics and starting point of the learner, together with a thorough knowledge of the field of enquiry' (Webster *et al.*, 1996, p. 151). They need to know, in regards to the children, when to support, to help and to leave them to work independently; this happens progressively over time, as outlined in Appendix 1. In this way, learning through enquiry is supportive and inclusive as all children work and achieve in their own ways. As noted above, they also need to know about the nature of subjects and the subject matter, even if they do not know all of them (and in geography and education there is always more to learn!). It is very important that teachers make the 'leap' into teaching and learning through enquiry early on; as through these experiences, we learn more about enquiry as a pedagogy. Once we are curious about the idea of enquiry, models, such as that in Figure 2.2, begin to make more sense.

This is not to say introducing enquiry is straightforward, as Roberts notes (2013b, p. 51):

EBL demands different approaches to pedagogy from those of traditional teaching. EBL requires teachers to establish a classroom culture which encourages students to question and study information critically and in which evidence and ideas are shared and open to scrutiny.

CASE STUDY 2.1 Past, present, future: 5–8 year olds, St James' National School

Children in the junior room in St James' undertook an enquiry about the school grounds. The children carried out a picture hunt around the school grounds to generate their thoughts and ideas about the school. The children were encouraged to ask questions about the school – including those about the past, present and future. The children's questions were both geographical and historical in nature:

- Why was the new school built?
- Where was the office in the old school?
- Are any of the old pupils still living in Stradbally?
- Why do we like school?
- Why was the yellow line painted?
- Who was the first principal?
- Why is the school called St James' National School?
- Why is there a rock outside our school?
- How old is the school?
- What will the school be like in the future?

As can be seen, children of all ages ask a range of questions; older and younger children asked both 'what' and 'why' questions of varied types. These questions were used as the basis of further lessons, as described in Case Study 5.2.

For enquiry to work in classrooms, teachers need to portray a sense of 'fascination' about geographical topics, setting up an atmosphere where awe and wonder is always present, and where they are prepared to say less! At the same time teachers need to plan activities to help children answer the questions that have emerged. The following examples portray these kinds of classrooms.

The process of learning through enquiry: examples from classrooms

The stages of enquiry are logical, and are actually common across disciplines, especially in geography, history and sciences, as outlined in Figure 2.2. As the case studies throughout this book reveal, it is not complex to enable learning through enquiry. The learning that goes on is multi-faceted, complex and hard to capture, but hopefully the photographs, children's work and their comments throughout this chapter and book will help.

Creating a need to know: generating ideas and questions. As Roberts notes, 'in much traditional teaching, information is given in answer to questions that students have never asked' and so children do not ask questions (Roberts, 2009, p. 183). In Ireland,

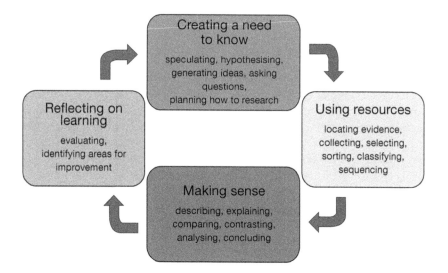

Figure 2.2 Learning through enquiry: the stages (adapted from Roberts, 2003; 2013a)

this scenario can still be found in classrooms although practices are changing (Waldron, 2003; Pike, 2007; Waldron *et al.*, 2009; Pike, 2012). On reflection, this makes little sense, as children are the learners and need and want to ask questions! As the theories and ideas above show, learning through enquiry builds on the idea that questions should frame the content of geography. Through selection of prompt material, teachers can allow these questions to be very open or to focus on particular curricular topics teachers need to cover. For example, as described in Case Study 2.2 and further in 9.4, when studying Brazil, the boys in Scoil Fhursa did not ask specifically about Rio 2016, but did ask lots of questions about sports, soccer and the World Cup. However, in providing stimulus material which included an artist's impressions of Rio 2016, the boys became very interested in the topic, as well as in their original questions.

There may also be times when a specific plan for geography is not really needed; teachers may simply wish the children to determine where their enquiries on a certain topic go. In most of the case studies in this book, such a stance meant that children's learning went beyond what was expected. This is possible with most curricula, and, generally, the nature of geography means that there are always choices to be made. However, teachers may want or need to have a teaching and learning plan when setting out on a topic. For example, when looking at a particular country we may want to have a focus, rather than trying to cover too much. In looking at the streetscape around the school, we may again want to have a plan. Also, if geography has been planned across the school, there will be certain foci different classes may have in their geography work.

So to start enquiry, teachers and children can choose certain items, to 'generate ideas'. These can include:

- the school, its grounds and the immediate locality;
- maps, globes or plans;
- photographs – aerial or views of people or places, etc.;

- newspapers or articles from online papers, etc.;
- media such as online videos, DVDs, TV programs;
- cartoons or other images.

This is just a selection of the materials that can be used, all of them have advantages and disadvantages; none of them should be the only resource used for a series of lessons. There are benefits and issues with the use of all of these resources. Images and cartoons are fantastic but need to be carefully selected, as discussed further in Chapters 9 and 10.

Starting enquiry: devising questions. Wood (2006, p. 26) argues that learners 'wishing to develop their capacity to enquire geographically' requires 'a clear capacity to question'. Most younger children need no prompts to ask questions! However, children may be discouraged from asking questions by adults, especially where the focus in classrooms is on covering courses, reaching targets, finishing books and/or revising for assessments. Overall, it is best to give children time to think about their questions, to start the process in a lesson but to leave questions on a whiteboard or sheet for children to think about and come back to. Beginning an enquiry by asking children to write down questions as homework is also a good idea.

There are many different strategies to use when devising questions for geographical enquiry, as shown in Case Studies 2.2 and 2.3, and can include the following approaches:

- *Children all suggest questions that are recorded on a flip chart or board*. These questions can then be discussed and the most 'important' ones decided on. These can become enquiry questions. This relatively unstructured way to encourage children to ask questions works because of its simplicity. However, working as a whole class may mean some children do not ask questions. For this reason it is best to do this activity with the children working in pairs or groups first, and then inviting contributions from others.
- *Children all write down their own question on scraps of paper or 'stickies'*. Children then look for 'question buddies', which is those with questions on a similar topic to themselves. They then generate 'enquiry questions' from what they have in the groups. Children in Newtown National School did this on their work on rocks – their questions are listed and sorted in Case Study 2.3. This strategy is very effective and generally works out very well.
- *Children, in groups or alone, have their own questions*. Children decide on enquiry questions from their own questions. This strategy works very well for children as they value their own questions very highly. It can, however, mean a lot of checking of questions for teachers.

All of the above strategies will mean that all children and their range of questions are included. Whatever their specific needs and abilities, all children can take part in these processes. This is an essential characteristic of enquiry; it is inclusive and democratic in nature. In all these cases, teachers should suggest questions that children may miss, for example when asking questions about a country children may neglect to ask 'What is life like in this place?', a question always featured on curricula for primary geography! Questions can, of course, be added to as the class proceeds through their enquiries.

Two frameworks commonly used to structure students' questions are the five Ws: Who, What, When, Why, Where (Nichols and Kinninment, 2001) and the Compass Rose, as shown in Figure 3.1, 'a framework for raising questions' (TIDE, 2009). Such tools have advantages but as Roberts notes, neither focus on the 'meaning of place, what ought to happen or from what viewpoint, they are not neutral; they influence what is seen and the geography that is constructed' (2009, p. 194). Furthermore, questions may be missed as they are too advanced or random for the frameworks – these may be the most interesting questions! So using a range of strategies, and providing thinking time is always important:

- *using resources*: locating evidence, collecting, selecting, sorting, classifying, sequencing;
- *making sense*: describing, explaining, comparing, contrasting, analysing, concluding.

Children should be given the opportunity to take their time, collect and evaluate data and use their thinking in making sense of the data collected. Data for enquiries can be sourced from many resources, such as:

- *maps*: any sort or scale of map (online or paper);
- *photographs*: online (Instagram, Flicker, sites from abroad, local sites), photo packs, photographs in textbooks, photographs from others;

(a)   (b)   (c)   (d)

Figure 2.3 Children's questions are the basis of all enquiry work in primary geography: (a) working together, (b) grouping the class's questions, (c) brainstorming as a class and (d) paired brainstorms

- *moving images*: video sharing sites such as YouTube, TV programmes;
- *information from and interactions with others*: interviews, online interactions (social media, Mystery Skypes, etc.), visitors to the classroom, interactions during fieldwork, radio programmes;
- *written accounts*: news stories, library books, literature, textbooks.

CASE STUDY 2.2 How should our area change in the future? Senior class, Scoil Fhursa

The boys in fifth and sixth class in Scoil Fhursa turned to their locality for some geography after investigating links with other places through their geography lessons, including Brazil and Hungary, as outlined in Chapter 8. The boys started off their work by talking and completing a grid with four sections:

- What would you tell someone about your area?
- What questions do you have about your area?
- What would you like to do in geography about your area?
- Anything else to add?

After a bit of moving around the room to sit in more logical groups, so children who lived near each other sat together, the boys came up with a number of questions, many of which were largely focused on the local environment. It was immediately apparent that an issue locally for the boys was an underpass, as they called it 'the tunnel' from near the school to the local shopping centre. The tunnel was built to help access between these two places, but had issues of graffiti and vandalism. The boys' main question initially was: 'Should the tunnel close?', however the boys were encouraged to ask broader questions and to consider:

- places in the locality apart from the tunnel;
- different peoples' views of changes in the locality;
- the history of the area.

From this, the boys' questions, with a bit of refining, became:

- What do people think of the area?
- Which places should change?
- Which places should not change?
- What is the area like?
- What do we think of the area?
- Why was Coolock built? How did it change?

The boys decided their overall questions should be 'How should our area change in the future?'. The rest of the boys' work on their locality and what it led to is described in Case Study 9.4.

www.scoilfhursa.ie/Scoil_Fhursa/Failte.html

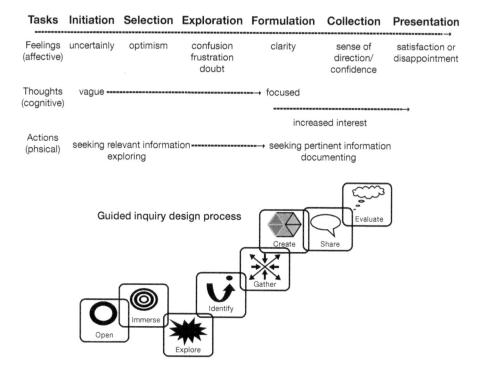

Tasks	Initiation	Selection	Exploration	Formulation	Collection	Presentation
Feelings (affective)	uncertainly	optimism	confusion frustration doubt	clarity	sense of direction/ confidence	satisfaction or disappointment
Thoughts (cognitive)	vague ···→ focused					
					increased interest	
Actions (phsical)	seeking relevant information ···········→ seeking pertinent information					
	exploring			documenting		

Guided inquiry design process

Figure 2.4 Working through enquiry – can mean that confusion is both allowed and valued! (Kuhlthau *et al.*, 2015)

As teachers, we can approach different topics with the strategies that work, although diagrams such as Figures 2.2 and 2.4 provide frameworks for learning through enquiry. Overall, some topics work as part of focused enquiries; others work well as a series of lessons each focused on different enquiry questions. This is largely dependent on the learning involved. For example, if children are used to finding out about countries and have the frameworks for thinking about places, as described in Chapter 8, then they can work relatively independently. If children in older classes are carrying out enquiries based on their locality, and have already worked locally before, again, they are more likely to be able to work independently but with the support of the teacher. As teachers, we must remember that confusion can be part of the process of enquiry, and this is not necessarily a bad thing! This is illustrated very well in the diagram in Figure 2.4, from Kuhlthau *et al.* (2015). With the support of each other and teachers, children will soon realise that confusion is part of the learning process, and that they will overcome it.

When referring to their level of independence, there will always be variations in the classes. Some children will always need the support of teachers and other staff, but will still be able to work through the enquiry frame. Teachers can provide encouragement through:

- *Support*: Some children need support from other children and adults to complete work. This can be achieved through working in groups, but will always involve the support of teachers and other staff.

- *Outcomes*: Some children will achieve higher standards in their work than others. However, it becomes very evident in working through enquiry that whatever the children's ability, they are able to think geographically. Often children achieve far more in geography than they may in other subjects, even if the evidence of their achievements are oral or pictorial rather than written.
- *Tasks*: For some children, their needs are such that they will only access the enquiry to a certain level. For example, children may be able to focus on the features of the locality, but not the processes of change occurring locally.

There are topics where the enquiry approach needs to be more structured. For example, in any type of decision-making activity, such as 'Where would a butterfly like to live in our school?' or 'How can we make our lane safer?', a reasonable amount of structure is needed for the different elements of the enquiry, not to mention supervision by adults for the fieldwork! In these types of enquiry, agreement of the enquiry questions is important, to allow the class to carry out activities associated with each question, as the following example, adapted from *Eco-Detectives Teacher's Resource Pack* (Pike 2011a), illustrates:

Key enquiry question

Where would a butterfly like to live in our school grounds?

Enquiry questions and possible activities:

What is a butterfly?

- looking at images/video of butterflies and talking about them;
- sorting images, describing the characteristics of butterflies.

What do butterflies do? (Where do they rest? Where do they live?)

- reading the *Hungry Caterpillar* by Eric Carle';
- watching butterflies life cycles (e.g. using Vimeo or YouTube);
- sequencing and drawing the stages of the lifecycle of a butterfly;
- making films of the lifecycle of a butterfly (e.g. using modelling clay, Lego, etc.);
- researching other animal lifecycles as a homework.

Where would a butterfly like to live in our school grounds?

- choosing a range of places a butterfly may like, deduced from the activities above;
- devising criteria – that is what would a butterfly need?
- selecting four possible places – agreeing these as a class;
- visiting places, drawing what butterflies would like and not like;
- visiting places, scoring places on the criteria decided above;
- designing perfect school grounds for a butterfly – then setting about creating it.

The key learning from this activity is that a good environment for butterflies is also good for us as humans.

For older children, enquiries will involve more text, but still include the practical elements. Resources need to be carefully selected by teachers and children. As Roberts notes, data in geography textbooks are less useful because they have already been interpreted for students, for example bullet points of key information or lists of advantages and disadvantages (Roberts, 2009, p. 184). While this makes for an attractive layout in a textbook, it is rather frustrating for teachers who would like their children to make sense of data themselves! In order to develop understanding, children need to do something with the information they gather. They need to relate it to what they know already, see relationships between different bits of information and play around with it in their minds, not simply put it on a worksheet without it even 'going through their brains' (Jones, quoted in Roberts, 2003). Research on language and learning (Barnes and Todd, 1995; D'Arcy, 1989) suggests that the role of exploratory talk and writing is crucial in the process of making sense. As outlined in Chapter 3, there is also evidence that such processes improve children's achievements in reading.

Figure 2.5 shows some examples of activities children may do to collect data:

- Boys from St Joseph's Boys' National School collected images of patterns in and around Dungarvan Harbour as part of a craft project – Chapter 6.
- Boys from St Patrick's Boys' National School used maps to help them to find out about the proposal to build/extend the light rail system in Dublin – Chapter 3.
- Girls from Drumcondra National School collected data (photographs, maps, words) on the changing features of Drumcondra as part of a project on landscape – Chapter 3.
- Girls from St Vincent de Paul GNS collated information about Australia – Chapter 8.

Independent enquiries. For older children and for certain topics, children are able to work independently, but in their groups, to help answer their enquiry questions for example:

- *Looking at places*: As outlined further in Chapter 8, children can collate a number of questions on a country or region, then proceed to answer these through their own research. Teachers must carefully check the children's questions, and collating them as a class works well. Often children think the first or most important aspect of a place to write about is the tourist attractions. Teachers need to enable children to ask question about the physical and human characteristics of places, as well as how places are changing.
- *Looking at events*: As outlined in Chapter 7, helping children to appreciate that there are causes, effects and responses to events means they have a framework for thinking geographically about events in the world.

These two types of enquiry lend themselves very well to children, in older classes, approaching enquiry learning through independent project type activity.

Figure 2.5 Collecting data for geographical enquiries can involve a range of activity: (a) taking photographs, (b) using maps and other data, (c) using non-fiction texts and (d) collecting data on fieldwork

Enquiry focused lessons. For younger children, for topics that are new to children and for a certain area of geography, it makes more sense to have lessons that are enquiry driven, but where children work through tasks to scaffold their learning through enquiry.

- *Looking at issues*: As discussed further in Chapter 7, where the boys in St Patrick's Boys' National School focused on Dublin's transport.
- *Looking at the locality*: As outlined in examples in Chapters 5 and 6.

Presenting findings

Presenting findings is an exciting stage of any enquiry, and the possibilities are endless. Children can plan how and to whom they will present their work, as shown in Figure 2.6. They need to think about:

- What are we sharing? Is it our learning or ideas for change, or action.
- How will we present our work?
- Who will we share our work with?
- How will we share our work?
- What will we do next?

Ways of presenting can include any or all of the following:

- making poster displays for classroom or corridor walls;
- organising presentations to the class, other classes, teachers and others in the school;
- sharing learning and ideas for change with the wider community, through events, social media, letters and so on.

(a) (b) (c) (d)

Figure 2.6 Children make sense of their enquiries and present their findings: (a) using writing frames, (b) presenting findings through posters, (c) making mind maps and (d) creating maps.

CASE STUDY 2.3 Generating enquiry questions: 10–12 year olds, Newtown National School

The children in fifth and sixth class and their teachers took part in a series of enquiry-based lessons on rocks and soils. After a 'rock hunt' outlined fully in Case Study 4.2, children's questions about rocks included a range of inquiries that certainly covered everything required in the primary curriculum in relation to the topic!

Here are some of the questions, although questions asked more than once have been omitted:

- How are rocks unique?
- How are rocks with holes formed?
- How are there so many rocks at the beach?
- How did rocks get their names?
- How do people benefit from rocks?
- How do rocks get different colours?
- Why are rocks important?
- What way do you use rocks?
- Where do you find such interesting rocks?
- Are rocks important to humans?
- Are there rocks on other planets?
- Can people get sick from some rocks?
- Can rocks help people?
- Do rocks go bad?
- How are rocks all so different?
- How are rocks formed?
- How do rocks get their colours?
- How is rock made?

The children's questions included the characteristics of rocks as well as the formation and uses of rocks. The questions covered everything relating to rocks from the curriculum and more! From these questions, the children spontaneously decided to group them into the following larger or enquiry questions. The children then grouped the questions, putting questions on similar themes together. After this, the children decided how to ask a 'big' or enquiry questions from their group of queries. In some cases, the question was already among the ones they had; in other cases, they came up with a question. So their enquiry questions became:

- Why do people study rocks?
- In what ways do people use rocks?
- Why do rocks have holes in them?
- Are rocks important to humans?
- How are rocks formed?
- How are rocks important to us?

These questions formed the basis of the activity outlined further in Case Study 4.2, and shown in Figure 4.5.

www.snbailenua.ie – @snbailenua

Planning and resourcing for enquiry

Enquiry is a driving force in learning geography; it allows for freedom for children and teachers in their learning experiences. However, teachers are very important in the enquiry process, and enquiry must be planned carefully across the school. Consideration must be given to age appropriate enquiries. The 1999 curriculum for geography in Ireland did this very well. The aspects of enquiry were set out, with examples for each age group, as shown in Appendix 1. In Australia, the questions for enquiry are stated for each class level; this has advantages in helping teachers gauge questions children should ask. However, this may not allow younger children to ask more challenging questions.

Resourcing learning through enquiry, in terms of guides and sources for teachers, is slightly problematic! There is no magic formula, pack or book that will enable children to learn through enquiry. Producing too many resources could, in fact, hinder enquiry in classrooms, as activities may become too prescriptive. 'Eco-detectives' is a resource pack of environmental and climate change enquiries for schools. The aim of the resource was to help children construct their knowledge about the environment and climate change and to take part in action to protect the environment. All activity is enquiry led and fieldwork based, using the locality of the school. It also enhances children's learning in geography and science, as well as other curriculum areas, particularly language, mathematics and SPHE. The resource does not cover everything that it is possible to discuss with children in these areas, but importantly it shows teachers how to enable learning through enquiry. The resource pack contains four booklets to help teachers plan and resource the enquiries, a CD-ROM containing interactive activities and resource material, separate enquiry process teacher and student guides, photo cards and a game; it is also available online.

Key questions

- **What journeys are made in our locality?**

- **How do we get to school?**

Outline. Children start an enquiry about travel in their locality. They consider how they make different journeys and how different types of travel might affect the environment. Teachers may provide children with the following prompt words: Travel, How, Why, What, Impact, Environment, Climate Change, Future, Car, Bike, Walk, Sustainable, Transport.

Preparation. Teachers should be familiar with the enquiry/investigation approaches for learning.

Learning outcomes. On completing these activities, all children will be able to:

- describe and map journeys made in the locality by people or animals, for example planes overhead, children being driven to school, bees flying and so on;
- devise questions about travel in the locality;
- decide on and collect data relating to travel in the locality; and
- present findings relating to travel in the locality and its environmental impact.

Resources. Clipboards/notebooks, investigation sheets: what journeys are made in our locality.

Learning activities

1   Children observe journeys made in the locality through fieldwork.

2   Children write down questions relating to travel in their locality on strips of scrap paper. Children sort questions into broad categories. Children develop 'big' questions about transport in their locality, for example:
   – How do people travel in the locality, including getting to school?
   – Why do people travel as they do?
   – What impact has this on the environment?

3   Children decide on data they will need to collect in order to answer their questions – this may include other activities in this resource pack.

4   Children collect the data; this may include mapping, surveys, interviews and so on.

5   Children decide on any action that is possible in their school and community from the information they have collected.

Children's reactions to learning through enquiry

To date, there has been little large-scale research relating to children's attitudes to learning through enquiry. There are however numerous small-scale projects that are very insightful. Smyth (2010) constructed a study where she enabled a class of children to carry out an enquiry on a river near to their school, involving children, teachers and parents in the process. The results were very interesting. The children were very enthusiastic about the work they did. They thought they learnt a lot from the work, especially as they had directed much of it. It was the reaction of the parents that was most insightful. Many of the parents had negative associations with primary geography. They remembered learning by rote and never taking part in fieldwork. As helpers for the river enquiry, they were impressed by the learning that occurred and the contribution the river enquiry made to their children's experiences of primary geography (see further Chapter 6).

Children at the upper end of their primary school experiences are able to reflect deeply about their learning (Green *et al.*, 2012). The boys of St Joseph's Boys' National School design and carry out enquiries on any topic of their choice each year for geography, history and science. Each term, there are competitions, and the boys' projects are completed and then judged by local enthusiasts. The enquiry element of the projects does vary from class to class, as would be expected. However, the boys' reactions to the work clearly show how much they value their independence in their learning:

> I did Venus because not that many people are talking about it. It was very interesting and fun. Doing this project I learned many different things. I also liked listening to my friends and their projects.

The children in St James' National School were very positive about their learning through enquiry, as described in Case Study 4.1:

> I liked making up questions that we wanted to answer, because that way the teachers could see what we wanted to learn about.

> I really enjoyed the work we did . . . I liked it when we made up questions and tried to find the answers.

Younger children are also able to express their ideas about their learning in geography. The 5- and 6-year-old children in Our Lady of Victories expressed their views of their work on climates as well as changing seasons, as shown in Case Study 5.3, by saying:

– I like it because I can see all the wonderful things.
– The yard because you learn about spring.
– I liked drawing the pictures.
– I liked drawing the animals.

The comments show that not only are children positive about their learning experiences in geography, but at all ages, they are also able to articulate why they hold these views.

Conclusions

Overall, learning through enquiry is a powerful way to conceptualise learning in primary geography. It means children enjoy geography and are challenged by it. The willingness to consider, facilitate and enable learning through enquiry in a classroom does involve us embracing a certain ethos; however, the benefits soon become evident as the following chapters illustrate.

Reflection and action

- How did you learn at school? What did you think of it?
- Have you ever learnt through enquiry? What was it like for you?
- Which ideas about enquiry appeal to you the most – those of Dewey, Freire or Bruner? Why?
- Drawing on the examples in this chapter, what do you think would be the benefits for children of learning through enquiry?
- What sort of ethos do you need to develop in your classroom when teaching through enquiry? How will you do this?
- What are the barriers to teaching through enquiry in your setting?
- What impact would learning through enquiry have on children's learning in other areas, including literacy and numeracy?

Further resources

Books on learning through enquiry

Coles, T. (2013) *Never Mind the Inspectors – Here's Punk Learning*. Carmarthen: Crown House Publishing.

Kuhlthau, C.K., Maniotes, L.K. and Caspari, A.K. (2015) *Guided Inquiry: Learning in the 21st Century (2nd Edition)*. Santa Barbara, CA: ABC CLIO/Libraries.

Roberts, M. (2003) *Learning Through Enquiry: Making Sense of Geography in the Key Stage 3 Classroom*. Sheffield: Geographical Association.

Roberts, M. (2013) *Geography Through Enquiry: Approaches to Teaching and Learning in the Secondary School*. Sheffield: Geographical Association.

Chapter 3

Learning through experience – the literacies of geography

> I loved doing the things with maps and making up our own maps. It was fun and I hope we do it again.
>
> Girl, 11

Geography provides many opportunities to develop literacies for children. This chapter is based on the following key thoughts:

- Children naturally use a range of ways to make sense of the world.
- Children need a range of literacies to negotiate the world – and these will change over time.
- A range of literacies can also be used in geography lessons.
- Geography can contribute significantly to children's understanding of the world through the use of literacies.

This chapter outlines:

- different literacies that can be used in geography lessons;
- learning in mathematics and geography;
- learning in language and geography; and
- learning spatially in and out of classrooms.

This chapter informs all others in the book, especially Chapters 5, 6 and 8 where opportunities for children to critically examine their schools, localities and the wider world are outlined, as well as Chapter 9, which specifically looks at children's participation in local communities.

Literacies in primary geography

There are many literacies that can enhance geography lessons for children, and, in turn, geography lessons can enhance children's literacies, including:

- *Geo-literacy*: the ability to locate, use and critique spatial information – all chapters.
- *Critical literacy*: the ability to think critically – all chapters.
- *Media literacy*: the ability to think critically about different types of media – Chapters 8 and 9.

- *Information literacy*: the ability to evaluate, locate, identify and effectively use – all chapters.
- *Technology literacy*: the ability to use technology effectively in several different ways – all chapters but particularly 8 and 9.
- *Political literacy*: the ability to actively participate in political matters – this chapter as well as Chapters 7 and 9.
- *Visual literacy*: the ability to critically read images – all chapters but especially Chapters 8 and 9.
- *Spatial literacies*: the ability to use and manipulate spatial information – all chapters.

In this chapter, the role of literacies within the framework of learning through enquiry will be outlined and exemplified, focusing on language, mathematics and spatial literacies. The types of activity characteristically found in well-planned geography lessons can contribute to many types of literacy:

- asking questions – and deciding how to answer them;
- using plans, maps and globes;
- giving oral, written or pictorial accounts and descriptions of environmental factors observed or studied;
- collecting information from a range of sources;
- observing accurately both inside and outside the classroom;
- predicting outcomes of an investigation;
- estimating, measuring and comparing;
- analysing objects and processes;
- sorting and grouping people, events and natural phenomena;
- recognising, describing and accounting for patterns;
- undertaking a range of outdoor tasks;
- displaying and reporting on completed project work and on work in progress;
- using elements of graphicacy;
- using interactive ICTs which enable the child to explore geographical themes and topics and complete a range of tasks, puzzles or problems;
- completing independent geographical research, recording and presenting the results;
- engaging in practical environmental investigation or enhancement.

This is an edited list of suggested assessments in geography from the Irish curriculum (DES/NCCA, 1999b, p. 93) but these suggestions are common to geography classes in many settings.

Literacy and primary geography

Geography always links with language, as geographers need to access many different types of information through language. Children need to use, create and re-present a range of information in their geographical enquiries. The range of language sources typically includes: maps, pictures, graphs, charts and geo-spatial representations of information, along with newspaper articles, flyers, articles in magazines, textbooks, stories and so on. When geography is taught through enquiry, there are many opportunities for children to develop their language skills through talking, reading and different forms of writing. This partnership between geography and language is stated in many curricula:

> Ireland (DES/NCCA, 1999b, p4): Many elements from the history, science and geography curricula may be explored concurrently, and much of the work involved will contribute to the development of the children's oral language, literacy numeracy and communication skills.

> USA (NGACBP/CCSSO, 2014): The Standards insist that instruction in reading, writing, speaking, listening, and language be a shared responsibility within the school. The K-5 standards include expectations for reading, writing, speaking, listening, and language applicable to a range of subjects, including but not limited to English Language Arts (ELA).

Many curricula also recognise the need for meaningful engagement with a range of literacies in childhood. Sometimes this is related to children's future needs as citizens and students, as the National Geographic website states (2015):

> ... geography is about preparing people to make the important individual and collective decisions we will all face in the 21st century.

Research on geography and the development of language shows the positive impact geography lessons have on children's language development in all dimensions. In the US, 5,300 students in over 100 classrooms across a range of settings in Arizona took part in a study to assess if Geo-literacy had an impact on reading scores. The use of Geo-literacy in Arizona is broad, and includes a range of dimensions of geography. The results of the study showed (Hinde *et al.*, 2007, p. 355):

> when teachers employed Geo-literacy lessons, their students' reading comprehension achievement improved. The significance of gain varied by grade level, but it is clear that when Geo-literacy was used, there was a positive trend in student achievement in reading comprehension.

The impact of the Geo-literacy programme was statistically significant in most class levels and in all class levels there was a positive impact on students' reading scores. The study also found that children were motivated to learn; in particular, children with specific learning needs in literacy were motivated to read and write more. The study concluded that when 'skilled teachers integrate across content areas, students gain' (2007, p. 358).

Geography provides contexts where children need, and want to use, their literacy skills. For example, Cleary (2008) found links between learning through enquiry and motivation to develop literacy, end where it occurred this motivation:

- opened up space for students to learn in ways that were congruent with their own ways of being;
- provided real audiences and purposes to express those ways of being;
- showed paths for identity construction through literacy;
- constructed two-way bridges to the mainstream world.

CASE STUDY 3.1 Pushkin Project on landscapes: all classes, Drumcondra National School

Drumcondra National School is a small urban primary school; there are 65 children in three classrooms, ranging in age from 4 to 13. Landscape was a very apt theme for the school, as they were about to undertake a temporary move to facilitate building work in their school. Their current building had changed marginally in the past 100 years – although lots of features within the building had changed significantly! The school decided to take part in the Pushkin Project and were keen to link up with geography education student teachers from St Patrick's College as the focus was partly geographical.

Each class took a slightly different perspective on the project; these are some of the activities they carried out:

- **Features and landscape**: The infant class (4–7 year olds) found out about the features of their landscape. The student teachers talked to the children about their views of their locality and focused on the children's views and changes in the locality. The children were particularly keen to find out where the student teachers went to 'school'! They visited the local churchyard, streets and college grounds, using picture frames as a device to focus their attention on the landscape. Back in the classroom, they created a mural of the features they had seen.

- **Our school – new and old**: The middle class (7–10 year olds) started by focusing on the new school building. They wrote down the many questions they had, some of which are shown in Figure 2.1. The children then carried out a 'description walk' around the school grounds, recording descriptive words on paper as well as taking photographs. Later, the children read Seamus Heaney's poem 'Digging', focusing on the descriptive words used by the poet. They then wrote their own shape poems describing their school.

- **Changing landscapes**: The senior class (10–13 year olds) worked independently. To begin with they used maps of the locality to tell the students all about their locality. As the majority of the students lived in the same area as the children, the conversations were interesting, and the differing 'ethnogeographies' of the area were immediately apparent! With the students' support, the children decided to investigate the locality by planning a trail. Together they planned a route around the locality.

One of the student teachers reflected on the process on enquiry she facilitated:

> In enquiry learning children are responsible for processing the data they are working with in order to reach their own conclusions. The children's ideas on places and spaces were used as a starting point for all of the activities in the school . . . I got to know a lot about the children as a result of this and when it came to exploring the landscape, the one place I know the most about without having ever been there

was the scary space! I found it interesting to compare children's interpretations with my own upon finally seeing the space. The children were also given choices in certain activities, such as writing shape poems . . . I noticed that all the children were happy enough to get stuck into the activity regardless of ability. The element of choice allowed the children the comfort and freedom to express themselves and their views within their own comfort zones.

www.drumcondrans.scoilnet.ie, www.pushkintrust.com

As discussed in Chapter 2, learning through enquiry motivates children to engage in learning activities, including reading. Motivation is central to children's progression in literacy. As Guthrie states: 'engaged reading is a merger of motivation and thoughtfulness. Engaged readers seek to understand; they enjoy learning and they believe in their reading abilities' (2001). What's more, geography provides opportunities for children to become more literate, without necessarily thinking they are 'working'!

There are a range of tools and strategies in geography that provide opportunities to develop children's language through their thinking. One of these is the Development Compass Rose, as shown in Figure 3.1; this is a tool to encourage children's questioning. There are also a number of activities which can be broadly described as thinking skills activities, through which children consider important issues in geography. In these activities, children manipulate and sort pieces of cards on which words, sentences and/or photographs/pictures are presented.

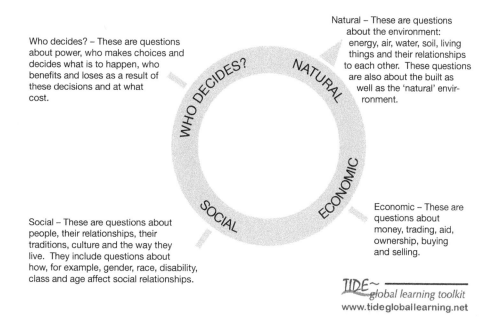

Natural – These are questions about the environment: energy, air, water, soil, living things and their relationships to each other. These questions are also about the built as well as the 'natural' environment.

Who decides? – These are questions about power, who makes choices and decides what is to happen, who benefits and loses as a result of these decisions and at what cost.

Social – These are questions about people, their relationships, their traditions, culture and the way they live. They include questions about how, for example, gender, race, disability, class and age affect social relationships.

Economic – These are questions about money, trading, aid, ownership, buying and selling.

TIDE~ global learning toolkit
www.tidegloballearning.net

Figure 3.1 Tools such as the Development Compass Rose encourage children to use language (TIDE, 2015)

- 'Mysteries' – children have to decide why something happened; these are usually used as a prompt for work about an event or issue. (See Table 3.1.)
- 'Dilemmas'/'Moral Dilemmas' – this is similar to a mystery but more personalised, in that the issue or event is tied to a particular person, for example: why is Batman in Rio? (See Table 7.3.)
- 'Odd One Out' decision-making activity – children decide which piece of information is the odd one out.
- 'Diamond Nine' ranking and sorting activity – children select pieces of information from 12 or more, then rank the information in a 1,2,3,2,1 formation.

While these types of activities can be very effective in lessons, they need to be used as part of the process of enquiry in classrooms. When this occurs, the activities provide opportunities for children to read, discuss, analyse, argue and make sense of information. Considering they are such a simple resource, they provide children with fantastic learning experiences. The most well designed activities can be used over a number of lessons and independently by children in their subsequent enquiry activity. Examples of these types of activities are included in Chapters 7, 8 and 9.

Some of the more specific ways children use language in geography is shown in Table 3.2. While each genre of language is used by every age group of children, in junior classes the children will be working orally in the genre as a precursor to writing in it.

It is evident that through interacting with a range of texts they meet in geography, children learn to write in different ways, although in reality these two aspects of learning

Table 3.1 Sample resource: Dilemma – Would Mrs Murphy move to Cavan?

Mrs Murphy has lived in Phibsborough for 50 years. She loves the areas.	There is an active retirement group in Cavan.
Mrs Murphy's daughter lives in Cavan. She only sees her once a month.	The Metro lines will be completed in 2020.
The new Metro lines will solve Dublin's transport problems.	Mr Murphy died in 1990.
The Metro company will give her E500,000 for her house.	Mr And Mrs O'Neill next door have moved house.
Mrs Murphy knows most of the people on her street and the shops in Drumcondra.	Dublin's population is over one million.
Mrs Murphy loves going to the theatre, with her neighbour.	Mrs Murphy likes going to the bakers and café in Drumcondra.
Mrs Murphy could buy a house in Cavan for E150,000.	Ranelagh has lots of pubs.
Mrs Murphy goes to the social club for over 60s once a week.	The fields next to Mrs Murphy's home are up for sale.
Mrs Murphy has two great friends in Cavan from her childhood holidays.	Mrs Murphy never goes out after dark.
Mrs Murphy used to go on holiday to Cavan when she was a child.	Mrs Murphy's daughter has a huge house.

Table 3.2 Genres of writing in geography lessons

Genre	Purpose	Activities
Descriptive writing	Children observe carefully and choose precise language. They take notice of sensory details and create comparisons (metaphors and similes) to make their writing more powerful.	• Comparing places • Descriptive places, people and patterns
Expository writing	Children collect and synthesise information. This writing is objective. Children use expository writing to give directions, sequence steps, compare one thing to another, explain causes and effects, or describe problems and solutions.	• Autobiographies • Positional language: directions, etc. • Posters • Reports and summaries
Journals and letters	Children write to themselves and to others. Their writing can be personal and less formal than other genres. They share news, explore new ideas and record notes.	• Various types of letters and notes • Email messages and posts • Learning logs and blogs • Personal journals
Narrative writing	Children tell and retell stories, they develop sequels for stories they have read, write stories about events in their own and other people's lives.	• Original short stories and narratives • Retellings of stories
Persuasive writing	Children present their position using appeals to logic, moral character and emotion and support it with examples and evidence.	• Advertisements • Letters to decison-makers • Persuasive letters

Source: Adapted from Tomkins, 2013.

work together. Geography provides children with great opportunities to develop their vocabulary through reading a wide range of material, as discussed further in Chapter 4. The writing children produce from their geographical enquiries can be varied: reports, news articles, posters, fact files and presentations. As shown in Chapter 2, these can be shared with the class, school and/or the wider communities, online or in person.

Numeracy and primary geography

There are strong parallels between primary geography and mathematics. As Dooley *et al.* (2014, p. 22) note:

> good mathematics pedagogy can be enacted when educators engage children in a variety of mathematically-related activities across different areas of learning. The activities should arise from children's interests, questions, concerns and everyday experiences (p. 22).

Dooley *et al.* (2014) outline many points about the mathematical learning environment that are also characteristic of geography:

• Tasks are designed based on children's current interests, but they also serve the long-term learning goals.

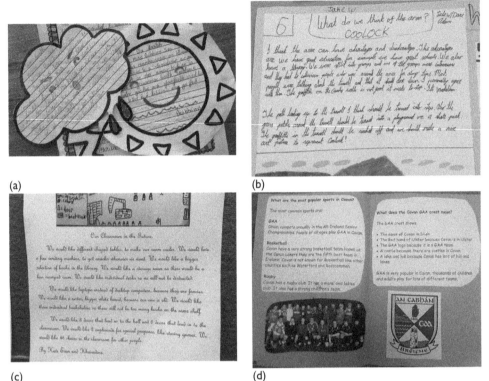

Figure 3.2 Children's writing in geography (a) describing weather phenomena in Irish, (b) expressing opinions about the locality, (c) speculating about the future and (d) describing places in scrapbook projects

- Children are given opportunities to engage in justification, argumentation and generalisation.
- A wide range of children's everyday activities, play and interests are used to engage, challenge and extend their mathematical knowledge and skills.
- Children are provided with opportunities to learn in a wide range of imaginative and real-world contexts, some of which integrate and connect mathematics with other activities and other activities with mathematics.
- Investigative-type activities that stem from children's interests and questions, give rise to the creation of models of the problem which can be generalised and used in other situations.
- Contexts that are rich in perceptual and social experiences are used to support the development of problem-solving and creative skills.

This list makes it very evident that there are many aspects of learning in mathematics that have strong parallels with how geography can be taught. The contribution of children to the learning process, supported by the expertise of the teacher, is essential for both subjects. The use of real world contexts, tied to children's lives but also taking children beyond their immediate experiences, is also essential in mathematics and geography.

Finally, opportunities to provide freedom for children to think deeply and reflect on their learning are evident in both subjects. All of these are evident before we even begin to think about the aspects of geography and mathematics that integrate effectively.

In both disciplines, there is a focus on how everyday aspects of the discipline should be the basis of learning. Everyday geography and mathematics can be used for their own sake as a basis of learning in the subject. Robinson and Koshy (2004, pp. 70–1) suggest that different levels of mathematical activity should be planned, all of which can be applied to geography:

- procedures – facts, skills and concepts;
- application – putting skills into practice, involving higher order thinking;
- elegance – making personal values and judgments on the activities carried out through procedures and applications.

These levels of mathematical activity can be enhanced very easily with a geographical angle, starting with procedures and moving through to elegance, as shown in these examples:

- **Example 1: Patterns in the school**. Children can carry out procedures to find patterns in and around the school as part of wider enquiries about patterns. This type of activity is particularly appropriate as a foundation for younger children and will give children a stronger sense of both space and place in their school environments.
- **Example 2: Shapes in the school**. Classrooms, corridors, halls and school grounds provide many opportunities for looking at characteristics of shapes. Picking out different shapes in the environment provides children with opportunities to really remember shapes that may only be seen on a sheet or textbook page. This can be extended to consider the limitations of the activities – what shapes cannot be found? Why?
- **Example 3: Length and measurement**. Lessons can come alive by using non-standard and standard measurements to find out lengths of different places in the school. Children can devise their own ways to do these activities and reflect on how they have worked. Older children could carry out enquiries, such as 'How can space be better used in our school?'. The opportunities for children to express their views on how places could be developed or simply left alone could be endless. This could also provide the opportunity for schools to link up with teachers and children from other schools to exchange experiences and practices.

Geographical investigations provide a rich context for children to manipulate many types of data:

- Where should we plant a tree in our school grounds?
- Do we need a new shopping centre?
- Where would a butterfly like to live in our school grounds?
- How can we encourage new business in our area?

(a)

(b)

(c)

(d)

Figure 3.3 Geography, art, mathematics and more – the CraftEd project at St Joseph's Boys' National School (a, b, c, d) finding patterns in the locality

CASE STUDY 3.2 CraftEd Project: 9–10 year olds, St Joseph's Boys' National School

Third class boys at St Joseph's took part in the 'CraftEd' project, with the theme 'locality'. Along with their teacher, they decided to do the project based on their own locality. Their ideas were to walk in the locality, to take photographs, to email them to the artist, to research tiles, to start sketchbooks and then to work with the craftsperson.

Patterns in the localty: The boys had an informative morning finding patterns in their locality. Using cameras, they observed the locality around the school, focusing on the streets of houses, the church and graveyard and a small park with a bandstand. The boys found many patterns in each place, and beyond, such as patterns in the water in the bay and across the bay on other buildings.

On their return to the classrooms, the boys had many positive things to say about their fieldwork, 'I noticed things that I usually just walk straight past.' and 'It was really fun and I learnt new things.' The comments from the boys once again indicate the difficulty children and adults have in segregating 'enjoyment' and 'learning'! The teacher also noted how many of the quieter boys had lots to say throughout the project.

Mapping our walk: For homework, the boys completed maps of their walk; these indicated the places the boys had seen on their way. Other activities the boys took part in after the walk included:

* researching patterns elsewhere, especially in relation to tiles;
* designing patterns, following Islamic designs;
* making a collage of the patterns found on their field trip;
* making maps of their route around the town.

The boys' work was featured online through a blog. The project shows the profound impact geographical and art activities in the locality can have on the boys' experiences at school. They described the field trip as 'exciting', 'fun' and 'interesting'; some even said they 'loved it' – powerful language when simply referring to a walk around a very familiar area.

http://stjosephscrafted.weebly.com

To answer all of these questions, data, including numerical data, is needed. Children, depending on their ages, may need to use the following types of numerical data:

* maps, images and plans;
* data they have recorded, for example scoring places in the school grounds for butterfly suitability;
* responses to questionnaires submitted to people they know;
* articles in local newspapers, national papers and online.

Case Study 3.3 shows how children used a range of such data to help them see the proposals and issues relating to transport in Dublin. The weighting shows how important each factor is – and so gives a better comparison of places. For Metro North, the 'west' route was good but simply did not have a high enough population density to warrant a light rail system. Older primary children will be able to think about and use a weighting system to help them to consider the relative importance of factors when making decisions.

Big data, big places. Generally, 'big' numerical data relates to other places in the world or to the scale of the globe itself. Through their atlases, textbooks and other resources, children will be able to find and discover many different types of data. This type of activity is most effective in context, as children are working on enquiries about particular countries or global topics, such as climate or trade. But also, how often do we leave children to look through atlases to find some random facts that appeal to them? For some of us, this is the reason we love geography (Catling *et al.*, 2010). This type of activity could also provide a need to know (Roberts, 2003; 2013a) for starting geographical enquiries. New versions of atlases can be found online through sites such as Worldmapper and Gapminder. These are really for second level students but are fascinating for primary children too. The work of Hans Rosling (2015) helps make sense of what the world is really like through data, encouraging us to see why the world is not as bad as we may think, and answering questions such as:

- Will saving poor children lead to over population?
- What was the greatest invention of the industrial revolution?

His site is excellent for teachers to use in their own research about global issues and places.

Enormous data, enormous places. In Ireland, space is part of the geography curriculum, and so provides the best opportunity to get thinking about enormous numbers.

Table 3.3 Sample resources: decision-making grids – junior classes and senior classes

Where would a butterfly like to live?			
Sunny	✓	✓	✓
Warm	✗	✓	✗
Shelters	✓	✗	✓
Flowers	✓	✓	✗
Quiet	✓	✗	✗
Add up	4	3	2

Where should Metro North go?

Positive factors	Weighting*	Central route		West route		East route	
High population density	10	10	100	5	50	7	70
Room for it to be built	8	5	40	9	72	7	56
Near education places	8	9	72	7	56	5	40
Minimum tunnelling	7	4	28	8	56	7	49
Passes housing estates	9	10	90	7	63	6	54
Links transport hubs	9	9	81	8	72	8	72
Links tourist attractions	4	9	36	5	20	7	28
Links with the airport	10	9	90	9	90	9	90
TOTAL	–	65	537	58	479	56	459

Even in our own Solar System, the distances are very difficult to comprehend. Research suggests that children have a lot of questions about space (Scoffham, 2013), and using the wealth of images and films on space is an excellent way to begin to answer some of their questions. Getting outside is essential to help children understand the real scale of the universe. Using pictures of planets and asking children to stand where they think the planets should be relative to each other is great fun. Then giving the children scaled images of

CASE STUDY 3.3 Does Dublin need a new Metro? 10–12 year olds, St Patrick's Boys' National School

Examining a local issue incorporates many aspects of geography as well as enhancing children's language and mathematical abilities. By drawing on local issues, the children are also interacting with local people and places in a meaningful way. Over the past 15 years, the Luas, a light rail system has been built in south Dublin. There have also been plans for Metro North and more recently Luas Cross City. The boys had a particular interest in the proposed Metro as the proposed route passes many of their personal places in the north of the city: homes, schools, GAA, football clubs and so on.

Asking enquiry questions and using enquiry approaches, they used photographs to devise questions they would like to ask about the Metro (as shown in Figure 3.4):

- How much money will it cost?
- Where will it go?
- How much will a ticket be?
- How can Ireland afford this when we owe €80bn?

Decison-making. Where will it go? The boys then proceeded to think about which route was best, including the decision-making grid shown in Figure 3.3. This brought together so many ideas from this chapter as boys were using their spatial, language and mathematical skills! They had to use the map of proposed routes to decide which route would be 'best'. They began by considering the following question – 'What would a new rail system need?' and used this to develop criteria to assist them in the decision-making process. Great discussions then took place, some of which are captured in the list below:

- locations: of stops, relative to their homes, of other types of stops, of familiar and unfamiliar places, etc.;
- distances: of routes, of what was underground/over ground, between stops, etc.;
- directions: the routes took, from their homes to the stops, etc.;
- densities: of people, buildings, transport, etc.;
- environmental issues: noise during construction, after construction, of existing transport, etc.

The full range of activities that the boys took part in are described in Chapter 6 as a model for looking at local issues in primary geography.

Figure 3.4 Mathematics and geography through local issues: (a) discussion about routes, (b, c) deciding on routes and (d) presenting arguments

the planets and getting them to stand where they really should be is informative! To do this properly, you will need 450 metres between the first and last child or planet – so it's best done in your local park or neighbouring fields to the school, unless your school grounds are large enough. Many children, and most adults, cannot actually comprehend numbers when it comes to space but they can learn a lot from trying!

Using data for a purpose in geography. After collecting data, children need to do something with it. In mathematics, this is termed data handling. In geography, this is about transforming information, which can be assessed in a number of ways, as can be seen in Figure 7.4. Even if we focus only on data handling, the opportunities for integrating and enhancing geography and mathematics are multiple and varied. All of these suggested activities should sit within appropriate geography topics, but can be explicitly mathematical:

Sorting and classifying data. One criterion, for example:

- What do leaves look like? Sorting leaves (green/not green).
- Where will we put our toys? Sorting toys into drawers in the classroom.

(a)   (b)

(c)   (d)

Figure 3.5 Thinking about enormous numbers: making the solar system at Drumcondra National School (a) children's initial ideas about the proportional size (b, c, d) walking the proportional distances of the solar system.

Two or more criteria, for example:

- Where will we play today? Choosing a place to play in the school – grass, garden, tarmac, trees, etc.
- Where is my favourite place? Talking and deciding on favourite places in the locality – park, river, woods, street, etc.
- How can we sort rocks? Playing with rocks and deciding how to sort them in different ways.

Children can also make supported decisions about how to set/solve problems, and represent and interpret data within geographical enquiries:

Representing data

- *Concrete objects*: children can sort toys into most favourites and least favourites then display what they have found out on shelves in the room.
- *Simple charts*: children can devise picture charts of holiday places, pets and so on.
- *Varied charts*: children can use Microsoft Excel or any other data handling package to make graphs of people's jobs, holiday places, soap opera places and so on.

Interpreting data

- *Selecting ways to present data*: children can easily make decisions about a very large number of graphs using computers to make graphs, and choose which represents their data best (see Chapter 4 for an example of this).
- *Interpreting charts, tables and graphs*: interpreting climate graphs from different places, using 'living graphs'.

Problems and data

- *To set problems*: children can use transport statistics from their own surveys, or those of others (such as the Census), to generate ideas for enquiry questions.
- *To solve problems*: children can use timetables of rubbish collections to work out the best times to go on a field trip.
- *To critically review data*: compare points of view, use newspapers reports, use the GapMinder website, etc.

Geography provides children with opportunities to question and critique data. Children can also be prompted to ask 'Who put these figures together?' and consider data from a critical view. The enquiry framework, as described in Chapter 2, ensures the opportunities for developing the many types of literacies described above. The following chapters outline theories and examples of these types of learning experiences grouped under broad themes of school, locality, places and global citizenship.

Spatial literacies and primary geography

Spatial literacy is the ability to be aware of oneself in space (National Research Council, 2006). It is an organised knowledge of objects in relation to oneself in space. Spatial awareness also involves understanding the relationship of these objects when there is a change of position.

Children and mapping – ideas, research and debates. As spatial awareness develops, the child will learn the concepts of direction, distance and location, as outlined in Table 3.4 and mapped out in Appendix 2. In this section, some of the arguments about spatial awareness and mapping in children are outlined before considering how to enhance children's abilities in these areas in primary geography.

Over the years, there has been much debate about the development of children's spatial awareness and mapping abilities, as well as their misconceptions with maps (Wiegand, 2006). The primary argument has been about children's ability to understand maps – is it natural and innate or learned. Blaut spent much of his working life arguing that mapping is innate and that the human mind supports map acquisition (Blaut, 1991; Blaut *et al.*, 2003). Blaut and colleagues used evidence from children's maps across cultures to support this argument, stating (1971, p. 393):

> Cross-cultural and developmental research on the untaught mapping abilities of children aged five through ten suggests that mapping behaviour is a normal and important process in human development, and that map learning begins long before the child encounters formal geography and cartography.

Table 3.4 Dimensions of spatial literacies: space, representation and reasoning

Space

Nature of spaces	Playing with blocks and mapping what is created. Making and using 2D and 3D maps and comparing them.
Calculating distance	Working out varied distances, e.g. across the school playground, from one town to another, etc.
Coordinate systems	Playing games with grids, such as snakes and ladders. Using the coordinate system on small-scale (OS/OSI) maps.

Representation

Relationships among views	Using photographs taken from different angles. Looking at places from different angles. Using aerial photographs and maps together. Using online maps with paper maps. Overlaying one map to another to investigate patterns.
Effect of projections	Critically comparing map projections. Deciding on the most appropriate map projection.
Principles of graphic design	Critically examining made and used maps: legibility, contrast, colour, keys and legends, etc.

Reasoning

Ways of thinking about distances	Working out the quickest ways around the school. Working out different distances using online maps.
Ability to extrapolate and interpolate	Working out whether a photograph was taken from high or low. Working out which slope is steeper on two parts of a map.
Making decisions	Deciding where is the best place for a picnic bench. Deciding on a route for a new transport link.

Roger Downs and colleagues drew on Piagetian theory to argue that mapping is a gradual, learned process (Downs and Stea, 1977; Downs *et al.*, 1988). As they state:

> Map understanding indeed begins early but it progresses through a complex and difficult sequence of developments that are simply not well understood at present. We argue for early beginnings but not early mastery of mapping.
>
> (Liben and Downs, 1997, p. 159)

Within this area of research are findings that are very important for geography lessons. First, it is evident that teaching makes a difference to children's spatial capabilities. For example, Catling found after a number of teaching activities, such as fieldwork, use of local maps and study of information from the local planning office, young people's maps of their local area improved (Catling, 1998). Catling concluded that it is 'vital to plan a range of active experiences so that local studies can develop young people's knowledge of local features, understanding of geographical ideas and the use of appropriate skills such as fieldwork and map work' (Catling, 1998, p,11). In Ireland, it was rare that children would make maps of any type, with more of an emphasis on learning of published maps (Pike, 2006). However, in recent years, there is evidence of a change in this pattern, and more balance between making and using maps is evident in classrooms (Pike, 2012), as can be seen by the range of maps in Figure 3.6. Furthermore, research with young primary children has found that the specific teaching of mapping has a positive impact on young people's spatial capabilities (Walsh, 2006; O'Neill, 2010).

Another consistent finding relating to spatial capabilities is that the more opportunities children have for free play in local environments, the more spatial knowledge they will have of that area (Hart, 1979; Matthews, 1987). In drawing together research evidence on young people's mapping, Matthews concludes that spatial knowledge develops from the well-known and develops unevenly over space, as a mosaic of places become familiar and is pieced together in the young person's mind. Such knowledge will range widely within any group of young people: 'within any group, there will be wide ranges of achievement in map-making, local knowledge, spatial awareness and the use of map conventions' (Matthews, 1992). Despite the importance of these findings, Catling and Matthews remain in a minority in linking children's experiences, attitudes and knowledge of local environments. Particularly relevant would be further examination of the influence of school and home on the development of these skills. Perhaps due to such debates over mapping, some believe that geography has not contributed as much as it could to the understanding of childhood experiences (Matthews and Limb, 1999; Aitken, 2001).

When children are involved in the types of activity described throughout this book, it is possible that the geographical element of what they do can be 'lost'. We need to remember that it is the spatial and graphicacy elements of lessons that make them geographical! In learning to think geographically, children need to use their graphicacy skills.

Enabling children to become more spatial. When these types of learning activity are designed for and with children, they will become spatially able. Children that are spatially able can (NRC, 2006):

- think spatially – knowing where, when, how and why to think spatially;
- practice spatial thinking in an informed way – having a broad and deep knowledge of spatial concepts and representations, the ability to use a variety of spatial ways of working and spatial capabilities for using spatial tools and technologies; and
- adopt a critical stance to spatial thinking – being able to evaluate the quality of spatial data; using spatial data to construct, articulate and reason a point of view in helping to answer enquiry questions.

To ensure children can think spatially, some steps can be taken in creating learning opportunities.

Making map-rich environments. There is no doubt that through creating map-rich learning environments, teachers can help children become spatially able. Teachers and children can source a wide variety of maps to use within their geographical enquiries and to display, including:

- *Picture maps*: maps and models made by children or maps in picture books are a great source of early maps for younger children.
- *Thematic maps*: these can include picture type maps such as tourist maps, maps from theme parks, for example, a map of Alton Towers, maps of Dublin and so on.
- *Street maps and road atlases*: A-Z maps, paper street maps, road atlases and GPS systems are all useful for local area and distant localities.

CASE STUDY 3.4 Using spatial and media literacies to develop global awareness and language: 11–12 year olds, St Patrick's Boys' National School

Some children were involved in a project for children with exceptional ability and were given time out of class to work with different teachers and visitors. In geography, the boys took part in a small project on the media.

Reporting the news. The boys started by looking through newspapers for anything that caught their eye. This process can be very informative for children as they then need to sort a lot of information such as adverts, opinion pieces and news stories. While the boys all had high reading ages, they still needed to work at their own pace and level: some will read articles, others will focus on headlines. At all ages, some children will need support from teachers for this type of activity.

Mapping the news. The boys recorded events on stickers and placed these on a globe and map. Without much prompting, the boys began to notice features and patterns in the news:

- There's a lot going on in Europe.
- Ebola is only in a few countries.
- There's 'nothing' in South America!

The boys then noted where the gaps were in the world map and set off to find out what was happening in these places. Teachers often use clips from the news or encourage classes to bring in papers for the topics they do. These are especially helpful when looking at geographical events; this is discussed further in Chapter 7. It is important to leave space in long-term planning to allow for news media and what is reported to be considered and critiqued. In our global world, children are constantly exposed to the news; as teachers, we can help them make sense of what is going on and understand why. We can also help them to move beyond those places that are represented in the headlines.

www.saintpats.ie

- *Ordnance Survey maps*: in Ireland, these include road maps, maps of Ireland in Irish, 1:50 000, 1: 25 000 and street maps, as well as custom maps centred on schools.
- *Plans from planning and architects' offices*: planning offices generally charge the public for these, but as a teacher you may be able to get them free! Online versions are always free. Online map databases from planning offices are a useful source of data for future change in a locality.
- *National and continental wall maps*: a range of maps are available in shops and online. A range of 'unexpected' maps, such as Pacific Centred maps can also be sourced online.

- *Globes and world maps*: all classrooms should have globes. Globes are very important in early years and infant classrooms to help children gain the concept of the earth as a sphere.
- *Historical maps, paper, online or on postcards*: many websites have historical maps. Many of these are posted on social media pages; remember to note copyright/source.
- *Public transport maps*: these are numerous and free and can be used for specific topics and make a great display.
- *Shipping charts*: shipping charts make for wonderful artwork, but are also useful for any work on the locality and coasts. Open Sea map offers a free online version: http://map.openseamap.org
- *Maps in newspapers, infographics and websites*: newspapers are one of the best sources of information for older classes. Maps from new sites and newspapers are a good source to generate ideas for enquiries. Children can create their own infographics: https://infogr.am
- *Maps in computer games and websites*: through the games they play online, children are very familiar with 3D maps and models, especially through simulation games such as Minecraft.

Enabling map rich experiences. Children will develop their spatial abilities through having the following types of incidental or planned spatial experiences:

- *Discussing locations*: leaving a toy under a desk and getting children to use locational language to discuss where it is. If children do this in smaller groups then there is more opportunity for them all to talk.
- *Using comparative terms*: mentioning which people are closer and who is further away from a classroom, such as: the lollipop man, Mr Bryne, is further away from us than Ms Kelly in the school office.
- *Talking about relationships*: showing a child that a book is under a chair or that a globe is on top of the shelf (if this is that case, you should move the globe so the children can look at it!).
- *Measuring distances*: a homework to find out how many paces it takes to walk the length or width of the back garden.
- *Giving directions*: asking a child to turn left out of the classroom. Displaying and using the points of the compass in conversations in the classroom.
- *Using new technologies and applications*: creating or finding GeoCaches (a worldwide treasure hunt) in the locality, using technology for orienteering.

These types of activities set the foundations for more complex spatial activities, the progression through which is shown in Appendix 2. Owens depicts the relative breadth and depth of experiences very well in Figure 3.6. The graph shows how some spatial information is more complex than others, and that children need a range of experiences with a range of maps and aerial photographs along with compasses, computer applications and other tools to help interpret maps. The graph also asks us to consider a wide range of maps, such as fantasy maps and story maps that are found in every classroom. During their time in primary school, children will become increasingly independent in their spatial activity. The suggested breakdown for using and making maps is outlined in Appendix 2. Often younger children have a huge interest in any type of map, and should

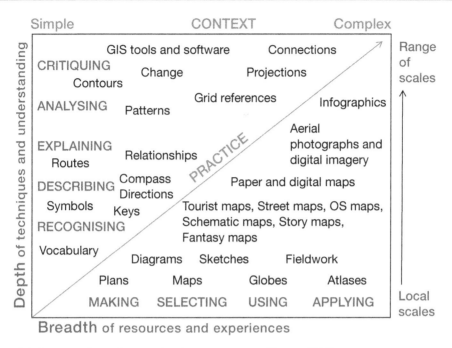

Figure 3.6 Degrees of complexity and scales in using maps (Owens, 2015)

be given opportunities to play with and use them. Overall, throughout primary education, children's spatial awareness develops through their use of the environment and their ability to make and use all sorts of maps. All of these activities will also contribute enormously to children's language and mathematical abilities.

Conclusions

Geography is a subject that makes a significant contribution to children's learning in many dimensions. This chapter has explored the main types of literacies used in geography lessons. However, there are other forms of literacy explored through the chapters of this book.

Reflection and action

- List all the types of literacies children can develop in primary geography. How can you enhance these in your teaching?
- What is the balance of making and using maps in your school? How can it be made more balanced?
- How literacy rich is your classroom and school? Are the types of literacy described in this chapter used, in context for children?

- Specifically for younger children:

    - Can they use a map or plan of the school and begin to make sense of it?
    - Is there a map of the locality of the school, with associated photographs in the school or classroom?
    - Can the children use and see globes to help them 'picture' the world? Can they examine the globe freely in their own way and time – or is it 'out of reach'?

Further resources

Language

Dolan, A. (2013) *You, Me and Diversity*. London: Institute of Education Press.
Martin, F. and Owens, P. (2008) *Caring for our World: ESD for 4–8 year olds*. Sheffield: Geographical Association.
Ruane, B., Kavanagh, A.M., Waldron, F., Dillon, S., Maunsell, C. and Prunty, A. (2010) *Young Pupils' Engagement With Issues of Global Justice*. Dublin: Centre for Human Rights and Citizenship Education, SPD and Trócaire.

Michael Rosen blogs and writes articles which critic policy and practice in education, but also suggest alternatives! www.michaelrosen.co.uk

Write to Read is a school- and community-based professional development model to enable teachers and community educators to deliver high quality literacy programmes for children. It adopts an evidence-based, holistic approach to literacy issues to meet the literacy needs of children in order to build their motivation, engagement, agency, creativity and higher-order thinking skills. The programme places great importance on the need to develop children's literacy skills in context, using other subjects as a way into reading and writing in different ways. www.writetoread.ie.

A selection of publishers with many fiction books on geographical themes:

Random House: www.randomhousekids.com
Walker Books: www.walker.co.uk

Mapping

Prunty, J. And Clarke, H.B. (2011) *Reading the Maps: A Guide to the Irish Historic Towns Atlas*. Dublin: Royal Irish Academy.
   This book will help any reader understand the development of settlements over time, and is essential reading for any teacher of geography or history in Ireland.
Wiegand, P. (2006) *Learning and Teaching with Maps*. London: Routledge.
   Patrick Wiegand's writing, and specifically this book, inform every aspect of using and making maps with children.

There are many online sites with maps and teaching resources. These are the key ones, all of which are worth following on social media.

Dublin Dashboard: www.dublindashboard.ie

Gapminder: www.gapminder.org

GeoCaching: www.geocaching.com

Ordnance Survey Ireland: www.osi.ie

Ordnance Survey UK: www.ordnancesurvey.co.uk

Scoilnet Maps: http://maps.scoilnet.ie

Stanfords: www.stanfords.co.uk

Worldmapper: www.worldmapper.org

National Geographic: online atlas/globe: http://maps.nationalgeographic.com/map-machine

Peter's projection map of the world: www.developmenteducation.ie/media/documents/Trocaire_Peters_World_Maps.pdf

Barbara Petchenik Children Map Drawing Competition: bi-annual mapping competition is run http://icaci.org/petchenik/

Wikipedia has a very visual outline of different map projections and how they are created: http://en.wikipedia.org/wiki/Map_projection

Arts and imagination

CraftEd: the programme gives primary school children and teachers an exciting opportunity to explore their creativity and learn new skills by working with professional craftspeople: www.learncraftdesign.com/learn/crafted.

Chapter 4

Fabulous geography – avoiding dull learning in geography

> Geography is maps countries rivers lakes and landscapes it's a wide variety and it's my favourite subject so far. It is also drawing maps landscapes etc. Going on fieldtrips is geography as well as five different subjects.
>
> Girl, age 12

This chapter aims to help teachers make geography interesting for all children, through enquiry frameworks and through connecting children's learning to their experiences.

The chapter is based on the following key thoughts:

- Geography is a fascinating subject that helps children understand essential concepts and perspectives about people and places.
- Involving children in decisions about what and how geography is taught is the key to making the subject engaging and challenging for them.
- Involving children in the learning process can increase their well-being in school.
- Teachers determine the level of children's engagement in decison-making about their geographical learning.

This chapter outlines:

- attitudes to geography of children and teachers;
- ways to make geography interesting and engaging; and
- examples of potentially boring topics in geography, and how they can be made engaging.

Views of geography

Geography is a common curricular subject, and so is familiar to the general public – adults and children. Views of geography can be extreme; people tend to love it or hate it. In fact, research reveals a range of views when children or adults are asked about geography (Gerber, 2001; Waldron *et al.*, 2008; Kitchen, 2013). Some readers of this book may be geography 'lovers' or 'haters'. Whatever your views, it is important to remember that the children you teach will also have differing views. Gerber carried out a substantial study with members of various professional groups and found participants in the study were very positive about the role of geography. Both the perception of and reason for studying geography varied between groups (Gerber, 2001). Generally, like all other school subjects, whether people like the subject or not depends largely on their experiences of it at school.

Children's views

Children in primary school have a wide range of opinions about geography, and this seems to be the case wherever the questions are asked. Research into geography in Irish primary schools revealed a somewhat limited perception of the subject on the part of teachers and children. Table 4.1 draws on a 2003 research project in which 200 children were asked 'What is geography?' (Pike, 2006). In 2013, this was repeated along with the questions, 'What do you do in geography?' and 'What do you think of geography?'. In 2003, the children's responses revealed a content driven subject, predominantly textbook-led, which drew on a small range of methodologies. However, when this survey was repeated ten years later, there was evidence of change in children's experiences, exemplified in Figure 4.1 (Pike, 2013b). Rote learning in geography was evident in the children's definitions in 2003 but not in 2013. In 2003, not one child mentioned fieldwork and only four mentioned any type of project work, with two of those referring to the lack of such work. In 2013, children referred to their locality and the wider world, and specifically to fieldwork experiences. These two features indicate a change in geography in line with the curriculum changes. Overall by 2013, the experiences of children appeared to be much more diverse, reflecting the implementation of the new 1999 curriculum (DES/NCCA, 1999a). In some classrooms, it appeared geography was

Table 4.1 Children's attitudes to geography

–   Geography is a lesson of nature like all around us. It is mostly about Ireland like I know off by heart there are 32 counties. Here are some things that we learn about in geography: Countries, rivers, capitals, mountains, counties, what type of weather there is like mild, moist, hot, cold. In my class, our teacher sometimes gives us a little test where we have to mark in things like countries, counties, capitals and Islands. The questions sometimes can be very hard or very easy. <div align="right">Girl, fifth class, urban girls' school, 2003</div>
–   Geography is a subject we do it in school and the name of it is World Wise 3. When we do geography we find out about the ups and downs of maps. <div align="right">Boy, fifth class, urban boys' school, 2003</div>
–   Geography is thinking about the world and thinking about the people in it. And about how we followed the journey of an avocado from South America to Ireland and then we made Guacamole with it! It's about doing projects on Italy and how the mountains formed. <div align="right">Girl, fifth class, mixed urban DEIS school, 2012</div>
–   Geography is a subject that you learn about countries and places and stuff like that. We do projects on the countries. We learn loads about them. We learn about their cultures, food, dances and cultures. <div align="right">Girl, fifth class, large urban all girls' school, 2012</div>

Source: Pike, 2006, 2012.

(a)   (b)

(c)   (d)

Figure 4.1 Making imaginative maps inspires children to be geographers (a) community models, (b) maps of the locality (c) imaginary maps inspired by fieldwork and (d) maps from stories

more in alignment with this enquiry-based curriculum than those sampled in 2003. In both studies, a wide range of practices in terms of teaching and learning were evident from the teachers.

In the research, the strongest finding from the children's responses was that teachers and the activities they facilitate in the classroom were the most important factors influencing children's attitudes to geography. And so, it appears there is much to celebrate in the changes in primary geography in the past ten years in some Irish classrooms. In these classrooms, children were most positive about geography; they liked it and even referred to 'loving' it! In other classrooms, children's experiences were more limited, but overall, it appeared geography had become a more interesting subject for children over the ten years. Such findings are common; Norman and Harrison found although children had rather straightforward concepts of geography, they were very clear on the types of activity they liked in geography, namely active, collaborative lessons rather than passive activity (2004). Based on her work with second level children in England, Kitchen (2013) has summarised the influences on children's ideas of geography (Figure 4.2). Her findings reveal the range of influences on children's views as well as their differing lived experiences in classrooms.

Despite these findings, it should be noted that all the studies of children's learning in and opinions of geography have found that these children express a range of views and experiences, even within the same classroom. For example, I found that children in the

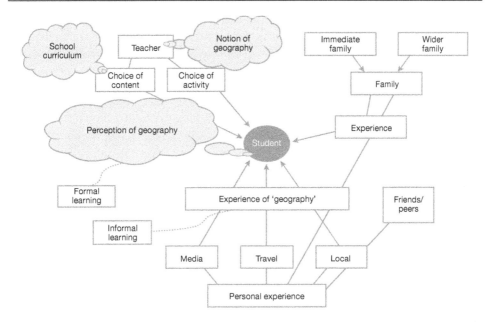

Figure 4.2 The many influences on children and their view of geography (Kitchen, 2013)

same class had varied opinions of geography, even when they had been in the same class all the way through primary school (Pike, 2006; 2012). I also found that children offered different accounts of what they did in geography too.

Teachers' views

Within the teaching profession new and established, teachers feel geography is an important subject for children to study. In an all-Ireland longitudinal study of the 2004–2008 cohort of Bachelor of Education students, it was found that student teachers who liked geography believed it was an important subject for primary children to learn. Even those who reported hating geography still thought it was an important subject for children to learn (Waldron *et al.*, 2009). The student teachers were idealistic and creative in their ideas on how geography should be taught (Waldron *et al.*, 2009). The majority of ITE students thought geography was an important subject for children to learn, and felt confident to teach it. Student teachers who participated in the study reported a variety of experiences of geography at primary and second level. They really valued any form of independent work, as well as fieldwork. There were particular aspects of content that were enjoyed, such as learning about places and people in different countries. Unfortunately, experiences of learning by rote and learning large amounts of content was also evident (Waldron *et al.*, 2009). The dominance of practices such as the rote learning of facts and place names seems particularly characteristic of geography classrooms in the Republic of Ireland. The research found little evidence of similar practices in Northern Ireland (*Waldron et al.*, 2009), and Catling's work on children's ideas of geography in English schools found no mention of such activities (2002, p. 363). Almost one in ten students who participated in the Becoming a Teacher study commented on the negative impact of teacher characteristics on their learning, interest and motivation. Student teachers' negative experiences of their own teachers included comments such as: 'boring', 'uninterested', 'unenthusiastic', 'awful', 'bad', 'poor' and 'terrible' (Waldron *et al.*, 2009, p. 52):

> ... text books ancient, dull, irrelevant, classes long with lots of writing/copying from the board in silence. Never remember learning anything interesting e.g. about weather/counties – all about definitions.

> Possibly the worst teacher I ever had for Leaving Certificate. His level of enthusiasm, interest and drive was abysmal; he really didn't inspire us to work hard or study.

As is evident from the quotes above, it is important that student teachers need time to develop positive ideas about the subject, before they teach it. Even research with geography teacher educators has found that their interest in geography was prompted by a range of very different experiences (Greenwood, 2010). Overall it seems, the way content is presented to children needs to be carefully considered by teachers. However, while content is important, it is not enough to focus on that alone. As Hopwood argues (2011, p. 40):

> We must face up to the fact that conceptions of geography education cannot be straightforwardly (re)shaped by simply changing what is taught or how. Young people lie at the heart of geography's future and must play a role in shaping it.

The boys in St Joseph's Boys' National School had very positive views on the subject, and were particularly positive about their annual Young Geographer Competition (Figure 4.3):

> It was cool to see what other people found out about and it was fun and interesting.

> I loved looking up the pictures on the computer. I loved writing out the information.

> I did the project because I enjoy a good challenge that gets me to learn and do a lot of research on the subject.

The competition runs each year, and the boys are very enthusiastic about the project and the learning experiences associated with it. Each year, I note how the experiences of researching, analysing and presenting their findings positively influences the children's learning and confidence. Children in St James' National School had quite definite views on geography too, as one child said:

> I like it because we go to the Fenor Bog and we go down the village. I don't like doing tests about soils. I like it when we do about countries and we did about China. Once we got to cook curry. And when we do projects. We rubbed rocks and held it.

So, even the most potentially boring topic can seem really interesting when teachers make the topic relevant to the children and put the children at the centre of the learning

Figure 4.3 The Young Geographer Competition, St Joseph's Boys' National School (a, c) presenting work, (b) a completed project and (d) an awards day.

CASE STUDY 4.1 What jobs do people do in our area? 8–12 year olds, St James' National School

People and work is a topic that can be taught in a number of ways. It can be made very relevant to children's lives, as well as expanding their understanding of work, trade and businesses, as suggested in the curriculum (1999b, pp. 90–1):

> Interviewing people who live or work in the area: Learning about the lives, concerns and attitudes of the people who live and work in a place an important aspect of exploring the area . . . interviews, particularly if they include visits to the work-place, can significantly enhance the child's understanding of the activities and conditions involved in particular occupations.

However, sometimes the vocabulary can be off-putting and terms such as 'location' and 'industry' can make it appear dull rather than exciting. In St James', this was a topic that the children had not studied before; however, they had strong knowledge about businesses, through family connections, and some families had experienced unemployment.

The children had excellent ideas on how to learn about people and work from the outset. Some of those ideas were:

- deciding how to attract businesses to their area;
- finding out about products made in their area;
- visiting a factory and finding out how things are made; and
- planning a new business for the area and deciding where it could go.

Activities were then designed around these questions, including:

Generating ideas/Brainstorming a product. To generate ideas about the topic, the children put their favourite item in the centre of a page. They then brainstormed all the products that go into that item. As can be seen from Figure 4.7, this activity encourages children to consider the huge range of products and processes involved in bringing their favourite item into their possession.

This activity works well with both very young children and older children! The teacher can use the following prompt to get children to think about each component: 'Do you think it grows or does it come from the ground?'. Children are amazed that plastic comes from oil, but others already know it – so the children are constantly learning from each other. It is very worthwhile to use one of the numerous videos on YouTube showing how products are made, as oil to plastic is rather abstract for some children to 'picture'.

Asking questions (see Chapter 2 for more examples). Children asked a range of questions; these were written on scraps of paper and then grouped. From each group of questions, the larger questions emerged. This sort of activity is one of the best ways to use children's questions effectively. The main questions included:

- What types of jobs do people we know do? – 18 questions
- What jobs earn the most and least money? – 5 questions
- What jobs could we do without? – 6 questions
- What happens in a factory? – 15 questions
- Random questions – 6 questions

Process of making products. This can be carried out creatively by using the children's ideas, and the children's construction of the stages of production must be at the centre of the activity. This transforms the activity from being pretty dull to a truly child-centred process. For example, the children in St James' National School (Figure 4.4) carried out the following:

- They listed different jobs involved in making a product on scraps of paper (Figure 4.4a).
- They grouped these in all sorts of ways: indoor/outdoor, well paid/not paid and so on. When carrying out this activity, children may also come up with jobs for different genders, different ages and so on. It is important that the images and resources we use for subsequent activities challenge any stereotypes that emerge.

- They were encouraged to group the jobs into 'making things' and 'providing a service', the teacher pulled out slips of paper with 'farming' and 'fishing' and asked, 'What is special about these ones?'. The children noted these jobs involve 'taking resources' from the earth, as one girl said, 'Those people all take things from the earth!'
- They were then told the names for the first category, 'primary', they guessed the second, 'secondary' and were told the third, 'tertiary' and the fourth 'quaternary'.

Interviews with workers. Children interviewed family and friends to find out about their jobs; this was a homework and the children were given over a week to do it. Drawing on people in the locality, children can interview family and friends about the work they have done or currently do; their questions were: What is the occupation? What did/do you do in your occupation? What did/do you like about it? What qualifications or experience did you need to get the job?

Presentations on occupations. Children presented their findings as a single slide on PowerPoint. They had not used this package before, and really enjoyed experimenting with their work. As one child said: 'I've always seen that orange 'P' and even knew it was so exciting!' The posters were printed, with one copy being displayed in the classroom, and another being presented back to the friend or family interviewed.

Survey of occupations. Children carried out a survey of the whole school to find out what type of jobs emerged across the school. The interview data was to be shared among the children. The children then used Microsoft Excel to make graphs and dropped these into Word to make simple information pages.

Making chocolate. The children watched a video about making chocolate. Then, on a second viewing, they made notes of different activities on scraps of paper. These were then sorted into inputs, outputs and processes and then made up into the annotated diagrams, one of which is shown in Figure 4.7d.

Visit to a factory. Nemeton, a local TV company, agreed that the children could visit. The children had a wonderful morning being shown around, and finding out about the process of making a programme for broadcast.

The children were very positive about all the work they did during this topic both in relation to their learning and how they learned, as their comments indicate:

I liked it when we made up the questions and tried to find the answers.

I was surprised about the PowerPoint because you could do so much with it.

It was really interesting when we looked at the aerial photograph.

I liked making my graphs and showing how many people work in primary, secondary and tertiary.

My favourite part was visiting the TV company, Nemeton.

Figure 4.4 An enquiry about people and work: what jobs do people do in our area? (a) generating ideas, (b) enhancing spatial skills, (c) collecting data and (d) consolidating learning through fieldwork to a local television company, Nemeton TV

process. We also need to think how we can tie children's learning to their everyday experiences, while at the same time, expanding their horizons. This may seem like a tall order but the case studies in this chapter show how those considerations can transform potentially boring topics into exciting ones.

Changing geography – some considerations for action

Changes in curriculum and classroom practice, as exemplified in Chapter 1, give an insight to how geography has been viewed as a school subject; this in turn goes some way to explain the experiences of geography for some of those entering teacher education. In Ireland, there has been a tradition of primary children being expected to know names and locations of towns, cities and counties in their country, as well as key physical features. This is a significant factor in some teachers not liking geography – as a learner or teacher. Interestingly, rote learning has never been part of the curriculum (DES, 1971; DES/NCCA, 1999b), but stems from the 'capes and bays' and 'payment by results' requirements of schools in general as outlined in Chapter 1. This approach to geography really does need to change; far too much time is spent learning material that is not remembered as it does not make sense or have a context for children. There are four considerations teachers can make to ensure geography is never boring. These considerations simply involve thinking about learning rather than teaching. They are shown in the following sections.

Linking children's lives and their geographical experiences

First, children are involved in numerous interests and hobbies, such as sports, maintaining friendships, playing computer games, travel and community activity, as well as simply 'hanging out' with their friends. These experiences and their experiences in geography lessons should be linked. Children's lives are inherently geographical (Catling, 2003; Martin, 2008, Pike, 2011), as they have a wealth of experiences every day with people and places. These experiences have a positive impact on many aspects of the quality of children's present lives (Greene and Hogan, 2005) and their learning (Catling, 2003). Examples include their spatial skills (Wiegand, 2006) and social skills (Chawla, 2002), as well as their development as citizens (Catling, 2003; Valentine, 2000), their agency and action (Punch, 2000; Christensen and O'Brien, 2003; Olwig and Gulløv, 2004; Pike, 2010) and their identity formation (Matthews *et al.*, 2000; Valentine, 2000). There is also an ongoing debate about the actions of children in and out of school (Valentine, 1996; O'Keeffe and O'Beirne, 2015). While some argue we should return to the 'good old days' where children did as they were told, others argue children's lives have improved beyond recognition. The reality is more complex, as Kirchberg (2000) summarises; children and young people have changed, not necessarily for the better or worse, just changed. As outlined in Table 4.2, children's personalities are more open, confident and independent. Children's role in decison-making in schools and classrooms is also more evident. The case studies of classrooms in this and other chapters exemplify how this change in children is a huge benefit in geography lessons as children are more able to engage with the world around them.

These changes in young people mean their agency in making decisions can be harnessed in teaching and learning geography (Catling, 2003; Pike 2011; Roberts, 2013b). When teaching geography, the changing characteristics of learners, as outlined

Table 4.2 Ambivalences in children and young people's characteristics

more self-confident	more egotistical
more independent	more self-willed
more open	more reserved
more experienced	more overtaxed
more performance-oriented	more fixed on marks
more individualistic	more heterogeneous
more lively	more restless
more grown-up	less idealistic
more well-informed	more opinionated
more spontaneous	more emotional
more open-minded	more distractible

Source: Kirchberg, 2000, p. 6.

above, can be drawn on to enrich the subject and learning experiences. Geography is a subject full of debate, opinion and controversies, ideally placed to engage children.

Attempting to make such topics interesting and relevant for children is nothing new; since the 1970s, the Geographical Association and others were concerned with Economic and Industrial awareness, and there were curriculum developed projects promoting innovative ways to teach the topic (e.g. Corney, 1985).

CASE STUDY 4.2 An enquiry on rocks and soils: why are rocks important to us? 10–12 year olds, Newtown National School

Rocks and soils are another topic that can be boring. However, it can also be one of the best topics for using the children's local environment. When considered like this, the topic changes in nature. Newtown National School is a small school in rural Waterford. The school continually draws on local and global links to enhance children's learning. Through the use of technology, especially using social media (Twitter) and online phone calls (Mystery Skype), the children's experiences are constantly widened. The school values the local area also – the children took part in a local place names project and produced an enormous display of the wealth of place name associated with their locality. Children in Newtown National School were experts of some aspects of rocks, as they lived in a beautiful area near to the Comeragh Mountains and Copper Coast. They had recently studied volcanoes, so were aware that rocks could change dramatically!

Generating ideas. To start their work on rocks, the children went outside to collect samples of rocks (see Figure 4.5a). Rather conveniently, a lorry load of gravel arrived in the middle of this activity! Within the confines of the school grounds, the children found a large variety of rocks of each of the three main types: igneous, sedimentary and metamorphic. At this stage, these terms were not used with the children (see consideration D below). Stimulus materials can have an obvious or obscure relationship to what is being studied and should enable students to connect new learning to their own experiences. The use of the rocks did this very well, especially as the children found them rather than the teachers sourcing the material. Even the adults present were surprised at the range of rocks found in the school grounds and noted that the children found far more than adults would anyway!

Starting enquiry. The children eventually brought the rocks inside and with little prompting began to sort the rocks (Figure 4.5b). Some also made impromptu rock art! The children devised criteria for how they sorted the rocks. These criteria included: feel, weight, appearance and even smell. From these categories, the children were ready to hear the names for the types of rocks, although some children knew them already. The amount of language involved in this stage of their enquiry was quite outstanding; it occurred at all types of levels as outlined in Table 4.4. All of this discussion and questioning gave rise to a revised outline scheme of work shown in Table 4.3. Arising from the children's activity, they devised questions on rocks in pairs. These were then grouped until there were two groups of children with five or six main questions each. The children were great thinkers and took control of the activity, for example by putting the main questions on yellow post-it notes!

Enquiry activities. The children carried out various activities to answer all their questions, including:

- Rock experiments (Figure 4.5c): the children researched and carried out experiments on rocks to test their properties.
- Fieldwork at Kilmacthomas Workhouse (Figure 4.5d): a local historian and comedian showed the children around the workhouse! Other adults who were present, including parents, helped the children notice features of the workhouse.
- Finding out about properties of rocks: using photographs of rocks and their uses children matched up images and found out rocks were used far more than they thought!

Within these activities there were a wide range of descriptive activities taking place, as outlined in Table 4.4.

www.snbailenua.ie

(a)

(b)

(c)

(d)

Figure 4.5 An enquiry on rocks: why are rocks important to us? (a) generating ideas, (b) sorting and asking questions, (c) collecting data in class and (d) linking learning through fieldwork

Table 4.3 Gaining and using place knowledge in geography

	Life skills	Knowledge of the world	Understanding of people and places
Gaining place knowledge in school	• Map reading and way finding in digital and paper forms. • Making maps and plans, in digital and paper forms, including 2D and 3D maps and plans. • Developing the ability to make sense of information.	• Developing an awareness and understanding of distant places and environments. • Building a framework of place knowledge. • Investigating characteristics of major rivers, mountains and cities.	• Developing an understanding of spatial relationships at a range of scales.
Using place knowledge in school and afterwards	• Observing and interpreting the environment. • Understanding and interpreting pictures of places. • Communicating findings in maps, drawings, charts and diagrams. • Discussing issues and problems with others. • Critical and creative thinking.	• Recognising how people from all over the world are linked through travel and trade. • Developing an appreciation of other peoples and cultures. • Recognising the need for a just and equitable society.	• Undertaking fieldwork, enquiries and active exploration of the locality. • Exploring landscapes, settlements and human activity. • Considering local issues, including environmental issues. • Becoming a global citizen with multi-cultural understanding.

Source: Adapted from GA, 2015a.

Enabling learning through enquiry

Throughout this book, the use of enquiry as a key learning strategy is emphasised and exemplified. Simply starting off a topic by asking children 'What would you like to know about this topic?' is both empowering and enabling. Examples of this are shown in Case Studies 4.1 and 4.2.

Ensure learning about places occurs in a context

Places, locations and names of places are essential components of geography. Any of us working as geographers will often be asked capitals and countries and be expected to know all such questions in any quiz! This 'Who wants to be a Millionaire' view of geography is part of the public perception of geography. But it is only a small part of geography. As outlined in Chapter 1, Lambert (2004) makes the distinction between geography's *vocabulary* (an apparently endless list of place-names) and its *grammar* (the concepts and theories that help us make sense of all those places). Both of these dimensions are important but work together to help children understand the world. In Ireland, the curriculum recognises the harm rote learning can do and specifically states children should learn about places in context as part of rich geographical experiences, which hints at the past ills in primary geography:

- **A sense of space**. Mere rote memorisation of the names of physical features, towns and countries contributes little to this learning process which is concerned with the development of a very distinctive geographical skill (DES/NCCA, 1999a, p. 10).
- **Human environments**. Mere rote memorisation of the names of cities, towns and countries does not enhance children's geographical understanding (DES/NCCA, 1999b, p. 13).
- **Key questions about other places**. An emphasis on enquiry, investigation and critical comparison rather than the rote acquisition of descriptions of exotic locations is recommended (DES/NCCA, 1999b, p117).

As the curriculum notes, children learn place names and locations in many ways. They often learn about places when not at school, through the news, travel or links with other places. It is this incidental learning of places that teachers can and should encourage by creating a map-rich teaching environment.

The acquisition and use of place knowledge are not mutually exclusive; children acquire knowledge and use it in different ways seamlessly. When children hear about a place or find it on a map, they then refer to other linked knowledge or ask questions in connection to that place. For this reason, I would argue it is important that place knowledge is best not taught in an isolated way. It should be flagged and celebrated for what it is, but then be used to help children develop all the skills and aptitudes outlined in Figure 4.1 above. The use of maps and plans is discussed in every chapter of this book, but particularly in relation to topical geography (Chapter 7) and places (Chapter 8).

Making geography more challenging

From the case studies in this chapter, it is evident that the study of rocks and soils, earthquakes and countries can all be taught in a way to make them interesting! Using Bloom's taxonomy of education objectives can be useful here (see Table 4.4) – not because it shows a level of thinking that should develop as children get older but because it shows how children, of all ages, are capable of differing types of thinking in geography. For example, 5 and 6 year olds in Our Lady of Victories School were able to apply what they had learnt about polar exploration, specifically about Tom Crean, into making cups of instant hot chocolate – with no milk! The children had discovered that explorers have to use items similar to convenience foods and were applying that knowledge to their activity. This is an example of how all children can analyse information and apply their knowledge to different situations, so Bloom is a useful tool for helping us to consider the value of types of thinking in geography. The work carried out by the children on exploration and polar lands is described more fully in Case Study 5.3.

Enabling learning of concepts through skills not vocabulary

Geography when taught as outlined in the its curriculum provides many opportunities for children to engage with an enormous range of vocabulary, these words provide children with opportunities to learn about many concepts beyond their own experiences, and develop their vocabulary in three tiers (Beck *et al.*, 2002):

- *Tier one words*: basic words, often known as 'high frequency words':
  - rarely require specific learning as children use them anyway, but can be used geographically;
  - *examples*: happy, walk, jump, hop, slide, girl, boy, dog, park.
- *Tier two words*: high frequency words, found across a variety of subject areas or domains:
  - using and learning these words can add dramatically to a student's use of language, and happens constantly during geography lessons;
  - *examples*: coincidence, industrious, fortunate.
- *Tier three words*: consist of words whose frequency of use is quite low and often limited to specific subject areas:
  - best learned when a specific need arises, ideally when concepts have been observed, worked out and understood, as outlined in this chapter;
  - *examples*: peninsular, erosion, sustainable, meander.

Children can be put off by geography when having to learn lots of vocabulary out of any context (Pike, 2006; Pike, 2013b). Sometimes, teachers simply use too many geographical terms, and think children need to know all the terms before starting a topic.

Table 4.4 Levels of thinking in describing as applied to the topic of rocks and soils

Level	Description	Thinking	Questions from children
Knowledge	• Remembering names and terms relating to rocks and soils	• Sharing names and definitions of rocks/soils • Labelling rocks	• What is the name of this rock?
Comprehension	• Understanding the meaning of rock and soil terms	• Describing the characteristics of rocks • Talking about where different rocks are found	• How are igneous rocks made? • How are rocks made?
Application	• Ability to apply knowledge to a new situation	• Thinking about different uses of rocks in the locality • Talking about the uses of rocks in a variety of everyday objects	• Why do some rocks have holes in them?
Analysis	• Breaking down knowledge into parts and seeing the relationships between the parts	• Inferring why certain rocks are used in particular ways	• Why do people need rocks? • How do people benefit from rocks?
Synthesis	• Creatively applying knowledge to new situations	• Thinking about rocks in unfamiliar places	• Would people survive without rocks?

Source: Using Bloom *et al.*, 1956.

Figure 4.6 Using every day ICT packages to enhance learning in geography (a) online maps, (b) sharing learning via social and educational media, (c) using tablets and (d) geographical information systems

This is not true. Rather than telling children geographical vocabulary, terms can arise from the work and the children's ideas, questions and activities. Sparking an interest in a topic means children will want to know the language of what they are studying, and they then learn more terms! In this way the definitions and concepts have arisen from the children's own work. It was very noticeable in St James' National School that the children automatically used the terms primary, secondary and tertiary after they had constructed their understanding of the concept, and then the knowledge of the terms.

People and work. To help children understand products and jobs as part of a process, children can be introduced to the terms primary, secondary and tertiary using the idea of 'delaying vocabulary', see Case Study 4.1. From this process the types of jobs arise: primary, secondary and tertiary. Conceptually, children need to know these stages to understand the importance of the process of making goods and services. Challenging children to think about research and development jobs is also good, and to use the term 'quaternary'. Hopefully, at the end, children will also note how primary, secondary and tertiary is a chain of processes – and that's why geographers divide occupations up like this! This can be reinforced by the children watching any of a number of videos available on YouTube of products being made and picking out the processes. This activity could be a great enhancing/reinforcing homework too.

What do I want children to get out of this?

- To work together as geographers: to ask geographical questions, to experiment with rocks and soils, to take part in fieldwork, to know types of rocks and soils, to recognise types of rocks in the environment, to recognise the value of rocks and soils, to understand the process and impact of processing rock into different products.

Enquiry questions

- How are rocks formed?
- What happens to rocks?
- How are rocks used?
- How do people benefit from rocks?
- Would people survive without rocks?
- How do rocks and soils affect people?
- Is there any bad use for rocks?
- Why is rock and roll called rock and roll?

GEOGRAPHY
Geography Rocks!

Key Enquiry Question
How do rocks shape our world?

Geography primary concepts
Change, features, processes
Geography secondary concepts
The rock cycle (initial understanding)
Types of rocks and soils
Geography skills *incl enquiry and fieldwork*
Fieldwork: Workhouse, village and school grounds
Enquiry: all aspects

Curriculum – Geography
- Enquiry: all aspects
- Local environment
- Rocks and soils
- People and work, transport

Curriculum – Other
- History: uses of rocks in past in locality
- Mathematics: sorting data
- English: descriptive language, categorising rocks, listening to accounts of the past, presenting on findings
- Science: rocks and soils – properties/investigation

Resources
- Rocks and soils: schools' rock pack
- School rock set
- School building
- Rock and soil school survey sheet
- Children's devices: cameras, iPhones, etc.
- Children's materials for rock experiments
- School grounds and buildings
- Sandpaper, cups, buckets, water, etc.

Sample activities
- Generating ideas through school fieldwork then examining/sorting rocks found.
- Devising enquiry questions: asking 'random' questions, grouping into enquiry questions, etc.
- Homework: investigate possible experiments from YouTube, etc.
- Investigating the properties of rocks through experimentation.
- Investigating the properties of rock experiments – homework.
- Fieldwork: Trip to Kilmacthomas Workhouse – looking at uses of stone in workhouse (alongside other activities!)
- Investigating how rocks are used in the broader locality – near school, on way home, etc.
- Homework then fieldwork: changing nature of rocks in the locality – evidence of physical processes in locality of school.
- Mystery Skype or Skype to geologist.

Homework
- Bring in rocks, survey on types of rocks in and about homes, questioning people about rocks – how used, last time used, etc.

Differentiation
- By outcome: question devising – children to develop different experiments.
- By task: recording of properties. LA children: examining the properties of rocks, describing rocks in the locality.

Figure 4.7 Outline plan for a series of lessons and homework on rocks – a second version adapted after children devised enquiry questions

Butterflies, food and plants. As part of our work on teaching and learning about places and locations, students have to investigate their own questions about butterflies in college, this year first year student teachers came up with questions such as:

- What do butterflies eat?
- How long do they live?
- Where do butterflies like to rest?
- Where do butterflies like to live?
- What do butterflies do?
- How do butterflies live and die?

As we walked around different possible places for butterflies, we stopped off at the herb planters along the college drive. Here we picked herbs, smelled them and discussed what they reminded us of, but we did not name them. Lots of stories of mojitos, grandparents' homes and Christmas dinners are told. We then name the herbs, but only when we have thought about them. For the students, this makes a very simple point: do not bombard children with terms and names without a context or conceptual framework. Get the children interested, and then they will want and need to know the names of features, processes and places in geography.

Conclusions

No topic in geography or any other subject needs to be boring! This is revealed through research (Waldron *et al.*, 2009; Kitchen, 2013; Pike, 2013b) over time and in different places. Some of you reading this book may be geography 'lovers' or 'haters'. Whatever your views, it is important to remember the children you teach will have differing views. However, it's also important to remember that with a focus on the children and their interests and questions, you can ensure they like, and are challenged by, any geographical activity they do! The examples above make it clear that when we start with the children, and their need to know (Roberts, 2003, 2013a), we are on to a winner!

Reflection and action

- What influences your ideas and opinions about geography? How have they affected your ideas, views and practices in geography?
- What boring geography do you do? How can you change it?
- Should geography always be exciting? What is more important: engagement, challenge, content, approaches or fun?
- How can you involve your class in more decison-making about the geography they do in class? What could you do tomorrow, this term, this year?

Further resources

Books on making learning interesting

As this chapter outlines, the key to avoiding boring geography is making learning relevant to children's lives, these books develop these ideas further, showing how teachers' main consideration should be the children they teach:

Coles, T. (2014) *Never Mind the Inspectors, Here's Punk Learning*. Carmarthen: Independent Thinking Press an imprint of Crown House Publishing.
Gilbert, I. (2012) *Why Do I Need a Teacher When I Have Google?* Carmarthen: Independent Thinking Press.

Online resources

There are a number of sites that promote a different approach to learning geography, although these are primarily for older children; they are great for inspiration – to help you realise you do not have to teach geography in the ways you learnt it!

Juicy Geography: www.juicygeography.co.uk
Global Trek: http://teacher.scholastic.com/activities/globaltrek
National Geographic: http://kids.nationalgeographic.com

Sites related to specific topics

Products, Justice and Sustainability: http://followthethings.com
Fashion and Justice: http://fashionrevolution.org
Sustainable Drainage: www.susdrain.org
Rocks and Soils/Earth Sciences: www.esta-uk.net

Books to inspire younger children about geography

Mizielinska, A. and Mizielinski, D. (2013) *Maps*. Dorking: Big Picture Press.
Petty, K. (2000) *What a Wonderful World Book*. London: Bodley Head

Chapter 5

Our school, our world – primary geography through the school grounds

Geography is all about personal connections to the outdoors, so I conduct lessons outside as often as possible, even if the learning intentions do not involve a specific link to the environment in which the lesson is taking place. I firmly believe that any time spent outside gives children the opportunity to notice things about their environment that they may not have previously considered.

Student teacher

The school and its grounds provide a wealth of opportunities for learning in geography. This chapter outlines research and practice relating to the use of the school grounds in primary geography.

The chapter draws on the following ideas:

- Children value their schools and grounds as a place for learning, playing and 'being'.
- The school and its grounds are a key resource in primary geography and should be used frequently in lessons.
- Many concepts and skills can be developed in school grounds for all classes.

This chapters outlines:

- ideas and research about children and their school grounds;
- ways to use the school grounds in primary geography;
- learning in the school grounds in younger classes, older classes and whole school approaches in primary geography; and
- issues over the use of school grounds for geography and other subjects.

This chapter focuses on the geographical learning that can take place in the school buildings, the school grounds and the immediate area of the school, using examples from a range of schools. Chapter 6 complements this chapter as it looks at how children can investigate issues immediately in the areas of their school, and Chapter 9 takes the idea of children's action in their locality further.

There is no doubt that over the past 20 years school grounds have developed considerably. I notice the development and 'un-development' of their outdoor areas, particularly:

- wild areas, including long grass, ponds and natural hedgerows;
- school allotments with vegetable, fruit and grains;
- seating areas, such as mini-amphitheatres and benches;
- play equipment, such as swings and climbing frames;
- environmental areas, including recycling and compost bins;
- areas to attract wildlife, such as bird feeders, wormeries and bug hotels;
- commemorative areas, such as gardens of inclusion, tepees and celebration murals; and
- indoor/outdoor areas, often beneath awning, where children move between areas freely.

CASE STUDY 5.1 Children's views on school grounds, 9–11 year olds, St Joseph's Boys' National School

St Joseph's school has 127 children from Ireland, England, Hungary, Poland, Lithuania, China and Benin. Their motto is 'Ní neart go cur le chéile', which translates into 'There is no strength without unity'. The school has a very strong ethos of inclusion, evident from first visiting the school.

The school grounds. Once any visitor ventures beyond the school's front gates, they see the grounds are a fascinating mix of spaces, as shown in Figure 5.1. The first area is the Garden of Inclusion, a special place recognising all the cultures and nationalities represented in the school, as well as a little history of the school, as it includes flags, restored school benches, mosaics and beautiful plantings. The boys were evidently very proud of the garden as they described each element of the space. We continued around the perimeter of the school and stopped at the front fence, a significant place as the boys have great memories of watching various cycling and running races coming past their school.

The boys' views. The boys talked at length about the use of the tarmac areas of the school grounds, to adults just a 'yard', but the boys revealed exactly who played which games of soccer where, and where you could go if you wished not to play soccer. Next, across the tarmac is a 'wild' area where rotting logs and bird feeders encourage a variety of creatures to inhabit. Despite the newness of this area, it is used for mini beast hunts and plenty have been found. Behind the school was an area used mainly for grass and planting, where there were flower and vegetable beds. Here, even the space between a new security fence and the school building had been used as a sheltered spot for growing rhubarb. Another bed was in the shape of the Star of David, illustrating cultural awareness even in gardening! On all the beds were the ends of pencils and egg shells – a clue to the extensive use of compost bins in the school, with each class contributing.

Work in progress. Not every element of the school grounds has been successful. To date the wormery has not worked well, illustrating that the grounds of St Joseph's are a 'work in progress'. The support of the boys, staff and parents show what can be done in a small urban school with limited outdoor space.

www.stjosephsprimary.ie

Figure 5.1 The many uses of school grounds: (a) indoor/outdoor spaces, (b) native hedgerow planting, (c) decorated yards and (d) outdoor classrooms

Some schools are just beginning to realise the potential of their school grounds (as shown in Figure 5.1); others have been using them for many years. Reasons for using the school grounds can include enhancing learning, but many teachers also go outside 'for a change', or because their classrooms are too small! Using the outdoors makes perfect sense, as Malone and Tranter (2003) argue:

It makes good pedagogical sense to provide real life environmental experiences for children drawing on their natural curiosity . . . Why learn about frogs from a book or a computer screen when you could have them in a pond outside your window?

Children's school grounds – ideas and research

Children are deeply involved with the physical environments they live within (Hart, 1979; Chawla, 2002; Catling, 2003; Pike, 2011; Casey, 2003). The history of school grounds is also important for children; whether they have family links to the school or not, they will have a sense of the school in the past. This wealth of knowledge and sense of place can be drawn on for history and geography lessons, as outlined in the case studies in this chapter.

Whether playing soccer, playing hide and seek or making daisy chains, children have great interest with their school grounds, as shown in Figures 5.1 and 5.2. As Titman notes, school grounds, particularly playgrounds, are places for play and many more uses (1994), as shown in the example of St Joseph's Boys' National School above. This is true even for a single child who will carry out different activities with others, or alone in different parts of the school grounds. As Catling notes, a playground is a 'daily part of children's lives, and it is a geographical environment, a physical and social 'world' in which to examine spatial use, conflict and development' (Catling, 2003, pp. 197–8). A useful way to think of what school grounds offer children (and other members of the school community) is that of 'affordances'. Affordances are defined as what the environment 'offers or furnishes an individual with; they are the social meaning of the environment or persons within the environment' (Gibson, 1979, p. 127). Affordances are varied and may include both items and people, and may be repellent or attractive (Clark and Uzzell, 2006, p. 177). Kyttä, by assessing children's independent mobility and their actualisation of affordances, created a model, in which she described a

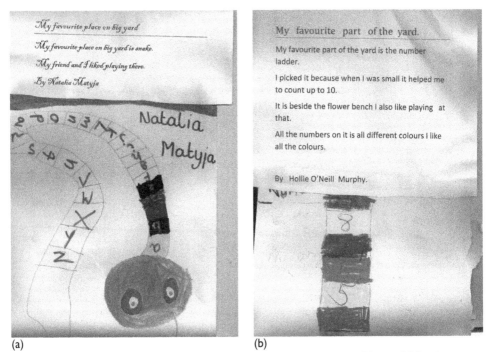

(a)   (b)

Figure 5.2 Views of the school grounds – (a, b) 8 year olds, Warrenmount National School

Table 5.1 Kyttä's model of affordances applied to school grounds

Degree of independent mobility	Number of realised affordances	
	Low	*High*
Low	**CELL** Due to mobility restrictions, children cannot find affordances. The ignorance of affordances tends to decrease the motivation to move around and explore the environment (e.g. a school yard where children are banned from running).	**GLASSHOUSE** In spite of mobility restrictions the environment appears to be a rich source of affordances. The awareness of affordances can be based on second hand information (e.g. a school garden with no free access).
High	**WASTELAND** Possibilities for mobility reveal only the dullness of the environment (e.g. a tarmac yard for playing games).	**BULLERBY** Possibilities for independent mobility reveal the many affordances. The actualisation of affordances motivates further exploration and mobility in the environment. (e.g. school 'wild areas' with loose material for using at any time of the day, including breaks).

Source: Adapted from: Kyttä, 2006, p. 146.

hypothetical, ideal, child friendly environment, entitled the 'Bullerby', based on the idea of a Swedish 'noisy village' (Kyttä, 2006, p. 141), as shown in Table 5.1. Kyttä's scenarios are found in other researches on play. Environments that children can change and mould offer many opportunities for learning and collaborative behaviours (Hart, 1979; Moore and Wong 1997; Chawla, 2002; Blades, 2006). Furthermore, research finds that children prefer and use playgrounds with high degrees of challenge, novelty and complexity (Fjørtoft and Sageie 2000).

However, many schools are very well kept; they have clearly defined areas (usually tarmac and grass) for play, and other areas such as gardens, parking spaces and paths. Some schools have developed beautifully wild and growing areas for children's learning but these areas are sometimes 'out-of-bounds' and fenced off for children except for formal class time. Other schools have differing and overlapping areas, areas for play and learning that may include tarmac areas, but also outdoor arenas, stepping stones, bird hives, bug hotels and perhaps a few hens too! These developments occur in all sorts of schools; in fact, the schools in the photographs in Figure 5.1 show that even where the weather is changeable and spaces tight, schools can create wonderful environments with and for children, for playing and socializing, as well as many geographical opportunities. However, it is also argued that children's views of school grounds are not always heard and the potential of them not always realised (Catling, 2003). Thomson, researching adult/child interactions in school grounds, found children wished for changes in them, namely adventure playgrounds, mums on duty, games from home, but they mostly wanted less regulation, less 'don'ts' and more 'dos' (2007). While researching gender differences in play, Flynn noted the restricted nature of children's play in Irish school yards, and suggested more of a range of games be available for children, such as rounders, chess and so on. (2001). Thomson suggested that play or yard time be used to develop children's

CASE STUDY 5.2 Past, present, future: 5–8 year olds, St James' National School

In the junior room of St James', the school was to be the focus of some geography work, as shown in Figure 5.3a and b.

Generating ideas. My first day in the school was subject to the weather – and so some indoor/outdoor geography took place! The children discussed a range of photographs of the school grounds. There were 16 photographs that had been copied into PowerPoint and then printed off 4 to a page and laminated. Finally, the four pages of photographs were held together with string. This provides children with an attractive set of pictures to use in a number of ways for school-based geography. Over time, they can be replaced and the old ones become a geography and history resource!

Fieldwork – our school. The children used photographs taken outside or elsewhere to decide on their favourite places. The children worked independently, but the teacher was there to help/advice. Like the boys in St Joseph's Boys' National School, the children were overwhelmingly positive about their school. The children chose a range of places as their favourites, including the field, space for playing soccer and a painted stone made by children in the past at the entrance of the school, as shown in Figure 5.3. Some places chosen were more unique, for example Liam chose the window of the old school, as he fondly remembered doing the Christmas play inside. Even though they were just starting their enquiry, the children were using geographical and descriptive language, expressing their opinions about places and being able to say why they felt that way:

> My favourite place is the corner of the field. I like it because it is cosy. I like to watch the boys playing football.

> My favourite place is in the hole in the wall, because we made a fairy house. We leave presents and notes for the fairies, sometimes they reply.

> I like the window. If you look from the other side it is inside and it reminds me of doing our play. I want to do a play next year.

Our favourite places. As found elsewhere, it was evident the children's valued places were personal to them. The painted stone would only just be noticed by adults but to the children it told them about past pupils, who they know as teenagers. The children's real and imagined worlds collided in their work, for example when writing about fairies. The following week the children found the places in the photographs as a treasure hunt. They also decided on their favourite place once again. The children were encouraged to ask questions about the school – including those about the past, present and future. The children's questions were both geographical and historical in nature, these are just some of those asked:

- Why was the new school built?
- Where was the office in the old school?

- Are any of the old pupils still living in Stradbally?
- Why do we like school?
- Why was the yellow line painted?
- How old is the school?
- Who was the first principal?
- Why is the school called St James' National School?
- Why is there a rock outside our school?
- What will the school be like in the future?

As can be seen, children of all ages ask a range of questions, older and younger children ask what and why questions of varying degrees of openness. The children then found out the answers to these questions by:

- observing the school and finding old and new features;
- using photographs of the school in the past – comparing the school then and now; and
- interviewing people from the school (past and present): teachers, grandparents, parents.

All aspects of these activities were informative and interesting for the children. They were delighted to interview visitors. They also took great delight in the old photographs of the school, including one of the school's first computer bought in 1980 for £1000!

appreciation and knowledge of the natural and built environment (2007), and geography lessons are the perfect opportunity for such activity!

Learning in the school and its grounds

The immediate area around the school, including the school grounds or yards, can contribute hugely to children's learning, as outlined in the case studies in this chapter. It is evident that learning happens when children interact with their surroundings over extended time periods, at home or school (Hart, 1979; Moore, 1986; Adams and Ingham, 1998; Nundy, 1999). Titman (1994, p. 58) identified four elements children looked for in the school grounds she studied:

- A place for *doing*, which offers opportunities for physical activities, for 'doing' all kinds of things, and which recognises children's needs to extend themselves, develop new skills, to find challenges and take risks.
- A place for *thinking*, which provides intellectual stimulation, things which they could discover and study and learn about, by themselves and with friends, which allows them to explore and discover and understand more about the world they live in.
- A place for *feeling*, which presents colour, beauty and interest, which engenders a sense of ownership and pride and belonging, in which children can be small without

Figure 5.3 School grounds enquiries (a, b) our school past, present and future and (c, d) finding signs of spring

feeling vulnerable, where they can care for the place and people in it and feel cared for themselves.

• A place for *being*, which allows children to 'be' themselves, which recognises their individuality, their need to have a private persona in a public place, for privacy, for being alone with friends, for being quiet outside of the classroom, for being a child.

Her elements provide a very useful framework for schools to consider how they can use their school grounds. They show that the possibilities for using the school grounds are endless. Teachers need to think carefully for every topic they teach about how to use the school grounds. Most importantly, teachers can ask the children for ideas about how they would like to do this.

Planning for the use of the school grounds in geography

The remainder of this chapter will focus on possibilities for different ages in the school grounds, while recognising all activity can be adapted for different ages depending on planning and the children's interests. This final section of the chapter will help teachers to negotiate barriers to using the school grounds, and suggests practical ways to develop grounds for learning. However, in geography, it is important that children be working as geographers and learning geography when outside, through:

Children *doing* geography:

- asking questions about the school – past, present and future;
- observing and collecting data on different places in the school grounds;
- interacting with people in the school and its grounds;
- recording places and people, through words, sound, pictures and video.

Children *thinking* geographically:

- analysing sources on the school in the past through discussion, comparing them with now;
- working out why features are located where they are;
- recording patterns in the school grounds, such as people visiting, busy and quiet times, etc.

Children *feeling* geographically:

- observing and recording natural features in the school grounds;
- expressing opinions about places in the school and the grounds;
- talking about the future of the school, drawing preferred futures of the school.

Children *being* geographers:

- using maps and plans of the school;
- making maps and plans of the past, present and future school;
- debating the futures of the school based on data collected from other activities.

These types of activities are exemplified in the case studies in this and the next chapter. In fact, there are very many ways to use the school grounds in expected/unexpected ways. A good framework to think of activity in the school grounds is to consider whether the use of the grounds is core or supplementary.

Core activities. These are activities where the best way to do them is outside in the school grounds. Signs of Spring Projects has been developed in a number of different places over a number of years. One, initiated by the website Seomra Ranga, uses social media where children simply record signs of spring, usually through photographs or words and post them to social media. The children use the hashtag #spring or #antearrach so other schools can easily track down the posts. Needless to say, with the success of the project, it has been expanded to include Autumn. This project is so simple but meaningful, and it has to take place outdoors! Any of these activities could involve one, two or more trips outside to generate ideas, answer questions and collect data. Other activities can use the school grounds for exploring some aspects of a topic or theme. Examples of core outdoor activities can include:

What features are in our school grounds (this chapter)?

- observing, and then drawing features;
- talking about likes/dislikes and justifying their thoughts;
- predicting the future of the school and its grounds, over short and long terms.

What are rocks? How are they used (see Chapter 4)?

- collecting and sorting rocks;
- observing the use of rocks in the school grounds;
- predicting and assessing the changes in rocks in the school buildings and explaining why these changes occur.

Where does water go in the environment (DES/NCCA, 1999c, p. 92)?

- observing water in the school grounds – asking questions about water;
- predicting where water will go – then following water to find out what happens to it;
- considering how the water cycle can be slowed – to replicate natural water movements.

What will the weather do today? What weather patterns are there?

- predicting the weather from observations;
- measuring the weather;
- analysing the features that affect the weather (micro-climates);
- considering how and why weather is becoming more changeable.

Supplementary activities. There are all sorts of opportunities to use the school grounds in geography (and other subjects) where the outdoor activity is not essential but will enhance the children's experiences, including their learning. For example, children could be investigating what happens to the sun during the day and at night, and using the school grounds will help them understand the concept of how the earth moves. The lesson plan in Appendix 9 is a good example of this. This lesson could be taught entirely inside, however, the lesson is enhanced by going outside to work out where the sun 'goes' at night. Without this experience, it is likely that not all the children would understand the rather complex concept the teacher would like them to understand. The sample lesson allows children's voices to be heard and acted on in a number of ways, as the children decide on the questions at the start of the lesson. They also help make decisions about how their works will be displayed at the end of the lesson. Examples of supplementary outdoor activities are projects that use the school and its grounds occasionally through a topic to help children understand certain concepts or develop particular skills:

What does the sun do at night (Appendix 9)?

- reading stories about the sun, asking questions about the sun and shadows;
- investigating patterns the sun makes in the school grounds;
- talking about where the sun goes at night when outside.

What is Brazil like? How is it changing (Chapter 7)?

- observe changes in the school area;
- decide where the changes are in Figure 3.1 (see Chapter 6);
- observe changes in a DVD/YouTube clip on Brazil – and sort changes into categories on the Development Compass Rose.

What are the effects of hurricanes (Chapter 7)?

* asking questions promoted by photographs of hurricanes;
* working out why it rains, and why hurricanes form on the school grounds;
* imagining the impact of a hurricane in our locality;
* research activity on recent hurricanes.

What jobs do people do in our area (Chapter 4)?

* note down jobs visible (primary and secondary evidence) in the school;
* Categorise jobs – see Case Study 4.1;
* look up jobs in the local papers – again categorise them;
* mapping jobs in the local area on a large scale map – looking for patterns about which jobs are where.

Some specific activities on particular topics for younger and older classes are outlined in the following sections, derived from practice in St James' National School and Scoil Fhursa.

There are many other activities children can take part in within their school grounds, which should sit easily within medium term plans:

* *I-spy*: very young children can describe features by their colour or letter sound rather than letter. This game helps children recognise features in the school and its grounds;
* *sight*: observing features, waiting for and observing events, stating opinions of places, drawing places;
* *sound*: being silent and listening, describing sounds, asking questions about the sources of sounds, making a sound map;
* *smells*: finding lovely and horrible smells, testing the smell of different plants, testing the smells of rocks and soil;
* *taste*: tasting food grown in the school, finding out where different food are grown, tasting food inside and outside.

There are also many games children will play anyway, these include:

* *feelings*: taking a sensory walk, choosing favourite places, walks with partners;
* *hide and seek*: a fantastic way to recognise children's spaces and places in the school grounds.

In many school, grounds have been developed to include all sorts of materials and structures for children to play in and with, such as:

* *loose playthings*: tyres, sand, water, skipping ropes, books, etc.;
* *structures*: climbing frames, sheds (can become shops, dens, reading spaces, etc.);
* *indoor/outdoor*: many schools are developing 'indoor/outdoor' spaces beneath awnings, enabling children to move between areas freely.

These types of activities help children recognise and describe geographical features and processes in their immediate surroundings.

Learning in the school grounds – younger classes

Early years geography is enhanced and developed in many dimensions in the school grounds (Martin and Owens, 2008). The most important aspect of learning in the school grounds for younger children is play. Play is valuable as it is an enjoyable activity and a learning process, in which children can take part without instructions. Play contributes to many areas of children's learning and well-being, including problem solving, experimentation, communication, cooperation, creativity, personal responsibility, creativity and imagination. The type, quality and diversity of children's play in school grounds directly affects the type, quality and diversity of children's play in general? (Moore *et al.*, 1992). There is compelling evidence across varying research projects that the combination of playing and being outdoors delivers benefits to children in many ways. One example is the work of Herrington and Studtmann who found that when children played in an environment with an open grassy area planted with shrubs, children played through fantasy

---

CASE STUDY 5.3 Spring is coming: how can we tell?
5–6 year olds, Our Lady of Victories Infant School

Following on from their work on polar explorers (Chapter 8), the children in Senior Infants (5 and 6 year olds) investigated the seasons, as shown in Figure 5.3c and d.

- **What happens in spring?** To begin with, they found out about what happens in spring by talking about a range of photographs. Their teacher gradually introduced the photographs to the children, who were all grouped around one large table (Figure 5.4a).
- **What signs of spring can we find?** They then went out into the school grounds to find signs of spring (Figure 5.4a and b).

The children found the following signs:

- buds on plants – although some were from the year before;
- grass growing – although not too much!
- birds singing – in the mature trees around the school;
- flowers growing – such as snowdrops and daffodils.

For the children, some of the features and processes they saw were familiar to them, but others were new. Also the children were able to see that some signs were not as they expected, for example plants that had grown from the previous year were not a sign of this year's spring. They could not find any puddles as it had not rained, but generally, they were able to note that spring was coming, slowly.

- **What did we find out today?** When the children drew and talked about the signs of spring they had seen, there were some rather creative responses, such as sightings of sunflowers and rabbits!

http://olvinfants.ie/index.php/antarctic-adventures-in-room-7

play. When their play areas were dominated by structures rather than natural elements, they established social hierarchy by means of physical competence. Fjørtoft and Sageie also agreed that natural environments are better than purpose built playgrounds because they stimulate more diverse and creative play (2000).

Young children are interested in their immediate areas, and this interest can be harnessed in lesson planning. Children's understanding of their world can be opened up through their concrete experiences in and around the school. The activities the children took part in at St James' National School were described as geography, however, they also encompassed many other areas of development for children. The activities also drew on the principles of slow pedagogy (Payne and Wattchow, 2009), as the children were asked to go to their favourite place and just stay there a while. Interestingly in most cases the children chose different places outside as opposed to those they had planned when inside!

What was also evident during this time was that thoughts and research elsewhere were true of the children in St James', as they shared their views of their school grounds with each other and their teachers. Crucially, for the development of their language in geography, children were able to say why they liked particular places. The children revealed the multiple uses of the spaces (Catling, 2003), used in different ways by different children at different times. For example, a wall to bounce a ball over was also a seat as well as a space to leave items for fairies. The children went alone to some places but for some this was difficult as their favourite activity was a group one, namely playing football.

It is very important to consider the timing of any outdoor work in schools, especially with younger classes. Give the children plenty of time to do the activities – do not try to plan too much as even the experience of being outside with their friends is a learning experience. It is important to ensure the children have something to do and use along the way to help them with their learning. Empty frames or bags to collect things work very well with younger children. All children enjoy the responsibility of using clipboards and even where children are not required to write anything, a piece of paper on a clipboard can be used for random thoughts and notes. In fact, I have found that when children are asked *not* to write, they can end up filling pages! In other situations, the children may have writing or drawing frames to complete.

Learning in the school grounds – older classes

Using the school grounds does not have to be restricted to the younger children. From ages 7 and upwards, children are more capable of working independently in groups on longer tasks in their school grounds. Teachers and children can plan a number of activities for groups to carry out. At this age, the use of the school grounds can really help children understand some quite complex ideas that they will revisit late in their geographical experiences, as children can use the school and its grounds to help understand big ideas in geography:

Change. What are seasons? Why do they change?

- examining changes through the seasons in plants in the school grounds;
- discussing what happens to the sun at night;
- watching shadows during the day to explore night and day.

Interactions. Who helps our school? What do they do?

- recording visitors to the school, using the visitor book;
- watching and talking to people who visit the school during the day;
- interviewing people who work in the school;
- unseen people who help us – in other places in the world.

Movement. Where have animals come from? Where are they going next?

- feeding animals, such as birds, in the school grounds;
- asking questions about the movements and migrations of birds;
- studying migration patterns online of birds.

Justice. What products can we buy locally? What products come from elsewhere? Who makes them?

- asking questions about where foods in our lunches come from;
- asking where foods in the supermarket come from: 'one week' homework;
- mapping locations: investigating how foods are produced and by whom;
- critically examining trade, including fair trade.

Figure 5.4 Using the school grounds can start small (a) number lines, (b) colour palettes, (c) locations for mini-beasts and (d) unusual finds – snowdrops become 'snow covered mountains'

Through the spiral curriculum, these ideas help children to develop their thinking and so will help them understand more complex versions of these big ideas later in their lives. However, these activities are also useful and fulfilling in their own right! The case studies and photographs above show the excitement that can be generated through the use of the school grounds. The development of enquiry questions by the children in St James' show just how many ideas can be explored by using or starting out by using the school grounds.

Issues over the use of school grounds

Despite the obvious benefits of the use and development of the spaces in and around schools, there are still schools where children have very limited experiences in their school grounds. The issues appear to be the lack of affordances in school grounds, lack of use of school grounds and the severe restrictions put on children during breaks.

- *Lack of the use of school grounds.* Some schools use their school grounds, whereas others may not. Often a particular teacher takes responsibility for the use of the grounds. Many schools have wonderful grounds that are used in many ways. School staff need time to consider how they can use their grounds for educational purposes; continued professional development (CPD) hours or days can be used to help teachers think about this. Often a change in mindset of considering the classroom as the main place where learning takes place is all that is needed.
- *Lack of affordances in school grounds.* Some school grounds may lack the affordances that give rise to geographical learning; they may be simple yards of tarmac and grass. However, as teachers, we should ask the children their views, show them other school yards and so on, and so begin to look through their eyes at school yards. As described above, the tarmac yard at St Joseph's Boys' National School, actually had all sorts of spaces and meanings for the boys in the school. We should ask ourselves:
  - What do my children think of their yards? Ask them what they think, visit another local school and so on.
  - What do they like? What would they change?
  - What would they like to play with during break times? (loose materials, such as sand and wood are often popular)
  - School grounds are always a work in progress, even those that are developed over decades of work. Figure 5.4 shows how small resource changes can be introduced to facilitate outdoor learning experiences.
- *Restrictions on children's movement in school grounds.* There are still schools where the grounds are simply tarmac yards with little scope for anything but running around. There are schools where the children are not allowed to run around for 'safety' or 'insurance' reasons. Reports of 'no running' policies during break time in 40 per cent of schools in Counties Cork and Kerry (Murray and Millar, 2005) attracted media attention in Ireland (RTE, 2005). However, the minister for education at the time described the growing trend for schools introducing 'no running' policies at lunch time for fear of litigation as 'ludicrous' (RTE, 2005). In fact, many schools still subscribe to the 'surplus energy theory', first proposed by the psychologist Herbert Spencer (*Principles of Psychology* (1855); see Malone and Tranter, 2003) and see breaks only as a time to 'run free'.

All of these factors can restrict the use of school grounds, however, often schools are simply too preoccupied with other priorities to focus on use of the school yard. Often the use and associated development (or 'un-development') of school grounds needs a leader to guide others and help the entire school community to see the possibilities in the type of activity described in this chapter.

Conclusions

School grounds are one of the most important resources for primary geography, whatever state of development they are in. The use of the school grounds as a main focus within a series of lessons or as an incidental learning opportunity is essential for children. The benefits of such activities are clear in terms of learning and well-being for children. For teachers, it also makes a welcome change from the classroom environment.

Reflection and action

- How does your school use its outdoor space in primary geography?
- How could children and teachers plan to develop the use of the outdoors in geography in the next few years?
- What activity could take place in each class level – planned and not so planned?
- How can the barriers to using outdoor spaces in geography be overcome?
- Who can help the school develop the use of the outdoors?

Further resources

Books

There are many books on using the school grounds and other outdoor spaces in primary schools for teachers and children:

Martin, F., and Owen, P. (2008) *Caring for our World: A Practical Guide for ESD for ages 4–8*. Sheffield, Geographical Association.
Robertson, J. (2014) *Dirty Teaching: A Beginner's Guide to Learning Outdoors*. Carmarthen: Independent Thinking Press.

Online sites

Centre for Human Rights and Citizenship, through St Patrick's College, regularly publishes resources for schools all thoroughly researched and piloted with children in schools: www.spd.dcu.ie/chrce.

INTO Magazine frequently features the use of school grounds. Articles have included the use of nature in the school grounds and how schools are using 'yard time' for more variety of activity: www.into.ie; www.playworks.org/sites/default/files/09Mar15_ School_Yard-2_0.pdf.

Learning Through Landscapes recognises that every child benefits from stimulating outdoor learning and play in their education. They aim to enable children to connect with nature, be more active, be more engaged with their learning, develop their social skills and have fun! www.ltl.org.uk.

Forest School uses the woods and forests as a means to build independence and self-esteem in children and young adults. Topics are cross-curriculum including the natural environment. However, the personal skills are considered highly valuable, such as teamwork and problem solving. Earth force Education offers Forest School training in Ireland. www.forestschools.com; www.earthforceeducation.com.

Willow Wonder run by Beth Murphy use heritage craft skills to promote Green Craft/Art/Natural Spaces inspired by nature working with nature. Based in Kildare, they have worked with many schools and colleges to create enhanced green spaces in schools grounds: www.willowwonder.net.

Chapter 6

Our geographical locality – primary geography through the locality

Geography affects children's daily lives – geography is life! The children can interact with their own geography by making maps of their locality, observing patterns and behaviours in the environment, discussing and offering solutions for local and national issues.

Geography Teacher Educator

Geography on their own localities, including fieldwork, is one of the most significant and engaging activities children and teachers can take part in during lessons. This chapter outlines research and practice relating to the use of the locality in primary geography, using case studies from various schools and classrooms.

This chapter is based on the following key thoughts:

- The importance of living in and interacting with the locality for children.
- The values and benefits of teaching and learning geography about and within the locality.
- Children's development and learning related to geography in the locality.
- Auditing and planning for the use of the locality in primary geography.

Throughout the chapter, the terms 'locality' and 'local area' are used referring to the area near children's homes and schools, recognising these areas may not be the same spaces. The term 'local learning' is also used to refer to learning 'about and within the locality of the school' (Pike, 2011b). This learning can act as a source of studying for all aspects of geography, as well as many other subjects and opportunities.

The chapter outlines:

- children's everyday geographies as a source for learning geography;
- planning locality geography with children at the centre of the process;
- approaching locality geography planning in a progressive and collegial way; and
- using the resources, including people and places, of the locality for geography.

In looking at the locality, this chapter interacts significantly with most others in this book, particularly Chapter 2 on enquiry, Chapter 5 on the school and its grounds, and Chapter 7 on teaching geography through issues.

Children and their localities

Wherever they live, children value and use their local area in a large number of ways and develop complex but real relationships with their local environments (Hart, 1979; Chawla, 2002; Spencer and Blades, 2006; Pike, 2011). In all settings for children's lives, there will be range of places and spaces within a locality that children will know and use. Children's localities are part of their everyday lives (Chawla, 2002; Catling, 2003; Pike, 2011). Children's 'every day geographies' or 'ethno-geographies' are very important to them. As Martin states (2008, p. 369):

> through interacting in a myriad of daily-life activities, children already think and, more specifically, they think geographically.

CASE STUDY 6.1 Learning in the locality and beyond, all ages – St Joseph's National School

The boys in St Joseph's have come to understand complex concepts such as changes in land use, the flora and fauna in ecosystems and sustainability issues, when their learning enables them to use areas in and around the school itself.

Some examples of local learning the boys have undertaken include:

- **Art project, with geography**. CraftEd project on pattern, as described in Case Study 3.2.

- **Environmental Education/Green Flag**. Working towards their fourth Green Flag on transport: including auditing travel to work and taking part in cycling proficiency lessons.

- **Sustainability/cycle training**. The boys receive free training on cycling through Go Dungarvan/Waterford Sports Partnership, which encourages independent mobility in the locality.

- **EU/Comenius project**. The school has taken part in a Pleased to Meet You Project over two years with schools across Europe, sharing information about their locality and their learning.

- **Geography/weather station**. The school set up a Davis Vantage Vue wireless weather station in their ecological garden. The station measures all aspects of ether and sends the data wirelessly to a data logger within the school. This information is displayed on the school website and used in lessons.

- **Gardens**. The school also enhances learning outside through their Garden of Inclusion, the Ecological Garden and other zones in the schools grounds, all of which are featured on their website.

www.stjosephsprimary.ie

Figure 6.1 The locality and primary geography: built and natural environments (a) Kilmacthomas Workhouse, (b) Drumcondra Road, Dublin, (c) Devonshire Bridge and Colligan River, Dungarvan, Waterford and (d) Stradbally Cove, Waterford.

Research evidence shows that there are many natural and built places children use and value in the local area for their day-to-day lives and that the range of places used is broad (Matthews, 1992; Chawla, 2002; Pike, 2011).

- Natural spaces and places in the locality:
  - *natural*: beaches, lakes and seas, fields, hills/mountains, rivers/streams, woods/forests;
  - *built 'green' areas*: dens, parks, public 'greens', sports fields.
- Built spaces and places in the locality:
  - *everyday spaces*: houses, shops, churches and church yards;
  - *commercial places*: bowling alleys, cinemas, food outlets/restaurants, local shops, shopping centres, sports clubs (swimming pools, halls, etc.);
  - *community facilities*: churches, clubs (hurling, football, soccer, etc.);
  - *sports clubs*: swimming pools, halls, tennis clubs, youth clubs.
- People in the locality:
  - *familiar people*: family in the locality, friends of all ages, youth workers, neighbours and other local residents;
  - *less familiar people*: adults: neighbours, teenagers, older children, younger children.

Children value local people and places, including shops, green spaces and sports facilities, not simply because of what they provide in terms of facilities but also as a place to meet friends. In all areas, children find places with 'rural' and 'urban' characteristics appealing to use, and any local place that has a number of affordances, and therefore open to multiple uses, will be very popular with children. The most popular place I found for all children was a local shop: a place to buy products, to meet friends, to hang out and a point from which to go and do other activities in the locality. In any locality, there is a wealth of these types of places, spaces and people to draw upon for primary geography. The use of these places can be a spring board for many geography activities.

Children's learning in their locality

The use of local places and people is a well-established practice in education. Key education theorists (Dewey, 1954; Piaget, 1956; Bruner, 1986; Vygotsky, 1986) all refer to children's learning in their local environment and social contexts. For example, Piaget valued children's complex environmental interactions, viewing such interactions as contributing towards children's intellectual development. Dewey's work strongly informs the use of the locality in geography learning. Dewey strongly encouraged teachers to relate children's learning to the real world. One hundred years on, his work helps us as teachers to appreciate that using spaces outdoors and planning fieldwork can enhance

---

CASE STUDY 6.2 What features are in our village? 9–13 year olds, St James' National School

St James' National School is situated in a perfect location for all types of fieldwork, as the village has a shop, two pubs, soccer and GAA grounds, as well as beaches, woods and a small stream. As one of their final activities in geography, the children in the senior room drew on all of these features when they conducted an enquiry based on their geographies of the village, as outlined in Figure 6.2.

- **Asking enquiry questions**: They used enquiry approaches to come up with a main enquiry question for their work, simply 'What features are in our village?'

- **Our village – fieldwork**: The children walked around the village with no concrete plans, deciding on places to visit at each point with their teacher. The teacher knew the area well and was aware of any possible hazards. Interestingly, although the children were not asked to write anything, they wrote endlessly in each place they visited! They also discussed the characteristics of each place, their likes and dislikes and their thoughts for the future. Two boys created this list of their views:

  - We think the playground should open soon.
  - We don't think they should have pulled up the plants in the village.
  - We liked the way they painted the houses.
  - There should be a better echo in the ball alley.

- We think there should be a toy shop in the village.
- We think our granddad did a good job of cutting the grass in the village.
- We think the signs should be bigger.

- **Our village – the past**: The following week a local resident, and author of a book on the history of the village, took the children on a walk around significant places for him.

- **Presenting our findings**: On returning to the classroom, they were asked how they would like to present their findings. There was a lengthy discussion! Eventually after considering graphs, posters and articles, the children decided to create a timeline of the village, to which they would add to over time.

The children really enjoyed the work in the village, as one child said:

> The project was great because we had lots of choices, like the question and where we went on the fieldwork. It was really interesting to meet people and find out about the village in the past, and how it had changed.

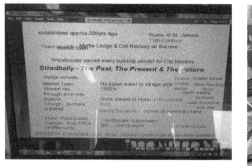

Figure 6.2 A child led enquiry: what features are in our village? St James' National School

our children's learning. Whether they are learning about the changing nature of their school and its buildings, exploring habitats or examining weathering around school grounds, their knowledge and understanding can be improved by planning outdoor experiences in schools.

Research has linked children's experiences in the locality and the quality of their present lives (Greene and Hogan, 2005) and their learning (Catling, 2003; Martin, 2008; Pike, 2011). Locality-based learning has also been linked to children's agency (Christensen and O'Brien, 2003; Olwig and Gulløv, 2003) and to the development of their identities (Valentine, 1996; Matthews *et al.*, 2000). Research has also focused on the importance of children's interactions with natural environments (Louv, 2010; Zelenski *et al.*, 2015) and their concerns about the future of their localities (Hicks, 2006). Within schools, there is a growing body of evidence that using the locality of the school can enhance children's learning, because:

- children really enjoy learning in their locality;
- children can learn in a variety of ways in their locality;
- children can learn new geographical concepts and skills in their localities;
- where children have positive views of their locality, children welcome their teachers valuing their area as much as they do;
- where children have negative views of their locality, these may be improved by taking part in geography activity in the locality;
- learning in the locality within geography lessons is a welcome change from classroom-based school activities;
- learning in and about the locality in geography can have huge positive impacts on other areas of learning in the curriculum; and
- relationships between teachers and children are enhanced through local fieldwork.

Overall, it is becoming increasingly evident that learning in and about the locality can have positive impacts on all elements of children's lives. A report by the Scottish Natural Heritage found that compared to indoor settings, outdoor lessons resulted in the significant enhancement of: 'challenge and enjoyment', 'personalisation', 'relevance', 'breadth' and 'progression' (Mannion *et al.*, 2015). The overall report findings were generally positive, although concerns were expressed about experiences for some children:

- Outdoor provision increases learner engagement and enhances educational experience.
- Schools and preschools have increased their average outdoor durations since 2006 but provision is unevenly spread and further substantial increases are realistically achievable.
- Schools in deprived areas face greater challenges in providing for learning outdoors, and pupils attending schools in more deprived areas were less likely to be in receipt of a residential outdoor experience, and were more likely to experience shorter outdoor events.
- Many schools were beginning to use local areas more, enabling them to provide low-cost, teacher-led provisions outdoors.

Table 6.1 Correlation between children's independent mobility, well-being and PISA scores

Country	Independent mobility*	Achievement in reading, mathematics and science**	Well-being***	Low health complaints***	Daily physical activity****
Finland	1	1	3	3	2
Germany	2	5	8	1	4
Norway	3	4	4	6	7
Sweden	4	6	1	7	6
Japan	5	2	N/A	N/A	N/A
Denmark	6	9	4	4	9
England	7	10	8	8	3
France	8	8	9	9	8
Israel	9	13	N/A	N/A	N/A
Sri Lanka	10	N/A	N/A	N/A	N/A
Brazil	11	14	N/A	N/A	N/A
Ireland	12	7	6	5	1
Australia	13	3	N/A	N/A	N/A
Portugal	14	11	11	2	5
Italy	15	12	5	10	10
South Africa	16	N/A	N/A	N/A	N/A

* Level of independent mobility enjoyed by a child, weighted for age. ** Programme for International Student Assessment (PISA) data. *** UNICEF based on a composite index of child welfare in wealthy countries. **** Moderate and/or Vigorous Physical Activity (MPVA) data

Source: O'Keefe and O'Beirne, 2015.

- Outdoor provisions were helping schools and preschools address many aspects of the 'Curriculum for Excellence' including health and wellbeing and sustainable development.

The Children's Mobility study linked children's independent use of the locality, well-being and their abilities across the curriculum. A multiple country study found that there was a correlation between the PISA scores of children in particular countries and their independent mobility, as can be seen in Table 6.1. The countries where children were doing relatively well in reading, mathematics and science were those where children were more likely to be travelling to and from school and around their locality independently (O'Keeffe and O'Beirne, 2015). Although further studies are required, it does appear that when children are able to negotiate such daily tasks they do learn more than adults may think from such experiences.

Benefits of local learning and learning in geography

The benefits of local learning can be broken down into cognitive and affective domains of learning, with significant overlap between these.

First, there is evidence that local learning, whether within a school context or not, brings affective benefits to children; these include an enjoyment of learning, positive attitudes to learning, developed self-identity and increased likelihood of active citizenship. For example, research consistently reveals children like learning about their local environment (Ballantyne and Packer, 2002; Biddulph and Adey, 2004; Pike, 2011). In England, Nundy found these benefits were both cognitive and affective, with each of these reinforcing the other. His research showed that experiencing learning in ways that use multiple methods and resources, including local fieldwork, makes connections in the brain, helping children to develop higher order cognitive and affective structures. These processes can be far more complex than learning in more traditional classroom based ways (Nundy, 1999). Learning in the locality can significantly improve children's ability to work independently, as they can plan meaningful enquiries on local features and processes, with the support of their teachers. There are so many topics in geography that can be enhanced by the use of the locality, as outlined on Table 6.2. These activities can be used with all different age groups, as appropriate.

Second, the locality of the school can also be used to help children understand geographical concepts within their locality, for example:

- *Development*: How has our area changed? An investigation into how the locality of the school had changed in recent years, and what may happen in the future.

Table 6.2 Activities and learning in local environments

Foci of local learning	Examples of activity
Learning about nature	• Caring for animals, plants, recycling, gardening • Physical processes in rivers, beaches, etc.
Learning about society	• Community-based gardening initiatives • Finding out about local issues
Learning about nature–society interactions	• Recycling, composting, farming • Visits to outdoor nature centres
Learning about oneself	• Fulfilment through adventure education • Enquiry on home area
Learning about working with others	• Small-group fieldwork • Interviewing professionals and residents
Learning new skills	• Fieldwork in school grounds • Identifying pollutants in a water basin
Learning about conservation	• Focused activities on city farms • Waste audits in locality
Learning about influencing society	• Campaigning on controversial issues
Learning research skills	• Action research during fieldwork

Source: Adapted from: Hart, 1992; Pike, 2011.

- *Decison-making*: Where would a butterfly like to live in our school grounds? An enquiry deciding where would be the best place for a caterpillar/butterfly and realising good places for wildlife are also good for us.
- *Sustainability*: How can we care for our locality? An investigation into the different people that care for the local area, and those who do not.
- *Place/location*: Where are our favourite places in the locality? An investigation finding and describing features and locations in the area around the school.

Finally, the locality can be used to help children understand major concepts in geography that they will revisit later. This draws on the ideas of Jerome Bruner, who stated that 'we begin with the hypothesis that any subject can be taught effectively in some intellectually honest form to any child at any stage of development' (Bruner 1960, p. 33). For example, by using the locality as a prompt for:

- learning about hurricanes by using the locality to revise about how rain and wind are formed;
- learning about characteristics of the localities before comparing their locality to a distant locality;
- observing signs of development in the locality of the school to help understand the concept of development, before examining the concept of development in the wider world;
- considering their own views on local changes, before considering the views of others about a change in a less familiar place.

Examples of these ideas are shown in each of the case studies shown in this chapter and in Chapter 7.

Third, learning in the locality also has a positive impact on children's spatial capabilities. For example, Catling found that after a number of teaching activities, such as fieldwork, use of local maps and study of information from the local planning office, young people's maps of their local area improved (1998). He concluded that it is 'vital to plan a range of active experiences so that local studies can develop young people's knowledge of local features, understanding of geographical ideas and the use of appropriate skills such as fieldwork and map work' (Catling, 1998, p. 11). Turning specifically to mapping within work on the school and its grounds, research with young primary children has found that the specific teaching of mapping in the school has a positive impact on young people's spatial capabilities (Walsh, 2006). Bacon also found a series of enquiry-based lessons on maps and mapping had an impact on children's ability to produce accurate maps of their own (Bacon and Matthews, 2014). It appears that work on the locality, incorporating the making and using of maps, is also particularity effective at transforming children's views of geography (Smyth, 2010; Pike, 2011).

For example, the children in St James' were making and using maps to help them answer their enquiry questions. However, the learning was two way, as the children's ideas helped the adults present learn more about the children's places, or their ethno-geographies (Martin, 2005; 2008). For example, their 'wishing pond' was actually a stream that passed through the main street in the village, but it was where they gathered at the end of school and threw stones into the river and made wishes or generally played around.

CASE STUDY 6.3 Mapping our village: what features can we see? 5–8 year olds, St James National School

As part of their work on the past, present and future of their school, the children carried out further work on their locality, as shown in Figure 6.3:

Fieldwork. What features can we see? Why are they here? The children started their investigation with a walk around the areas near the school, the intended outcome of which was to take a journey and then map the journey, however intended and unintended outcomes included:

- Observing a range of features, including man-made and natural, as well as those difficult to categorise (such as gravel on the road).
- Observing and discussing features that were 'new' (a new house, sign, etc.) and 'old' (the medieval church ruin, the school itself, the old school teacher's house).
- Taking special note of features that had changed very recently (a house in the process of renovation, new signage, etc.).
- Observing and discussing why features in the locality had changed, such as why the teacher's house was sold.
- Collecting artefacts in all the above places to use to make a 'journey stick' map.

The children led the fieldwork in the locality, as they had decided where the class should go. Places visited during the fieldwork included:

- *The wishing tree*: The children had decided that the first place to go was 'the wishing tree' in the churchyard, where the children all make their wishes (Figure 6.2a). (The class teacher had named the tree some years before.)
- *Homes on the lane*: The children moved on to the houses in the lane discussing all the points listed above.
- *The stream*: The next stop was one of the children's favourite places, the stream at the bottom of the lane. Here the children stopped and spoke of how they liked meeting here and jumping in the stream.
- *The square*: Finally the children went to the village square and noted the very newest and oldest things they could see. They collected their items together and compared what they had found (Figure 6.3b).

Making 3D journey stick maps. The children used their collected material to make 'journey stick' maps. These are wooden twigs or long pieces of string to which children attach items collected on a journey (Figure 6.2c). When completed, the children have actually produced a map or timeline of their journey.

The maps had different values for the children, one child noted how it helped her remember the journey they had made:

> When I came to draw my map it was hard because the things had disappeared from my head but when I looked at my journey stick I remembered them all.

Children were asked to think about their experiences of drawing the maps and some found it easy or easier than before; others found it 'hard'. One child had never drawn a map before and found it hard to get started. In the end she drew the map shown in Figure 6.3d; as can be seen she was very proud of her map!

(a)   (b)
(c)   (d)

Figure 6.3 Using the locality in primary geography: (a, b) walking and talking, (c) collecting data and (d) making maps

Through these activities, the children's spatial abilities and mapping developed together; this is why primary curricula place equal emphasis on children making and using maps. Generally, guidance suggests that making familiar and local maps should be emphasised in younger years, and using maps should be emphasised in older years, as outlined in Appendix 2; although, children of all ages do benefit from both making and using maps of all different places. As Catling (2003) notes, for all of us mapping is important:

> To make sense of the features and layout of our immediate and the wider world, we map it, both to see where things are and to help us understand . . . the variety of natural and human processes at work.

Table 6.3 Examples of children's learning in their local environments

Cognitive development	Affective development
• Ability to carry out enquiry/investigation based on the locality	• Responding and reacting to locality
	• Valuing locality
• Knowledge of features and processes in the locality	• Expressing ideas and opinions
	• Organisation of personal values and attitudes
• Development of spatial awareness and abilities	• Appreciating the opinions and attitudes of others in the locality
• Understanding and analysis of local physical processes	• Participation in local decison-making
• Understanding and analysis of local human processes	• Resolving conflicts with or between others
	• Appreciating diverse opinions
• Application of learning about locality to other places	• Managing and avoiding risks
• Evaluation of local physical and human processes within and beyond the locality	

Source: Adapted from Pike, 2011b.

As outlined in Chapter 2, the types of maps children can make include: picture maps, model maps, maps with construction toys, messy maps, journey stick maps, journey string maps and collage maps. This list is not exhaustive, and children themselves will come up with even more possibilities. Journey sticks, as described in Case Study 6.3, work particularly well; it draws on a technique used by North American Indians in which they used physical artefacts attached to a stick in the field during a journey. The idea behind this is that the items on the journey stick will reinforce the memory of being in the particular places and also instil a deeper sense of place due to the construction of the journey stick by the children. Therefore, for the children the activity develops cognitive and affective mapping and engages the learners at deeper levels than simply talking or drawing (Whittle, 2006). As Martin notes, the skill of teachers is to recognise the features in 'different cultural and social contexts (children's geographies) that were common to all types of geographical thinking (i.e., the universal elements) and to make connections between the two for the learners.'(Martin, 2008)

There is also evidence that local learning in geography contributes to positive outcomes in the affective domains of learning (Nundy, 1999; Rickson *et al.*, 2004; Pike, 2011). The Review of Outdoor Learning by Rickson *et al.*, includes many references to the transformative value of all types of outdoor learning for children and young people. Smyth (2010), working with children and parents in one school, found that using the locality through enquiry did not readily occur to teachers when planning geography lessons.

- *Pre-fieldwork*: 'I think geography should be based more outdoors. It would make it way more interesting. It's way too boring reading from a textbook'.
- *Post-fieldwork*: 'The best part of the experience was when we visited the river, it was really good because you could understand the features of the river that you learned in the classroom.'

Over a number of weeks, Smyth designed a number of enquiry-based tasks centred on a stream close to the school. Her most important finding was that children really enjoyed and learned from the experience of enquiry-based fieldwork in the locality of their school. The project was transformative for the children, as can be seen from the comments in Table 6.4. For the children's parents, the school project revealed the power of primary geography as a subject to allow children the opportunity to learn differently from their own experiences.

The interaction between learning and enjoyment is complex. However, researchers have found that young people enjoy subjects more when active methodologies, such as fieldwork, are used in learning at school, including when learning in geography (Biddulph and Adey, 2004; Pike, 2013b). They also found that children not only enjoyed fieldwork but could accurately recall what they had learned and that where children did not do fieldwork they regretted it.

Planning learning in and about the locality in geography

The possibilities of learning geography in the locality are many and can usually involve developing knowledge and understanding of human and physical processes through fieldwork. Fieldwork in the locality can also be used to develop other aspects of children's learning, including:

*   geographical and generic skills;
*   language and literacy skills;
*   attitudes to learning and to their locality;
*   friendships, relationship with teachers and other adults;
*   the ability to work alone and with others;
*   appreciation of their local environment and community.

Before whole school planning for local learning in primary geography, it is essential to audit the locality; this is an activity that can be very enjoyable for teachers, as it involves school planning through outdoor activity and will help teachers see the potential of the locality. This could also be carried out with a class in the school; for example, the oldest class in the school could carry out an audit in groups for the rest of the school. It must be remembered that the children in a school are the experts on its locality. Local areas of most schools contain some or all of the following, an audit for which can be found in Appendix 3:

*   streams or rivers;
*   houses: new, old, refurbishments and extensions;
*   beaches or lakes;
*   fields and farms;
*   roads and streets;
*   homes: houses, apartments, caravans, etc.;
*   industry: companies, buildings, etc.;
*   wild areas: woods, paths, etc.;
*   communications: wires, drains, etc.

CASE STUDY 6.4 How might our area change in the future? 10–12 year olds, Scoil Fhursa

The boys in Scoil Fhursa spent a number of geography lessons focusing on their locality, and a number looking at different places (penpals, Rio 2016, etc.).

Our area, our opinions. To begin with the boys brainstormed thoughts about their area and the following types of features and opinions were recorded:

- **My area**. Lots of kids, big park, sports centre, pitches, pharmacy, football club, Chipper and Chinese.
- **Good features**. The Shack youth club, friendly dogs.
- **Bad features**. Smoking, rubbish, vandalism, fires, rats.
- **What to do**. Traps to kills rats, clean up the paint, stop fires, cut down shrubs, restore the green.

During these initial brainstorms the boys asked questions such as:

- Why did they build the tunnel?
- Why did they only show the bad side (referring to a television documentary)?
- Why is there trouble?
- Why do people litter?

Devising enquiry questions. From these findings, the boys devised a number of enquiry questions and decided on their key enquiry question:

- What do people think?
- Which places should change?
- What is the area like?
- What do we think of the area?
- Why was Coolock built? How did it change?

These questions were negotiated between the teacher and the children. From this, the boys originally decided that their main question would be: 'Would the tunnel close down?'. They were encouraged to widen the focus of their question, to reflect the amount of work they were doing. The question then became: 'How might our area change in the future?'.

Collecting data. Their ideas for geography activities to answer their questions included: talking to people, doing surveys, walking around their area, looking on the internet and so on. The next week, the boys carried out a fieldwork survey on the area around the shopping centre (Figure 6.4). They worked in groups and each group focused on a different aspect of their enquiry:

- talking to local residents;
- taking photographs of features in the locality;
- recording their own thoughts on different places in the locality.

The boys completed a large amount of analysis and presented their work publicly, as described in Case Study 9.4.

Figure 6.4 Fieldwork on local issues: how could our area change in the future? (a) collecting data, (b) investigating local issues – the tunnel, (c) work completed and (d) still writing!

There are also a large number of resources that can help us plan about the locality, to enhance fieldwork opportunities:

- the Internet: local webpages, social media pages and accounts;
- local maps and plans: past, present and future (proposed developments);
- local newspapers and reports;
- local residents: older people, young people, parents, local councillors, etc.;
- photographs and paintings;
- oral history tapes and accounts from the Schools Folklore Collection;
- census returns and online information;
- local city, town and county planning office;
- local GIY, Transition Towns or Tidy Towns groups.

As teachers, we need to plan the stages of learning carefully with children, but also need to think of the practical arrangements for trips out of school. A thorough familiarity on the part of the teacher with the places to be visited and explored is essential (DES/NCCA, 1999c, p. 74). Appendix 5 includes a straightforward but useful risk assessment, using a numerical scale to assess and manage risk.

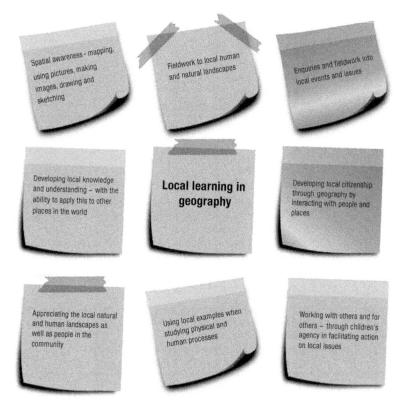

Figure 6.5 The possibilities of locality learning in geography

Before embarking on local geography fieldwork we must consider the following steps:

- get to know the environment thoroughly, using personal and continual professional development (CPD) time to explore the locality on foot;
- identify and note potential hazards, using a suitable template;
- consult:
  - principal/head teacher and if required board of management;
  - school policy on out-of-classroom activities;
  - safety statement;
  - other teachers, LSAa, SNAs and parent helpers;
  - parents/guardians/carers;
- choose and prepare for the enquiries and activities in which children will engage, with the children;
- consult safety guidelines in relevant curriculum/guidelines;
- prepare the children for the experience, include learning and behaviour expectations
  - plan and complete preparatory classroom work;
  - plan forthcoming work – agree simple contract of learning and behaviour;
- inform parents and obtain parental consent through letter/email at start of school year or for each trip – refer to school policies for guidance;

Table 6.4 A simple plan for a series of lessons on a local beach

Enquiry question	Possible activities
What can you see at the beach?	• Observe. List. Draw – features • Categorise objects into natural/manmade – touch/feel – living/dead – over/under land • Discuss **features** and **processes**
How are the features made?	
What is being worn away?	• Find evidence of erosion • Observe erosion • Discuss how and why material is worn away = **eroded**
What is being moved?	• Experiment with different materials in the sea – safety! Teacher to do experiments. Children must remain away from water. Or can be done in rock pools by children • Discuss how and why material is moved = **transported**
What is being dropped?	• Investigate what has been dropped at high and low watermark • Investigate what happens to materials of different weight, properties, etc. • Discuss how and why material is dropped = **deposited**
What are people doing about these processes?	• Investigate **beach management** • Make a list of erosion prevention • List hazards at the beach • Observe and list **safety features** at the beach • List ways the beach could be cared for

•   organise what the teacher and children should bring with them and do on the trip;
•   ensure adequate supervision by teachers, school staff and parent helpers;
•   complete follow-up work in classroom;
•   evaluate the learning experience;
•   ask children to write thank you notes to helpers and anyone they met on the visit.

One of the most essential stages listed above is the assessment of risk for any activity carried out with children outside. Three factors are central to determining whether or not the level of risk is acceptable or tolerable in a learning activity:

•   the likelihood of coming to harm;
•   the severity of that harm;
•   the benefits, rewards or outcomes of the activity.

A risk assessment template can be found in Appendix 5, this will help teachers have a realistic view of risk. However, an important consideration in carrying out local fieldwork is 'What are the benefits?' – when this is taken into account it is always apparent that the enormous benefits in doing geography fieldwork outweigh risks, once appropriate places for fieldwork are found (Ball *et al.*, 2013, p. 112).

Issues over using the locality with children

Unfortunately, there are reasons why children may not experience locality-based learning and fieldwork in primary classrooms. These can be related to large scale issues or to local practical issues. Studies over time and in different countries suggest that teacher's geographies and interests have an influence on whether the locality is used in geography lessons (Cummins, 2010; Pike, 2011b; 2013a). Researchers have documented numerous institutional, cultural and logistical barriers that have limited the amount and nature of outdoor learning (e.g. Comishan *et al.*, 2004; Ham and Sewing, 1988; Hart and Nolan, 1999; Rickinson *et al.*, 2004; Simmons, 1998). In their review of the literature on outdoor learning, Rickinson *et al.* (2004) summarise five key barriers to outdoor learning:

- fear and concern about young people's health and safety;
- teacher's confidence and expertise in teaching and learning outdoors;
- the requirements of school curricula;
- shortages of time, resources and support;
- wider changes within the education sector and beyond.

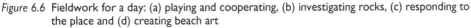

Figure 6.6 Fieldwork for a day: (a) playing and cooperating, (b) investigating rocks, (c) responding to the place and (d) creating beach art

A further issue may be the one outlined in Chapter 5, that the development and use of school grounds may ironically stop teachers using places beyond the school gates for geography.

The lack of opportunities for local geography, including fieldwork, that children may experience can be looked at from two perspectives. Children's localities and ideas may not be used in teaching geography, or may be used in a tokenistic way (Hart, 1992; Pike, 2011b) because adults do not wish to allow children to learn in such ways. Catling argues children are marginalised in their local neighbourhood and school environments and are also marginalised in the primary school geography curriculum (Catling, 2005). Although this is not the case in the Irish primary curriculum, it is the case in some classrooms and is certainly the case in many textbooks. Martin (2006) argues the English geography curriculum is dominated by a top-down approach, which values the academic voice but does little to recognise the non-specialist voice common to most primary teachers.

The locality may not appear 'geographical' to some teachers. Hence, Pike found that teachers with no strong interest in geography, and who were not from the locality, were less likely to use the locality in their teaching, let alone carry out fieldwork (2011). Often this is because of a lack of opportunities for teachers to work together to plan for primary geography. Cummins (2010) found that teachers in her study who were not from the area dismissed the local area as a site of learning as it was mainly housing estates. In these cases, it is important to note that teachers had received very little CPD in geography education and had never received any that was based on their own or any other school locality.

Again, this appears to be more evident when the teachers are from outside the area of the school. Even local teachers may not know the local people and places to explore. However, children use and think about places very differently compared to the way adults do (Catling, 2003; Pike, 2011). Also, teachers may not wish to address more difficult issues in local areas. As Catling (2005, p. 335) argues:

> '[children's] real world is kept at a safe distance from what must be learnt. It enables geographical topics to be taught comfortably . . . It stays with safe questions and safe answers, as well as avoiding controversy . . . [it] presents a potentially sanitized, almost cosmetically dressed, 'reality' for consumption by parents, governors and politicians.

Martin argues that the failure to link the everyday and school geography for children has been problematic (2008, p. 439):

> The discontinuity between children, their environmental experiences and the geography curriculum could be a key factor behind the decline in the status of, and standards in, geography over the last decade.

Conclusions

As Adams and Ingham (1998) note, research shows that children's experiences of their local environment can affect their future attitudes:

> There is a link between young people's experiences and perceptions of their environment and the attitudes they develop towards it. Where children are able to establish a strong connection with a neighbourhood and develop a feeling of ownership and engagement with it, while at the same time feeling a sense of belonging, they can develop a strong sense of place. This can only be based on first-hand, social and emotional experience, which is vital today when so much experience is second-hand and mediated, whether through programmed learning in school or the soap opera on television. The fostering of a sense of place will work against feelings of dispossession alienation.

Being familiar with the intricacies of local lanes, businesses and physical features provides teachers with the knowledge to share with children, or the confidence to allow children to construct, the knowledge through geographical enquiry in such places.

Reflection and action

- How does your school use the immediate locality in primary geography?
- How could you plan to develop the use of the immediate locality of the school in geography in the next few years?
- What activity could take place in each class level – planned and not so planned?
- How can the barriers to using the locality in geography be overcome?
- What local people and places can be drawn upon and used for primary geography?

Further resources

Reports and guidance

There are many reports and guidance booklets, from organisations such as:

The Council for Learning Outside the Classroom: www.lotc.org.uk
Play England: www.playengland.org.uk
Scottish Natural Heritage (SNH): www.snh.gov.uk

Journals

Children, Youth and Environments: www.jstor.org/action/showPublication?journal Code=chilyoutenvi&
Children's Geographies: www.tandfonline.com/toc/cchg20/current
Primary Geography: produced by the Geographical Association, it always features ideas for using the locality in primary geography lessons – www.geography.org.uk

Environmental Education Ireland

A group of educators in Ireland, interested in sharing ideas, stories and research around connecting people to nature, place and community through meeting up online and in person. Their social media account posts all sorts of events and articles relating to environmental education: www.facebook.com/groups/488656621217724.

Children and their localities

There is an international movement concerned with the loss of children's independent mobility in their localities. A number of websites and blogs feature interesting articles relevant to geography education, for example:

Mission Explore is an award winning project that encourages children to complete missions in their locality, in school or out: www.missionexplore.net.

Richard Louv writes a blog which features recent writings and selected articles, from the author of *Last Child in the Woods*: http://richardlouv.com.

Project Wild Thing is a growing movement of organisations and individuals who care deeply about the need for nature connected, free-range, roaming and outdoor playing kids in the 21st century: https://projectwildthing.com.

Chapter 7

Real geography – topical geography through issues and events

We also presented our projects to local TDs. It helped us to build up courage and not be afraid to talk to people on a stage or platform. I really enjoyed doing this project. It was amazing that we were able to get people to listen to us.

Boy, 11

The chapter is based on the following key thoughts:

- Be aware of the research in primary geography and related areas on children's views of places, events and issues.
- Create lessons based on events and issues, to incorporate several areas of geography as well as other subjects.
- Source resources on local, national and international issues and events, and plan learning activities around these with children.

This chapter outlines:

- How to make geography topical and interesting for children.
- How to use children's enquiry questions as the basis for issue- and event-based lessons.
- How learning about topical events and issues enhances children's experiences of geography and other subjects.
- How children can tackle controversial content and challenging pedagogies in geography lessons.
- How action and participation are logical conclusions to any class or fieldwork on events and issues.

The school and the locality also provide opportunities to study issues and events, and so this chapter enhances the ideas and examples in Chapters 5 and 6.

Children's engagement with geographical issues and events

Children are interested in issues in their locality and the wider world: they listen to adults talk, see the news, read papers and have a range of questions to ask. Children's lives are geographical (Catling, 2003; Martin, 2008) and so it is not surprising that their questions are also geographical:

- Where do flowers go in the winter?
- What animals live in the wood?
- Why is the park so messy today?
- Why is traffic always worse on Tuesdays?
- How long will it take for the new shopping centre to be built?
- What's the best country to live in?
- Why do tsunamis happen?
- Why is there fighting in some countries and not others?

As teachers, we can draw on this wealth of potential knowledge in geography lessons. We can also help children to develop their enquiry skills to answer their own questions (Roberts, 2003). We can also ensure children learn 'powerful knowledge' beyond their immediate experiences (Young, 2008) in topical geography. The school and local area provides a wealth of opportunities for this type of learning. In one area (Co. Waterford) featured in this book, local issues and events include:

- *School buildings*: making space for nature, for example planting, wild areas, ponds, etc.
- *Travel to school*: lack of footpaths, traffic problems, improvements of cycle lanes etc.
- *Deise Greenway*: the development of the Deise Greenway – a 30km extension to the local 10km cycle track to bring it from Dungarvan to Waterford along a disused railway route and the issues over the extension of the Greenway.
- *Traffic*: despite a multi-million pound EU grant on the cycle network around town, known as Go Dungarvan, traffic is still very heavy at rush hours and most journeys are less than 2km. However, the scheme has increased children's independent journeys to school.
- *Marina*: the proposal to build a marina in Dungarvan Harbour – a long-running issue but has not progressed to date.
- *Wind turbines*: the building of wind turbines in An Rinn, a rural Irish-speaking area. These have now been built and a wind turbine in Dungarvan at a multi-national company is still being debated.
- *Events*: there are many events in Waterford, which can be used as a source of geography lessons, such as the Waterford Festival of Food and the Tall Ships Festival, etc.

To check such local issues and events, we only need to open a newspaper application on our phone or pick up a newspaper. There are many ways we can become more aware of issues and events, and use these with children:

- *The school*: noting changes or proposed changes due to natural or human actions, for example features of spring and potential for tree planting, etc.
- *The locality*: noting any places and spaces with issues in the locality, such as new housing developments and sustainable developments such as community gardens, etc.
- *Local newspaper*: always look through the local paper for local geographical issues, such as new cycle routes and wind turbines, etc.

Figure 7.1 Local issues and events: an instant source of primary geography: (a, b) artist's impressions and (c, d) current work on Dublin's new light railway lines

- *National newspapers*: like or follow local and national newspapers on their social media accounts.
- *Online newspapers*: setting the homepage on their computer as a newspaper or news channel home page.
- *Radio*: listening to news channels on the radio in the mornings.
- *Television*: watch the news at least a few times a week.

Using topical geography is a very effective way for children to learn geography and much more! From my own experience of teaching, I have found that teaching through issues brings the following benefits for children and teachers:

- *Geographical learning*: make sense of events and issues, locally, nationally and globally.
- *Literacies and learning*: use all the literacies referred to in Chapter 2.
- *Children's citizenship*: realise and develop their own agency and roles in events and issues in the locality and wider world.
- *Values education*: begin to consider events and issues from the perspectives of others.
- *Human Rights education*: develop a rights perspective on events and issues.

Figure 7.2 Learning through geographical issues and events can enhance children's learning across the curriculum (a) world sports events, geography and mathematics, (b) personal geographies and histories, (c) local issues and language through letter writing and (d) water, geography and art

The photographs in Figure 7.2 show just some examples of these. The first of these are discussed below, with the final three being discussed further in Chapter 9.

In exploring issues and events locally and in the wider world, we can help children understand why they occur, and their impact. Even for younger children this is very important, as children hear about events in the news and need to understand them. It is also very important to help children make sense of the world and learn how to put events and issues in context in time and space. Children's fears are often exaggerated by avoiding issues, and part of our role as teachers is to help them negotiate the worlds they live in. In fact, many schools use social media, to find out about the news and share their own. Children learn all about the Internet through using it, as one child in Scoil Fhursa said:

> My favourite memory of this year: My favourite memory of the year would probably have to be when we got 500 followers on Twitter – by the way follow @MsToalsClass. The whole class cheered and we got TWO nights off homework!

Sites such as Storyful use social media to develop news stories for a global audience. Websites such as The Paper Boy feature newspapers from across the world.

Learning through geographical events

Although there has been little formal research about children's views of learning events in geography, it is evident that they are interested in this type of geography. To learn about events a relatively straight-forward framework can be used:

What do we want to know about this event?

- for homework, the children should bring in papers, articles and so on about the event;
- arrange time for free talk about pictures, news articles, cartoons, etc.;
- write down all the questions the children would like answered about the event;
- sort these questions into themes and decide on enquiry questions.

What were the causes?

- investigate enquiry questions – from children;
- use the school grounds to discuss and clarify why hurricanes occur drawing on past weather lessons;
- investigate the causes of the event using news reports, diagrams, infographics, etc.

What were the effects?

- investigate effects of the event using news reports, diagrams, infographics, social media, etc.;
- the children should sort effects into immediate and short-term effects; and then predict long-term effects.

How did or can people respond?

- investigate responses to the event using news reports, diagrams, infographics, etc.;
- the children should sort responses into immediate and short-term responses; and then predict long-term needs and responses;
- investigate the reporting of the event in different media;
- create a newspaper report from a newsroom simulation (see Geography Champions for examples).

CASE STUDY 7.1 Why do hurricanes happen? Hurricane Sandy: 8–12 year olds, St James' National School

Children in the senior class in St James' National School found out about Hurricane Sandy, not because it was part of what they were doing in geography but because it was a major news story. They carried out a range of activities as shown in Figure 7.3, including:

- **Generating ideas through discussion.** The children looked at photographs from the hurricane and discussed them, speculating about what had happened and why.

- **Starting enquiry**. The children asked questions about the event and sorted these into enquiry questions.
- **Assessing the news**. The children reviewed place names mentioned in newspaper reports and mapped these. From this activity, they realised that events in some places were reported more than those in other places. In the case of Hurricane Sandy, it only became international news when it affected the United States, even though there had been substantial damage and deaths in Haiti and Cuba before the storm hit the coast of North America.
- **Analysing information on the hurricane**. The children were encouraged to sort the information they had found by:
  - recording the causes, effects and responses to the hurricane in different places;
  - completing a news room simulation on the hurricane, where the balance of reporting was addressed by some of the children.

The children found the activities really interesting, and they helped the children make sense of the events and understand why such events happen.

(a)

(b)

(c)

(d)

Figure 7.3 Events in local or global news provide opportunities for children to work as geographers (a) World Cup – flags and locations, (b) Dublin Light Rail and Swift Bus proposals, (c) using newspapers and (d) investigating local issues

This framework can be adapted; for example we could start with the effects as a source for generating ideas. However, the framework ensures children can think through events effectively and logically, as the example in Case Study 7.1 exemplifies. Overall, teaching primary geography through events helps make it real for primary children. It also ties up many areas of the geography curriculum and helps enhance children's learning in many other ways.

Learning through geographical issues

A geographical issue is an important geographical topic or problem for debate or discussion. The 'Crick Report' (Advisory Group on Citizenship, 1998, p. 56) defined a controversial issue as:

> An issue about which there is no one fixed or universally held point of view. Such issues are those which commonly divide society and for which significant groups offer conflicting explanations and solutions.

Within this book and specifically this chapter, geographical issues are any proposed or ongoing action that people debate. The stories that we are generally interested in are those that people disagree over: elections, new developments, changes in the locality and so on. These are all issues that are also of interest to children. Studies by Oulton *et al.* (2004) and Cotton (2006) found teachers identify issues and teach them – but generally at second level; this is possibly because issues are complex. However, at primary level, children can examine a wide range of issues, appropriate for their ages:

- school, for example places for wildlife, views on the location of benches, trees, new classrooms, gardens, etc.;
- local, for example construction of a new shopping centre, change of land use of a school field;
- national, for example building of new roads, the extraction of oil and gas;
- global for example conflicts between countries, issues over sporting events.

Each week local, national and global issues are reported, discussed and debated in communities and in the media. Accordingly, the curriculum suggests that children from ages 8 and up should be enabled to: 'identify and discuss a local, national or global environmental issue' (DES/NCCA, 1999b, pp. 61, 77). The curriculum suggests examples of issues children can investigate such as litter, pollution, changes in flora and fauna, and the need for new roads, etc. For each of these, we need to think about the geographical learning behind the issue; we need to give children the opportunity to ask questions and then plan the respective activities for the solution. A framework for this could be:

What do we want to know about this issue?

- for homework, children should ring in papers, online accounts and images about the issue;
- arrange time for free talk about pictures, news articles, etc.;
- write down the enquiry questions the children would like answered.

What is going to happen?

- investigate enquiry questions – from children, assisted by teachers;
- investigate features of the issue, for example the features of a proposed development using videos and artists' impressions;
- use maps to discuss proposed change, expressing personal opinions;
- use tools such as a decision-making grid to create graphs on alternative options;
- groups can present findings to each other and to the class.

What might be the effects?

- use and sort cards to consider arguments for and against the issue;
- for homework, collect other people's opinions on the issue;
- collate data on opinions and sort them using Venn diagrams.

How are or will people respond?

- children could consider a dilemma, based on a person or group of people affected by the issue;
- the class could discuss the impact of the issue both on individuals and on groups of people;
- children could consider groups of people who would be for, against or undecided on the issue;
- groups could be allocated to represent different perspectives and form 'gossip circles' to discuss their views;
- groups could use a writing frame to present their case to the class;
- children could write a persuasive text, depending on their final thoughts.

Teaching through geographical issues touches on many areas of geography, as well as other subjects, and may go beyond the curriculum. Teaching through issues can develop children's geographical understanding as well as help them in other ways:

Geographical knowledge. Children's knowledge of places and processes improves as they find out about where the issues are taking place, as well as other places affected. They also find out about people as they examine who is involved in the issue and what they think or may think. For example, in exploring the development of cities for Olympic events, children learn much about the places in which these events occur, as outlined in Case Study 5.2. Younger children can really begin to understand concepts such as features and locations through their investigations in the school grounds and locality.

Geographical understanding. Teaching through issues develops more than simply knowledge. Children will develop deep understanding of how and why human and physical processes occur. For example, through examining 'How should our beach be managed?' children will not only learn about how beaches change through the processes of erosion, transportation and deposition but also about how it is difficult for people to come to agreements about how beaches are used and managed. For younger children, concepts such as change can be better understood through examining the school grounds and localities. For older children, in studying events such as the Olympic events through different activities, they learn about the complex processes that occur when decisions are made about places.

Literacies. In dealing with the real world, teaching through issues develops all areas of children's learning, including the essential areas of literacy and numeracy, in a meaningful way. Using a range of sources, such as newspapers, brochures and people, means children have to access different genres of speaking and writing. Furthermore, looking at issues provides children with opportunities to think critically about information they are given and about how different groups of people may or may not be heard in decison-making. Examples of activities children may take part in include:

- in groups, examining artists' impressions of a proposed development or drawing their own ideas about changes;
- in pairs, highlighting the for/against views of an issue in a newspaper article;
- as part of fieldwork, talking to other people about their views on the issue;
- individually, during fieldwork, imagining what a place may look like in the future.

Geography gives literacy lessons a wealth of rich material with which to work. In recording information, writing about different sides of debates and putting together accounts of what could or should happen, children access a whole range of different literacies.

CASE STUDY 7.2 Does Dublin need a new Metro?
11–12 year olds, St Patrick's Boys National School

As described fully in Case Study 3.3, and shown in Figure 7.4, the boys in St Patrick's Boys' National School had a particular interest in the Metro as the proposed route passed many of their places: homes, schools, clubs and so on.

Devising enquiry questions. Using enquiry approaches, they used photographs to begin to devise questions about the Metro that they would like answers to. These included:

- How much money will it cost?
- Where will it go?
- Where is the driver?
- What do people think of it?
- Where is it going to?
- What time of day is it?

As well as a large range of other questions! The questions were then consolidated into enquiry questions, with each lesson being based around the questions, as described in Case Study 3.3.

www.saintpats.ie

Figure 7.4 Learning more about Dublin's transport – A local issue with national implications (a) devising questions, (b, c) considering alternatives and (d) writing persuasively

Numeracy. Depending on how an issue is approached, there are also many opportunities for developing children's mathematical thinking within real life contexts, for example:

- in pairs, look up statistics to do with a development;
- in groups, examine the development using maps and plans;
- individually, as homework, collect differing opinions about a development.

Once the enquiry frame has been set up, children could take part in a project to present the views of different people. A good example of this is 'How can we make our lane safer?' in Chapter 7 as well as the work in Scoil Fhursa described in Case Studies 6.4 and 9.4. The type of activity described in Case Studies 3.3 and 7.2, by the boys in St Patrick's Boys' National School, can be developed and incorporated in to many other curriculum areas. The work could also lead to project-based enquiries with the children working more independently. As Tables 7.2 and 7.5 indicate, there are so many possibilities for learning about issues. Activities could include:

- surveying the area where the issue is taking place or is proposed;
- annotating maps showing the area, issues and/or proposed changes;

Table 7.1 Issues, key frameworks and concepts, children's possible enquiry questions and activities

Key enquiry question	Key geographical frameworks and concepts	Possible activities
Junior classes Where should we plant a tree in our school grounds?	• Asking geographical questions • Describing needs of trees • Selecting criteria for deciding what plants, specifically trees, need • Describing locations within the school grounds	• Children sort pictures using a Venn diagram of good and bad places to plant trees • Children ask questions about where trees can be planted • Children go in school grounds to good/ OK / bad places for trees in the school grounds • Children sort photographs of places for their trees and decide on the best place for a tree
Senior classes Do we need a new shopping centre?	• Asking geographical questions • Considering reasons for developments – social, economic, political, etc. • Recognising differing arguments for and against developments – and the difficulty in resolving such debates	• Children ask questions about a proposed shopping centre • Children use online maps to select places suitable for a shopping centre • Children sort other people's opinions using a scale of 'most in favour' through to 'least in favour' • Children interview existing shop owners about the impact on their takings should a new shopping centre open

CASE STUDY 7.3 How can we make our lane safer? 10–12 year olds, St James' National School

The staff and children in the senior class were concerned about traffic coming up and down the lane to the school. The lane was approximately 200 metres long, with 11 homes, a church, a shop and the school.

The issue. Some parents drove up and down the lane to the school to collect and drop their children; others dropped off or waited at the bottom of the lane. Many other people used the lane, including teachers, residents, churchgoers, community groups meeting in the hall and service people. A small number of parents and children walked to school.

The enquiry question. The children decided that the main question was: how can we make our lane safer?

The enquiry process. The children then decided which data they needed and, after much discussion, their ideas included:

• asking questions of different people: children, residents, parents, and so on, as shown in Figure 7.5 a and b;
• taking photographs along the lane at different times of day;
• making questionnaires;

- asking people their questions;
- using maps of the lane to come up with new plans for it.

The children had a wealth of information to make sense of (see Figure 7.5c and d) but worked steadily through it. As one girl said: 'Phew, that was hard work!'

Presenting findings. The children presented their data as graphs, text, maps and photographs. They included other people's opinions, including the residents of the lane, parents of children, and the children and teachers in the school. This was shared with parents in the school via a flyer and at a Parents' Association meeting.

As the sixth class girls said: 'We thought writing up our findings was challenging. It was complicated because we had to pull lots of information together, especially as we were doing it all on the computer. We were pleased with what we ended up with. We then made a flyer to give to people who live on and use the lane' (Green *et al.*, 2013).

The pulling together of the information for the children was complex and at times confusing. However, the children managed to work through this and collate and analyse all the data they had collected.

(a)   (b)

(c)   (d)

Figure 7.5 A local enquiry: how can we make our lane safer? (a, b) collecting data and (c, d) sorting, analysing and presenting data

- asking an expert to talk to the children during fieldwork or work with them in class, for example a local councillor or developer;
- designing and using questionnaires and interviews with people in the area, this can be used to present data using graphs, by hand or using data handling programmes.

There is also great potential for involving local decison-makers in the children's work. Teachers often invite local TDs/MPs and councillors in to hear children's views of their localities, as the boys in Scoil Fhursa did in Case Study 9.4. However, with no national framework for children's participation in local decison-making, such projects remain piecemeal. Internationally, there are examples of children being involved in locally-based projects as well as in national initiatives, but it does seem, as Percy-Smith indicates, that 'having a say' generally means 'having a say when it suits organizations and services' (2010). The use of the curriculum, along with some resources on children's localities and participation, would provide the necessary frames for helping to realise children's participation in their current and future communities. However, the most logical starting point for children's participation is to ask children to share their views about their current lives and future wishes, with no preconceived ideas – the ultimate in child centred curriculum planning! These ideas are described in Chapter 9.

Learning for the future – and present

As indicated above, it is argued that children should have the right to become involved in shaping 'their own futures and those of their communities' (Hart, 1992, p. 3). Following its ratification of the United Nations Convention on the Rights of the Child (UNCRC) in 1992, the state met its requirements in relation to the Convention by establishing the National Children's Office (NCO) in 2002 overseen by the Minister for Children, and in 2004 an office of the Ombudsman for Children (OCO). There has been an increased provision for children and associated evaluation and research on children's provision rights, such as the right to play and the provision of playground facilities (De Róiste and Dinneen, 2004). However, it has been argued that children's rights generally and particularly, the right to participation, have not been recognised in Ireland (Kilkelly, 2007). Like elsewhere, the focus in Ireland has tended to be on the collection of a selection of children's views, for example through Comhairle na nÓg (CnÓ) and Dáil na nÓg (DnÓ) (local and national children's councils). Despite such shortcomings, the Irish primary curriculum holds progressive and active views of children. It is argued that the concept of participation in the geography curriculum is limited to action within school; as Waldron has noted 'one gets the sense of comfortable and safe parameters being drawn around the concept of action' (Waldron, 2004, p. 222).

Frameworks for futures work are varied and engaging, presenting opportunities for children to differentiate between what will probably happen (probably futures) and what they would like to happen (preferable futures). This framework can be used with any age children, at any scale. For example, infant children may draw the future of their school playground; older children may consider the future of traffic management in their locality. As can be seen, many of the activities proposed in Tables 7.1 and 7.5 include a futures dimension (Hicks, 2006). On a school or local level, where changes are agreed with children, definite and visible action should be taken to avoid tokenism. Schools may consider asking parents to contribute resources such as time or physical resources such as benches and plants. As illustrated earlier, teachers or children can invite local decison-makers to hear children's views of their localities. Children can cause visible stress to council officials as they are asked challenging questions over future developments! These ideas are explored and exemplified in Chapter 9.

Looking at local issues lends itself to an enquiry approach to learning. Each lesson can be based around the key questions as in the example above. The work could also lead to project-based enquiries with the children working more independently. Use of local

---

CASE STUDY 7.4 What is the impact of Rio 2014 and 2016 on people and places? 10–12 year olds, Scoil Fhursa

The boys in Scoil Fhursa had a great interest in Brazil. This came from many sources – sports in Brazil, TV programmes and family connections.

Questions about Brazil. The boys brainstormed their questions about Brazil. They included the following questions written by two of the children:

- What do they eat?
- How do they have fun?
- How do they travel?
- What do they wear?
- What are their traditions?
- What does their money look like?
- How many times have they been in the World Cup?
- What other sports do they play? How do they train?

Over a number of lessons, the boys began to answer their questions by:

Looking large: patterns in Brazil. The boys used a range of maps to find out about the scale and complexities of Brazil. They used two maps at a time to find out about the country; this activity is described in Case Study 7.2.

Looking smaller: finding out about life in Brazil. Using photographs and the Internet the boys answered questions about life in Brazil. They used many of the types of activities described in Chapter 8.

The impact of the World Cup and Olympics. The boys completed a 'mystery' about batman in Rio. This was based on a newspaper story about protests in Rio, written in the *Guardian*, which supported the perspective of the people whose homes were being destroyed. Extra information in favour of the developments for Rio 2016 was sourced from the Rio 2016 website. From this, the boys saw the different sides of the arguments about the impact of the mass building and other infrastructural development for Rio 2016.

Finding out more. Interviewing a teacher from Brazil, about life in Manaus and surrounding towns.

(a)   (b)
(c)   (d)

Figure 7.6 The impact of Rio 2016 on people and places: (a) generating ideas, (b) discussing issues, (c) solving mysteries and (d) investigating possible futures

Reflections. The children recorded some of their learning through their blogs:

We have been workings in groups and trying to figure out about Brazil, like Rio, Favela do Metro. We figured out that the poor and the rich live beside each other . . .

In my opinion the favelas houses shouldn't be knocked down because homelessness is as bad as it is in Rio. The people that live there are probably living there since they were kids and the houses were probably left in there will from the owners of the houses . . .

Why do they have to move the poor people they should move the rich people because they can afford to live and buy a new house? If they could only move it to a much richer country. And I don't even think they should move anyone's houses because they have no right to move people's houses or property. They should buy their own landmarks to build the Olympic stadium and Rio football stadium. I know the Olympics are so important to so many people in every country of the world especially Brazil. They should run a really good protest about it and see what they say about it.

www.kidsblog.com/mstoalsclass

fieldwork will enhance learning, and local experts can be asked to talk to the children or work with them in class, for example a local councillor or developer. Another option is to meet the expert at the location of the issue. Children can put even the most prepared local councillor on the spot with their difficult questions! Children also want to know more about the issues people debate in their country and the wider world. They often have a strong sense of fairness and justice and want the 'right' series of events to happen to resolve issues. However, they may or may not be part of such discourse or processes. As topics for the classroom, issues are up-to-date, challenging and interesting for children. Issues can be local or global; they can be about things that may happen or may never happen and they are often difficult or impossible to resolve. All of these features mean they provide great geographical learning possibilities! Within such topics, different aspects of geography are combined: knowledge, understanding, skills, attitudes and values. Also such topics lend themselves to creative integration with other subjects, including mathematics. Finally, interesting resources on issues can be easily and often freely obtained!

Planning and resourcing for topical geography

For any topical geography, there is a wealth of people, places and materials that can be used, including:

- local newspapers (maps, photographs, peoples' opinions);
- national newspapers;
- local council offices (maps, plans, brochures);
- tourist offices (maps, plans, brochures, fliers);
- community development offices (people, maps, plans, brochures);
- local builders/developers (maps, plans, brochures, aerial photographs, people);
- local residents, companies and organisations (opinions, historical data, photographs).

Children can source and use newspaper headlines to generate their ideas about topical issues and events, before thinking of questions. Through geography and media, children can also review the different ways the same events and issues are discussed in different papers:

- What does the headline say?
- Who is it aiming to impress?
- What style of writing is it using?
- How are the issues/events then reported?
- What does the writer think of the issue?

Children can investigate newspapers further to see how events are reported, which page they are on and if they are even reported at all. There are a number of ways to differentiate this type of activity, where a lot of text is used:

- asking children to concentrate first on photographs and captions, then the articles themselves;
- pairing stronger and weaker readers together so they can support each other;
- reading with the children and helping them along;
- using a range of newspapers, some of which have a lower reading age.

Table 7.2 Headlines relating to Metro North, Dublin

- Digging up Dublin: Six years, two drills, one big traffic jam
- No Metro North ... but Sponge Bob still catches the train to Ballymun
- €200m Dart plan for airport is five times cheaper than Metro
- €2.5bn Metro North plan looks doomed as airport Dart project speeds up
- Multi-billion deals for Metro North to be signed in weeks
- Pedal power is on the rise with 87pc more city cyclists
- Calls for Metro North levies to be scrapped
- 'Green light' for Metro North is good news for Dublin City
- Bendy bus plan faces rough ride from councillors
- Cut-price plan for city Metro is 'unrealistic'
- Can Dublin's traffic control system handle the recovery?
- Metro North could be scrapped as Minister reveals transport options

Children can also make up their own newspapers or newspaper articles, linking this work strongly with literacy. Children in Scoil Íde in Corbally, Limerick are very media aware. They link up with other schools and events through social media. The children make news programmes and play them back to each other, developing all areas of their learning.

Using facts about a proposed development, teachers or children can compile arguments for and against a development. Using Venn type diagrams for this activity works very well, and children will discover that some points are hard to categorise and that there is not always a right or wrong answer. Information flyers from a variety of sources are a fantastic resource for primary geography. These can include information from developers, council and promoters. For example, the Metro North flyers provide some useful information for the development, which can be cut and pasted and then used for a set of cards for and against the development. Newspaper articles can help counterbalance arguments. For example, for Metro North, statements on each side of the argument could include:

- The Metro will be out of date by the time it is built.
- People will still use their cars.
- The lines will not be finished until 2017.
- The trams will be frequent.
- There may be damage to buildings and monuments.
- There will be lots of stops on the Metro lines.
- The Metro will be environmentally friendly.
- The trams will be fast.
- There will be more traffic congestion.
- The Metro will be underground for some of its route.
- The Metro system will be safe.
- The fares will be expensive.

Table 7.3 A geographical mystery: Why is Batman in Favela do Metrô, Rio?

- In Rio's favelas most residents have built their houses themselves over decades.
- Favela do Metrô was founded by workers employed in the construction of the Maracanã Metro Station 35 years ago.
- Residents of Favela do Metrô have set up barricades near their homes.
- In the 1960s and 1970s, communities were forcibly relocated to housing projects.
- Favelas were built by squatters due to lack of formal and affordable housing.
- Favela do Metrô's families were already moved under the city's 'improved' plan in 2010.
- There are also rumours that Vila do Metrô will become a shopping centre.
- 40,000 people in Rio are under threat of eviction due to the World Cup and Olympics.
- Families in Rio are filing complaints about the demolition of their houses.
- In 2010, Favela do Metrô families were moved 70km away.
- Residents hold demonstrations against evictions.
- Favela do Metrô was cleared in 2010, but new poorer residents moved into emptied housing.
- Vila do Metrô is located near to the famous Maracanã stadium, which will be used in Rio 2016 and was used for the World Cup 2014.

- Favelas are 'informal' communities often built by the residents.
- Favela do Metrô may become a complex with commercial units, a park, skate park, gym, playground and 400 trees.
- In 2010, the 700 families were evicted from their homes in Favela do Metrô.
- Favelas are neighbourhoods that usually have vibrant social lives and communities.
- Favelas often suffer from a lack of infrastructure and services.
- Residents of Favela do Metrô have been asked to leave, as living conditions are unsanitary.
- The redevelopment of Favela do Metrô will cost R$30.5m.
- Homes in the Favela do Metrô are being demolished.
- Batman arrived at the Favela do Metrô on 9 Jan 2014.
- Early on 8 Jan, City officials arrived at Favela do Metrô to demolish homes.
- Some favelas have been ruled by ruthless gangs.
- The 2016 Summer Olympics (Jogos
- Olímpicos de Verão de 2016) will be held in Rio de Janerio on 5 to 21 August 2016.
- The Popular Committee for the World Cup and Olympics, say 170,000, will be affected by removals by the 2016 Olympics, 30,000 in Rio.

Children can also try to explore an issue from the perspectives of others, using techniques from drama such as Teacher-in-role and Conscience Alley. Cards such as those above and in Table 7.4 can be introduced to help this process or may be used afterwards, as appropriate. Such 'mysteries' are simply information provided on cards; they start with a question which acts as the organising 'frame' for the task and provides motivation as a puzzle or problem to be solved. When designing them, try to make the questions relevant or puzzling to the children you are working with. The statements about Rio in the example contain a range of different types of information (such as general or background information as well as specific details). They can also contain 'red herrings' or irrelevant information. Children work in pairs or small groups to read and sort the statements, to solve the mystery. The role of the teachers is to support, by listening in and questioning the children and supporting discussions. Through the course of a

Table 7.4 Role play cards for an issue – note: do not tell the children what to think!

Drumcondra parents You are a group of parents from the local mother and toddler group on Home Farm Road. Your children are aged 0 to 4. Some of you have cars, some do not.	*Cultivate* You represent various organisations concerned with the sustainable development of Ireland, including cities such as Dublin. www.cultivate.ie
AA Ireland You represent AA Ireland, a lobbying group for motorists. You provide assistance and motoring advice to drivers in Ireland. www.aaireland.com	*Bus Eireann* You represent the drivers and owners of Bus Eireann. Many bus routes run along Drumcondra Road, including buses to the airport. www.buseireann.ie
Older residents You are a group of residents from across Drumcondra. Most of you have lived in the locality all of your lives. Some of you have cars but prefer not to use them as you have bus passes.	*Dublin Cycling campaign* You represent Dublin Cyclists who promoting cycling across the city. You also lobby local TDs and councillors to try and make Dublin more cyclist friendly. home.connect.ie/dcc/
Shop owners You are a group of shop owners and managers from Drumcondra Road. Your businesses include services, shops and restaurants. www.mydrumcondra.ie	*USI* You representative all students in third levels colleges in Dublin, most of whom travel by public transport to college. www.usi.ie
Local councillors You are the local councillors for Drumcondra. You represent the local people for different political parties. You all live in the local area, and many of you have children in local schools www.dcc.ie	*Local children* You live and go to school in Drumcondra, Drumcondra has lots of places to go and to play. The main road is very busy and sometimes cars go too fast on smaller roads.

mystery, children have to sort relevant from irrelevant information, make decisions and analyse the information. Eventually, they refine their explanations as they make connections between the different pieces of information. Often they do this with very little prompting; in fact, speaking less is the best thing the teacher can do with mysteries. These are just one of a group of Thinking Through Geography activities, which include dilemmas, odd one out and so on outlined in Chapter 3. I have always noted how these help children to think at higher levels in primary geography and this has been backed up by research (Karkdijk· *et al.*, 2013).

Role cards are pieces of card used to support children's thoughts in geography role play activities. The cards are carefully designed to prompt the children to think about what they are going to argue. Tools, such as the Development Compass Rose described in Chapter 2 and illustrated in Figure 3.1, can help children think about the different aspects of what they would like to say.

All of these types of resources can be made and amended as appropriate. There is also a number of websites that are listed at the end of this chapter, which post resources relating to geographical events and issues very regularly.

Table 7.5 Progression in examining issues across primary geography

Possible issues	Younger classes: Where should a tree be planted in our school?	Middle classes: Where can our skate park go?	Older classes: Should Dublin have a Metro system?
What's the issue? Why is it an issue?	Homework: Look at and describe the location and features of a tree. Discuss what trees need to grow. Examine different trees in the school/area. Talk about 'different views', using children's views as examples.	Review material about skate parks. Looking at websites about skate parks, e.g. Gorey, Co. Wexford, Southsea. Talk about what makes an issue. List who would have an opinion on the development of a skate park.	Look at images. Watch programmes/ promotional material. Talk about the issue. Use newspaper headlines to review what are the issues.
What is this place currently like?	Examine photographs of the school grounds. Pupil led walk around the school grounds to describe places through drawing and talking.	Use photographs of the locality. Pupil planned walk around the locality.	Look at sources: maps, plans, artists' impressions. Use Google maps to examine places and follow routes.
Where is it taking place?	Walking around the school to think about possible places to plant a tree.	Examine possible places for a park on a field trip walk.	Consider local routes during fieldwork. Examine overall route on maps
How do you feel about the issue?	Talk about their views in pairs. Share with class.	Talk about their views in pairs, groups and then as whole class.	Talk in pairs, about personal opinion.
Which groups or individuals are involved? What views do they hold?	Talk to other people about their ideas about trees in the school grounds: children, teachers, caretaker, principal etc.	Identify interested parties, from websites or television clips.	Homework: Collect views of one person on the Metro. Identify interested parties from newspaper cuttings or television clips.
What alternative solutions are there?	Identify possible places using a tick chart frame.	Identify and plan for alternative solutions.	Identify alternatives and evaluate from the (perceived) different perspectives of the interested parties.
How will a decision be made?	Class discussion on best site. Planting of the tree.	Role-play/simulation of a council meeting.	Role-play/simulation of a transport meeting.
What do you think the decision should be and why?	Paired discussion if the best places and other possible places.		Write up a newspaper article about final decision made.

Conclusions

The take up of teaching through topical issues is varied; unfortunately, there is evidence that children's experiences of geography may be shaped more by the structure and context of work programmes and textbooks than by topical geography in or beyond the locality (Catling, 2003; Devine, 2003; Waldron, 2003; Pike, 2006). Research with primary children and their teachers reveals that actively learning through issues is not commonly experienced in primary classrooms (Waldron, 2008; Pike, 2006; Pike, 2011b), although this does appear to be changing. The 2015 partial eclipse of the sun was studied by many schools, who posted up their pinhole cameras and images on social media. Sporting events, such as the World Cup and Olympics, have increasingly become topics for summer time lessons in geography.

Like all other activities in primary geography, children's learning about issues and events in geography should be planned across the school. Because of the nature of topical geography, however, information and resources can become out of date quickly. The best way to plan for issues and events is not to plan too much! Allow the children to ask the questions, guided by the frameworks in this chapter. Sometimes, topical geography may only be used incidentally; however, for all classes in primary school, it is a good idea to plan at least one topical theme during each year. Table 7.5 indicates how topical geography progresses through the school, with younger children considering single issues and older children considering many more issues or events from different perspectives.

Across a school, teachers and children can be involved in collating resources on issues and events that can be used in geography lessons. For example, newspapers are great sources of information, and local issues are normally found on the front page of the local paper. Teachers or children can also try local architects, building contractors and council offices. Often planners are so surprised that you are looking to teach something so topical that they give away maps, plans and other resources for free! Parents or friends may be working on projects or know someone who is. These provide a wealth of geographical and other material for children to use. Like many other chapters in this book, teaching geography using topical issues and events is simply a case of considering lessons from the children's interests and questions.

Reflection and action

- Why is it important for children to learn about issues and events?
- What issues or events would be of interest to children in your school?
- Where can you allocate time in geography (and literacy/mathematics) to incorporate lessons about local, national and international issues?
- Have you left 'space' in your planning to incorporate events that may happen in the course of a school year? If not, how can you do this?

Further resources

Online support for teachers

Geographical Association. The GA always post resources (maps, images, activities) for any major events in the news: www.geography.org.uk.

Teaching for the Future. David Hick's ideas and models are all available online. His two books on teaching for the future are also available here as free downloads: www.teaching4abetterworld.co.uk.

Sustainability Frontiers. This international alliance of sustainability and global educators seeking transformation of the human condition through repaired and restored earth connection: www.sutainabilityfrontiers.org.

Futures Education. This cross-curricular skills-based project work for 11–14 year olds is based on the theme of sustainability:www.nuffieldfoundation.org/nuffield-stem-futures.

Follow school discussions on Twitter by using hashtags such as #edchatie and #edchat.

An interesting perspective on teaching controversial issues from a non-governmental organisation can be found at www.oxfam.org.uk/education/?coolplanet/teachers/controversial_issues.

Chapter 8

Connecting geography – learning about places

> Before we did this work I hadn't a clue about life in Brazil and now I would be able to tell someone who didn't know about Brazil everything I learned. I would prefer to do this more often than do other subjects, it was very interesting.
>
> Boy, 10

This chapter brings ideas and debates about learning about places, particularly distant places, together. The focus is on how children can learn about places, and debates about knowledge of place and places are also presented.

The chapter is based on the following key thoughts:

- Children are naturally curious about places and people.
- Children's interests and choices should be the basis of planning for teaching places.
- Children appreciate looking at places in detail.

This chapter outlines:

- the research relating to children's knowledge of the world;
- how the global dimension, global citizenship and distant locality studies are geographical;
- children's view of places, especially distant places; and
- how to plan interesting lessons on different localities.

Throughout the chapter, examples of learning from classrooms will be used to exemplify the above; further information on resources are outlined at the end of the chapter. In looking at the places through enquiry, this chapter overlaps significantly with Chapter 2 on enquiry and Chapter 3 on developing literacies.

Places in primary geography

There are many reasons to give children the opportunity to learn about places. First, children are naturally curious about the world. They have questions to ask about different places (Scoffham, 2013); they see other places through storybooks and media; they also have real connections with other places through family and friends. Through looking

(a)   (b)

(c)   (d)

Figure 8.1 Children learning about places through spatial data (a) using maps, (b) global displays, (c) local displays and (d) using globes

at other places, children can develop essential skills such as empathy and a sense of justice (Norodhan, 2012; Oberman *et al.*, 2014). Children are entitled to learn about different places to develop their understanding of the interconnected world they live in (Catling and Willy, 2011), and the impact their actions have on others. Learning about other places gives children an opportunity to question why the world is as it is, to think critically and consider alternative situations and futures. In primary school curricula, children are encouraged to look at places that are different from their own. In Ireland, they are required to study a European and non-European country during their primary school years; this ensures that children take time to look at places that are different to their own country, while recognising the similarities places have. In both Australia and Ireland, the curriculum places a great importance on examining connections with different places, recognising the diversity of experiences and connections children have (DES/NCCS, 1999a; ACARA, 2011). A final reason to learn about different places is that it is very interesting to children, and the experience can provide, with teachers' scaffolding, many opportunities for children to pursue their own questions and interests in learning geographically.

These reasons for studying places are categorised into different but overlapping aspects of learning:

1   Knowledge of people and places

   • location and features of places;
   • awareness of the variety of people in places, including different ethnic, religious and linguistic groups;
   • awareness of the human and natural features of places.

2   Understanding of people and places

   • similarities and differences between and within places;
   • spatial patterns across localities, regions and countries;
   • awareness of the interdependence of people.

3   Skills to find out about people and places

   • enquiry skills: questioning, collecting data, critiquing data, evaluating work, etc.;
   • spatial awareness and skills;
   • using a range of resources to find out about people and places: textbooks, atlases, websites, TV, DVDs, photographs.

4   Attitudes and values in relation to people and places

   • Developing rounded and varied perceptions of different people and places.
   • Appreciating the value of diversity of people and their cultures and lifestyles.
   • Developing critical approaches to the use of resources for finding out about places.

CASE STUDY 8.1 Thinking places: 8–9 year olds, Warrenmount Girls' National School

The children in third class were fortunate to have a teacher from a contrasting place in Ireland, Ballina, Co. Mayo. Needless to say, with the teacher's great interest in geography and the girls' enthusiasm for learning, they were experts on Ballina! When the weather was checked for Dublin, Ballina was checked too; when the girls spoke about different places, Ballina always got a mention. The girls had also found out about Mayo when looking at contrasting places. However, it was the incidental nature of learning that seemed to be most meaningful for the children – and the idea of knowing about this different place made them curious about other places.

http://warrenmountNprimary.com

Debates about learning about different places

The debates about knowledge in learning geography have been argued very effectively over the years. There are three concepts of knowledge relevant in primary geography: absolutism, constructivism and realism. The definitions and examples of these outlined in Table 8.1 shows how all three concepts can be used in enabling children to learn about places (or any other concept) in geography.

A good example of how these concepts can be put into practice is shown in the work the boys of Scoil Fhursa carried out on Brazil, outlined in Case Study 7.4. Through enquiry approaches, they learnt many facts about Brazil, adding to their existing knowledge. However, they also constructed knowledge about changes in parts of Brazil because of the 2014 World Cup and 2016 Olympics. In fact, like all the examples of learning about places in this chapter, it was practically impossible to assess exactly what individual boys had learned as their knowledge was so varied in relation to both what they had learned and their views on the changing face of Brazil. However, the fact that months after they had the topic of Brazil completed they were still talking about it, was proof they had learned plenty!

Children's learning about different places in geography

Over the years, there have been a number of studies on how children gain their knowledge of places. Although as outlined in Chapter 3, despite years of research, including research in geography education, environmental psychology and neuroscience, we

Table 8.1 The conceptions of knowledge in relation to learning about Brazil

Definition	Absolutism: knowledge as external, fixed, universal and certain	Constructivism: knowledge as situated, ideological and relativist	Realism: knowledge as objective and fallible
Ontology	• Reality exists independently of what anyone knows, thinks or believes it is	• Reality is socially constructed – even if it is fixed learners still interpret it in their ways	• Reality exists independently of learners' knowledge but their knowledge and perceptions are a part of knowledge
Curriculum	• Traditional curriculum: content driven, value of subject knowledge	• Generic and integrated curriculum, usually featuring skills more than content	• Curriculum focused on engagement, subject to change
Examples of learning about Brazil	• Learning names of places in Brazil • Learning locations of features in Brazil • Knowing current new stories from Brazil	• Using maps to interpret patterns on climate, settlement etc. in Brazil • Examining the differing views about the developments associated with Rio 2016	• Devising enquiry questions about Brazil • Comparing children's days in Brazil • Inferring about life in Brazil from this • Carrying out a Mystery Skype with a school in Brazil

Source: Adapted from Firth, 2011.

still do not know exactly how we learn spatially. However, there have been some very interesting and informative studies on children's maps of the world. Wiegand's research showed the spatial capabilities of young children, revealing 'highly detailed and accurate world maps' by the children (1995, p. 27). Wiegand looked at the maps of children aged 4–11; their maps were analysed in relation to key variables, such as the spatial arrangement, shape and size/scale of places and categorised into five types, which became more detailed and accurate with age. However, there were misconceptions in the locations and shape of places in all the age groups. Harwood and Rawlings explored children's freehand sketch maps of the world (2001). Their research was carried out with 26 children, aged 10–11 years. Like Wiegand, their findings showed children were able to draw maps of the world but were more able to depict the location and size of continents than their shape. Harwood and Rawlings recommended that map skills should be taught alone, so that children and teachers can focus on these skills.

While such research and the maps produced by the children are fascinating, it does make an assumption: that children will draw all they know in a map. Anyone who has sat next to children as they draw knows this is not the case. Whether drawing a real or imagined picture or map, children will not include everything that is in their heads! Furthermore, children's maps never include all they know, as it would take days for them to draw them. In fact, research does show that children are, quite possibly, better able to draw maps of the world than adults. As teachers, it is very important to bear these thoughts in mind when making judgments of what children can do.

It is also essential for children to appreciate how their locality fits into the world; this understanding of nested hierarchies can take place over time. It was thought that children may not understand this concept, known as nested hierarchies, until they were 10 years old (Harwood and McShane, 1996). However, other research has found this may not be the case and younger children may understand the concept, depending on how place studies are introduced to them (Storey, 2005). There are many ways to help children understand how a locality fits into bigger places in the world. This can be done using two main approaches:

1 *specifically teaching the concept* – using addresses, news stories, discussion, maps;
2 *incidentally teaching the concept* – using news stories, activities about countries the children are doing anyway.

Whichever approach is adopted, it is important that maps (in atlases and online) are readily available for children to use. Time to look at maps in any form, without lots of instructions from adults, is very important, as children need time to construct their personal maps of the world.

Children's views of places can be broadly divided into local, national and global views of places. Research has been carried out in all these areas, although not all of it exclusively from a geography educational perspective. Research has revealed the complex but fascinating views young children have of the world and are able to engage in issues of global citizenship (Ruane *et al.*, 2010; Oberman *et al.*, 2013). The 2010 study focused on 3–6 year olds and the 2013 study on 7–10 year olds, and found children were able to:

- demonstrate the ability to think critically about people and places;
- draw on their previous experiences to think about similarities and differences between places and people; and
- empathise with people in places far from their own homes.

These findings reflect the learning of the children in Case Study 9.2. However, considering the children's exposure to media and advertising, it was not surprising that children also had stereotyped views of places, notably Africa, in relation to poverty. Some of the children's views remained despite teaching more varied views of African people and places over a number of weeks (Oberman *et al.*, 2013). This research indicates the importance of enabling children to read or see beyond images and texts they are presented with in class (Catling, 2003). They can consider the connections between local and global communities, between personal and political issues and carefully consider 'how power is exercised, circulated, negotiated, and reconstructed' (Botelho and Rudman, 2009, p. 31). As Botelho and Rudman note, the teacher is essential as they need to scaffold the children's learning, and take note and respond to dominant cultural assumptions in children's thinking and in the material they use in geography lessons.

CASE STUDY 8.2 **What is life like in India? 5–8 year olds, St James' National School**

The children in the junior room at St James' already knew about India as they had found out about some of the festivals.

Generating ideas. To begin with the children looked at photographs, spread on the floor. The discussion about the pictures took a long time – the children were paired up in a somewhat fluid way and simply wandered around talking to each other about the picture. This is one of many strategies to use with photographs, see below for more.

Asking questions. The children in the junior class, aged 5 to 8 years looked at a range of photographs, set out randomly on the floor. After around 30 minutes of discussion, they began to write down questions they had about India. As expected for children of these ages, the spelling was phonetic. It is included to show how children's thinking is often far beyond their spelling in geography:

- How many hours does it take to get to India?
- Are they very poor?
- What do children do in school?
- What do the kids have for lunch?
- Do qepl rid Elfins in Indea? (Do people ride elephants in India?)
- Are they hot in their clothes?
- Do babes wer sores? (Do babies wear saris?)
- What is it like in the houses?

- Do they have books?
- Do the kids play on the street?
- Do they have pet shops?
- Why do they thingk they will be an animic wen tey diy? (Why do they think they will be an animal when they die?)

Following this process, the children undertook a number of activities to find out more about India.

(i) All children – aged 5–8:

  - *Using photographs*: the children used the photographs to help answer some of their questions
  - *Watching video*: the children watched DVD clips on family life and communities in contrasting parts of India
  - *Using artefacts*: the children looked at items from India, including clothes, newspapers, travel brochures and images.

(ii) Older children – aged 6–8 (in the afternoon when the younger children had gone home):

  - *Mapping India*: the children investigated the range of landscapes in India, including mountains, coastlines, cities and rural areas. They were surprised to find snow and swimming pools in India.
  - *Food*: the children made Dhal (a stew using orange lentils, water, ginger, garlic, coriander and cumin). And ate it all. Not only did this tie up to the work the children had covered about family life, including foods, it was also an opportunity to do procedural writing for English.

The children were positive about their learning experiences. For the younger children, learning so deeply about a distant place was a new experience for them. There were some fantastic responses to the work from the younger children. One child, when asking the enquiry questions, asked: 'Do people live as long in India as they do in Ireland?' This question revealed a depth of both inquisitiveness and awareness of the world. In enabling children to learn through enquiry about less familiar places and people, we are providing the opportunities for such deep learning to occur. Although another child did say, on just the second day of the project: 'Can we do some proper work today?'

The children's activity is outlined fully in Appendix 8.

Figure 8.2 Learning about India (a) comparing each other to understand different and similar, (b) comparing a 'typical' day and (c, d) presenting findings in pictures

Approaches to learning about places

There are many approaches to learning about places in geography; as teachers, we need to consider how places fit together before we can start to teach about different places.

Where is this place? There are a number of ways to think about where a place is, one is where within a nested hierarchy it is, as described in Chapter 3. By asking children to write their address, they can begin to develop their ideas about where they are relative to other places. So thinking about Red Fraggle, she can usually be found at this location:

Ms Red Fraggle
Room E303   (place)
St Patrick's College   (address)
Drumcondra   (locality)
Dublin 9   (village/town/city)
Leinster   (province)
Republic of Ireland   (country)
Europe   (continent)

After this, we can continue if we like: Northern Hemisphere, The Earth, The Solar System and so on, as children often will! These places are an example of nested hierarchies, as described above, they 'fit' inside each other, rather like Russian dolls or stacking toys.

Red Fraggle has been on lots of adventures since she came to the college, modelling a simple but effective activity with children (as seen in Figure 8.3) to help them understand nested hierarchies and develop their understanding of places. Flat Stanley and Barnaby Bear are other mascots children can use. However, any mascot can be used in classes for activities such as the following:

- Children use their mascot as an extra pair of eyes during enquiries about the locality – what can Red Fraggle see?
- Children take turns to take the mascot home and share their everyday experiences, such as shopping, sports and classes out of school – where did Red Fraggle go? Google maps and photographs on whiteboards can be used to show where she went.
- Children or friends/relatives take Red Fraggle away on holiday or just for the weekend.

All of these activities help children to appreciate how one place fits into another, while remembering that this understanding develops faster in some children than others.

Children also need to appreciate the location and scale of places they ask questions about. Chapter 3 lists many more possibilities for creating a map rich environment in schools and classrooms. There are many ways to do this (see also Figure 8.1):

- *Online maps.* As described in the case studies, children need time to use online maps such as Bing and Google Maps. When this time is invested with younger children, they are soon able to use such online tools easily. The directions feature on online maps enables children to work out the best way to travel to places and to appreciate the size of places, for example by working out how they could travel across a country. Children can also consider what Google Maps does not tell them about the places they find out about.
- *Paper maps.* When studying a distant place, use maps of the place. This is easier for some places than others! A folded map of a country that is gradually unfolded lends a bit of mystery about generating ideas about places.
- *Atlases.* Despite huge advances in technology, paper atlases are still fascinating to children, but not when they are made to look at particular pages or memorize information from them. Allowing children time to use atlases, with appropriate scaffolding, and encouraging them to look for places themselves is rewarding and interesting, and also challenging. Over time they will realise when to use the contents page (for large areas, continents, themes, etc.) and when to use the index (to look for specific cities, features, etc.). This sort of approach to using atlases is particularly useful when all the children have different atlases! Atlases are essential for taking part in Mystery Skypes, where classrooms connect through online phone calls. This often leads to other activity, as described in the case studies in this chapter.
- *Globes.* The truest representation of the world, in terms of shapes, sizes and positions of countries, is a globe. It is essential that every class has a globe. This is especially so for junior classes, where children are beginning to conceptualise the world.

Figure 8.3
Mascots can travel near and far and
help children begin to understand
about the variety of places

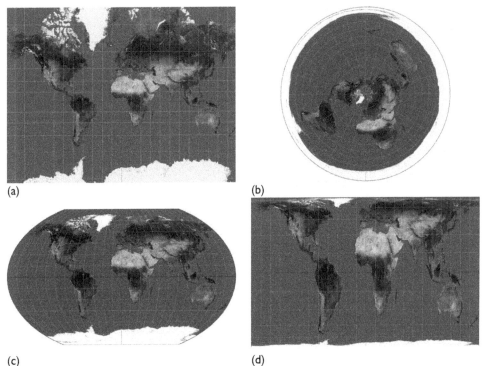

Figure 8.4 Projections of the world from globe to map (a) Mercator projection, (b) Azimuthal equidistant projection, (c) Kavraiskiy VII projection and (d) Gall-Peters projection

The world is portrayed in different ways on maps, depending on how the spherical globe is represented. This is simply because it is not possible to transfer information accurately from a sphere to a flat surface. There are different distortions that have to occur as a world map is created, these are:

*   Cylindrical Projection is best visualised by thinking of placing a screen around the globe in a cylinder shape, for example Figures 8.4a and d;
*   Conic Projection is created by placing a cone shaped screen on a globe, for example Figure 8.4c;
*   Plane Projection is created by placing an imaginary screen directly above or below a globe, for example Figure 8.4b.

The nature of map projections means that land masses are distorted and changed in size. For example, there are issues with a Mercator Projection map, in regard to the relative size of countries, for example on such a map it appears:

*   Alaska is nearly as large as the United States of America;
*   Greenland is roughly the same size as the continent of Africa;
*   Europe is slightly larger than South America;
*   Antarctica is the largest of all the continents.

CASE STUDY 8.3 Mystery Skypes and follow up activity: various schools

Mystery Skype is an educational game, invented by teachers, played by two classrooms on Skype. The aim of the game is to guess the location of the other classroom by asking each other a range of questions. Children use resources already in the classroom during the lessons, including:

- Maps, globes and atlases.
- White boards, flip charts – to record what they are finding out.
- Signs to direct the other class what they are up to – when the sound fails!

Mystery Skype works for all class levels, and is most effective when the phone call is used to lead to other activity. This could be:

- Exchanging letters describing life in each school, locality and/or country.
- Exchanging artefacts (concrete or online) from each country to give a sense of life in the places: newspapers, foods, information leaflets, school flyers, photographs and so on.
- Sharing learning in subjects, especially geography and history, to give a deeper sense of places.

Follow #mysteryskype online to see many examples of schools taking part in Mystery Skypes.

CASE STUDY 8.4 Kenya: people, places, food and connections: 5–8 year olds, Knockmahon National School

Before this unit, the children were already something of experts on food: they had already made different foods in school and some pupils' parents worked with food on farms, or in the local meat-processing factory.

What do we want to know? During a whole-class discussion on the topic, the children put forward questions that showed they had a particular interest in food sources and how foods were made. Following enquiry principles, these questions were used as the basis for planning the activities and were revisited regularly throughout the work.

How is food made? Children used materials from the Eco-Detectives resource (Pike, 2010) to sequence the production of bread. They found there were lots of stages in making bread, and the task involved a lot of discussion before they were satisfied that it was right. Hence, the activity developed children's language skills at the same time as developing their knowledge of the geographical processes involved in food production.

Where do bananas come from? Children in third to sixth class (8–12 years old) joined in the enquiry to look at how we get our bananas. Pupils looked at photographs from the Go Bananas (Oxfam, 2015 – bananas) resource pack and the Internet to work out all the stages of banana production. The pupils were astonished just how many people were involved in getting bananas to their homes and how little money went back to the farmers. The older pupils were able to begin to understand the reasons for this, and all the children improved their spatial awareness as they looked up places mentioned in the resource on world maps and in atlases.

Where do other foods come from? Next, children discussed and recorded where other foods came from – an activity some pupils found challenging. However, even the very youngest were able to understand the concept that a number of stages and products went into the production and delivery of the food they ate. They took pleasure in guessing what paper, plastic and tin were made of! By drawing on each other's knowledge and on us as teachers, the children discovered how complex making something as simple as a pot of yoghurt or a box of cereal could be. When asked what they thought of the work they had done, many children were still talking about what different foods and products were made from:

> I liked learning about how different foods are made because I live in an estate but my dad works on a farm.

> I liked learning about how food was made because I did not know all of that before.

During all the activities, and because the work was informed by their own questions, children were actively involved in the learning process and were often challenged by it too. We displayed photographs of the pupils carrying out the work in the classroom and noticed they were very proud of what they had achieved as well as being able to refer back to what they had learnt, and what they thought about the experience of learning about food.

What is life like in Kenya? As the children had studied food in different countries, we decided to get them to find out a little more about Kenya. Using the GA's Kaptalwana pack and other photographs to give a broader view of the country, children talked about different images of Kenya. They then used Google Maps to try and see more of Kenya's contrasts. The children set the overlays of the maps so they viewed satellite images and photographs people had taken. To begin with, they could just see the typical images of tourist attractions. But as they zoomed in, they soon saw images of every day features, such as shops and homes. The children ended their work by producing a display of their learning journey through these linked topics.

http://knockmahonns.wix.com/knockmahon

However, as a globe or the Gall-Peters' Projection shows:

- Alaska is about one third of the size of the United States of America.
- Greenland can fit inside Africa about 14 times.
- South America is nearly double the size of Europe.
- Antarctica is the second smallest continent.

Equal area maps, such as the Gall-Peters Projection, are designed to accurately reflect the sizes of countries and so this list is 'right'! The best activity to allow children the opportunity to understand this concept works with either an orange: can you make the peel flat? Or a ball and paper: can you cover the ball perfectly? These practical activities soon reveal the issues of map projections! After such a practical activity, using different types of world maps, especially on interactive white boards, is easily achieved in classrooms.

What is this place like? This simple question is one of the most engaging questions in primary geography! Children are intrigued by different places and this type of question is a way to find out all about the characteristics of places. A suggested list of themes children could explore is (DES/NCCA, 1999b, p. 75):

- location of places
- people and communities that live there: languages, art, culture, customs, traditions, clothes, play and pastimes, and leisure interests
- population changes
- some features of the natural environment
- interrelationships of the lives of people and these features
- homes and settlements, settled and nomadic lifestyles, major cities
- work and work-places, transport and communications
- similarities and differences between these places and Ireland
- trade, historic and other links these peoples have with Ireland.

There is no requirement that children should study all such aspects of the places they learn about. We can select a certain focus each time we look at a place; this is true of familiar and unfamiliar places. For example, some suggestions could be:

- India – culture and lifestyles with younger classes
- Italy – contrasting places with any class
- Japan – people and their work with older classes

If this approach is followed, opportunities should also be provided for a broad overview of the country as well. An alternative model might be that the children are grouped and can select certain aspects of the country to focus on. There are advantages and disadvantages of all the different ways to look at places. However, in finding out about places, children are using essential enquiry and research skills that they can replicate in many different ways. The approach of looking at places with a relational view of difference as described above should ensure children develop a rounded view of places other than their own communities.

Even when taking time to find out more about places, we do need to take care to go 'beneath the surface' when looking at places. This is why resources with a wealth of visual materials and activities such as Mystery Skypes are so good. There are generally three levels we can view different places and people, often compared to an iceberg:

- on the surface, like the top of an iceberg: features such as landmarks, traditional dress, 'typical' food;
- getting deeper, but still above the water: dress, clothes, traditions, daily foods and landscapes;
- below the surface, the part of the iceberg below the water: sources of and patterns of norms and traditions, relationships with the environment, concepts of food and notions of childhood.

Traditionally, geography lessons did not go much further than the surface learning; however, as children learn about fewer places in more detail, there is the freedom to go beyond the stereotyped images of places. Food is an excellent example of this; as children can see pictures of 'traditional' food, they can find out about the range of food eaten, or they can actually cook a range of foods eaten in a country, as this action can help them appreciate norms and values associated with foods. It may also make them a little more daring in their own food choices!

How does this place compare to where we live? Once we have seen the importance of looking in more depth about countries, it is also important to think about how we look at difference and similarity. Martin outlines essential considerations when learning

---

CASE STUDY 8.5 Investigating countries: 10–11 year olds, St Vincent de Paul Girls' National School

The girls in fifth class, learned about places in complex ways, considering places from a number of different perspectives. When studying India, they:

- Asked questions about India, and group these as enquiry questions.
- Made maps of places by pairing up back-to-back and describing how to draw a map of India to each other.
- Using a range of resources (maps, globes, books and the Internet) to find out about similarities and differences between Ireland and India.
- Using accounts of children's day (Chawla, 2002) to compare their days and think about similarities and differences at a deeper and more personal level.
- Taking part in recreations of a range of Indian festivals.

The children were fortunate that one of the girls was not only from India, she visited the country each year with her parents. There were many times when the children checked information with the girl. There were also girls in the class from other countries, and so the complexities and depth of comparisons were huge!

about places. She argues that there are different ways to view sameness-difference with children (2012a, b, 2013).

Binary views of sameness–difference. Where dominant groups hold power, there is a tendency to view groups of people as part of this or not. This creates a distinction of similar/different, where differences and similarities are simplified and generalised. This was evident in the 1990s in Ireland, where it was assumed people moving to the state from aboard during the economic boom or 'Celtic Tiger' would become 'one of our own' over time. Educationally, the danger of such an approach is that the 'assimilationist' model is an issue because there is the danger that important differences of the minority groups are ignored and what is chosen as similar (humanity) is decided by the dominant group. We are all the same because we are all human is arguably another way of saying 'you are (or should be) like us' (Martin, 2012, p. 5).

Diversity views of sameness–difference. As society moves on over time, there is more of a recognition of a diverse, plural society, with a value placed in these features. However, Martin argues, 'these differences are externalised and seen to be the property of the "other"', while the differences within the dominant group are submerged. Examples of this are when schools hold one-off events, such as drumming workshops or food tasting, without other learning to help children appreciate this is just one aspect of life in the 'other' place. Children need their geography lessons to expand on such events, and put them in a context of people and places to avoid them viewing otherness as quaint or strange.

Relational views of sameness–difference. Understood as relational difference is the starting point from which similarity might be understood. Rather than focusing on external points of comparison and contrast, here the difference is understood as elements of enacted, lived identity: difference within. The focus begins at the individual level, each shape understanding its own identity 'in relation to' the other shapes. What becomes important is not the object of understanding, but the relationships that enable understanding.

This model provides opportunities for us to think carefully about the language we use when talking about difference.

Planning and resourcing learning about places

The topic of resourcing places studies in geography takes time and effort but not necessarily lots of money. The scope devising enquiry questions based on images, music, maps or any number of resources is endless. Using a range of resources from different sources enables children to construct their own knowledge of places, with the combination of inference and information gained from resources enhances children's learning. However, teachers need to bear in mind that when schools are moving across from the sole use of textbooks to using a wider range of resources, it will take time to build up resources. For student teachers, relatively few resources can still be effective for teaching about places. Often I see student teachers design creative, enquiry driven lessons with simply an atlas, globe and books from the library and a range of photographs. It must be remembered that there are advantages and disadvantages to all resources, as outlined in Table 8.2.

Overall, some of the best resources to use are:

- *Commercial or NGO resource packs*: there are many resource packs on different countries and localities. These can also be used as a source for children to question the sources of information.

Table 8.2 Using different resources

Resource	Advantages	Disadvantages
Resource packs	• Many types are available • Allows for more in depth study • Good value for money per use	• Can be biased if produced by certain organizations • May not contain activities needed • May not be geographical
Photographs	• Very insightful and engaging source • Easy to obtain • Huge range of associated activities	• Need to take care over copyright and source • Need range of images to give balance • Images needed may be difficult to source
Textbooks	• All feature countries • Provide succinct information • Useful for generating ideas/ questions • Good for critiquing after a place is studied	• Becomes out-of-date rapidly • Skim the surface and simplify the complexities of places
Videos	• Great to give a 3D image of a place • Children not phased by difficult language! • Many TV programmes are suitable	• Difficult to obtain suitable ones for children. • Some can be very long • Language can be hard to access for SEN children
People	• Great to link with communities – face-to-face or online • Use of Mystery Skypes are very exciting for children	• May only give the 'surface view' of a place • Need time to brief people on how and what children are learning • Need time for children to develop questions
Maps	• They are fascinating • Easy to get hold of • Give a different insight into a place • Online maps and paper maps have different uses	• Expensive to buy • Date quickly • Teachers' knowledge of maps and cartography
News	• Makes geography relevant to children's lives • Easy to access via Internet	• Can be difficult for some children to access • Some news can be very disturbing
Stories	• Already available in classrooms	• Do not use real photographs of places in most cases. • Are only one version of descriptions of places
Brochures	• Often commercially produced	• Only show certain aspects of places, e.g. tourist attractions

Source: Adapted from Weldon, 2010.

- *Non-fiction and fiction texts*: school and local libraries often have a wealth of books that show different countries and localities within them. Some of these books are worth buying, as you will use them many times.
- *People living in the places*: relatives, friends and so on may be happy to collect and send everyday items. Student teachers may travel abroad for Erasmus and are a fantastic source of resources for place studies.
- *Teachers and pupils in other schools*: through school linkage projects, Mystery Skypes or just through existing friendships, schools can link up easily and exchange information about the place they live. Such links need to be built on and fostered to go beyond simple meetings.
- *Online resources*: there is a large number of websites that can help children find out about different places. Again children need to learn to view these with a critical stance, with the support of their teachers.

There are certain places in the world that are well resourced for teaching geography, including Kenya, India, St Lucia and Brazil. As teachers, decisions about where to teach will need to take into account what resources can be gathered easily, especially with so many other subjects to plan for! The various resource packs on places, as outlined in Table 8.2, can also act as a model for teachers to develop packs of their own on places using their own expertise and contacts to build up up-to-date resources on places. As outlined in the table, they are never perfect and often need to be supplemented with other materials, particularly photographs and other artefacts. However, this ca become a learning opportunity, as children can review:

- Who produced the resource?
- Who paid for the resource?
- If it is a commercial resource, what is their aim?
- Is it a government or NGO resource? Who are they? What were their world views, politics, agendas and so on?
- What images are portrayed in the resource? Are they accurate? Are they varied enough?

Green and Eco-Schools Programmes are excellent sources for enabling children's agency and action towards environmental awareness and care. However, many programmes and resources on the environment make little reference to the impact of our food choices on the emission of greenhouse gases. Furthermore, changes to old habits, travel, food and consumption need to be made now, by adults and children to reduce the impacts of climate change already happening across the globe, but especially in poorer countries.

Conclusions

Children love to learn about places, it is a feature of geography that is generally positive, when learners get the opportunity to delve deep and find out more than surface learning about places (Waldron *et al.*, 2009; Pike, 2013b). Resources can help children begin to see the world through different lenses and develop complex ideas about different places and people.

CASE STUDY 8.6 Polar places: 5–6 year olds, Our Lady of Victories Infant School

The children in Senior Infants investigated a wealth of aspects of the environments in polar regions, as shown in Figure 8.5. This included:

- **Polar play space**: The children and their teacher created a polar play space in the classroom, including a tent with equipment. The children also used other play activities such as designing ships for polar regions and dressing for polar regions.
- **Reading about polar regions**: The children looked at, and were read, a range of non-fiction and fiction books about polar regions. They also used atlases to find and describe polar places.
- **The life of explorers**: Finding out about the work of Irish explorers, Tom Crean and Ernest Shackleton, by visiting the Shackleton Exhibition, Dún Laoghaire.

As described in Chapter 5, it was evident the children were developing complex ideas about life in different times and places through these activities.

http://shackletonexhibition.com

(a) (b) (c) (d)

Figure 8.5 Recreating distant places (a) base camp, (b) drawing and writing about distant places, (c) comparing places and (d) designing a boat for polar regions

---

Reflection and action

- What places (locally, nationally, globally) are your children interested in?
- At what age should children start learning about other countries in geography? Before, simultaneously or after they have learnt about their own area?
- What links does your locality have with other places? How can these be drawn upon in primary geography?
- How should children learn about places: in more places in less detail or in fewer places, in more detail?
- How can your school ensure children gain a balanced view of different places in geography?

Further resources

Resources for teachers

Sustainability Frontiers: Sustainability Frontiers is an international alliance of sustainability and global educators seeking transformation of the human condition through repaired and restored earth connection: www.sustainabilityfrontiers.org.

Development Compass Rose: Questioning development involves taking a variety of factors into account when understanding a situation. The four 'domains' that the development compass rose encourages us to look at – and explore the links between – are: Economic, Natural, Political (Who decides?) and Social/Cultural: www.development education.ie/debates/_files/compass-rose.pdf.

Oxfam Education: Oxfam offers a huge range of ideas, resources and support for developing global learning in the classroom and the whole school. All of the resources here support Education for Global Citizenship – education that helps children understand their world and make a positive difference in it: www.oxfam.org.uk/education.

Global Learning Programme: This is a ground-breaking programme which will create a national network of like-minded schools, committed to equipping their students to make a positive contribution to a globalised world by helping their teachers to deliver effective teaching and learning about development and global issues for children ages 7–14: http://globaldimension.org.uk/glp.

Skype in the Classroom – Mystery Skypes: Allows children to connect with a wealth of different schools and individuals across the globe through Skype in the Classroom activities: https://education.skype.com.

Chimamanda Adichie: In 'The Danger of a Single Story', novelist Chimamanda Adichie tells the story of how she found her authentic cultural voice – and warns that if we hear only a single story about another person or country, we risk a critical misunderstanding: www.ted.com/talks/chimamanda_adichie_the_danger_of_a_single_ story.

Story books

There are many picture and story books to enhance primary geography lessons. As they are constantly being published, it is best to refer to sites rather than attempt to name them. Two excellent sites for suggestions are:

The Guardian Picture Books pages: www.theguardian.com/books/picture-books.

The Geographical Association Picture Books lists: www.geography.org.uk.

Mascots

Barnaby Bear: www.barnabybear.co.uk.
Flat Stanley: www.flatstanley.com

Many schools have their own mascot, many of which travel with children, parents and other people connected to schools.

Resources from the Centre for Human Rights and Citizenship (CHRCE) are referred to and listed at the end of Chapter 9

Chapter 9

Go geography – children's agency and action through geography

We worked on a project about our locality but it wasn't just geography, we learned history, photography and public speaking . . . We spoke about it on grandparents' day and TDs and councillors came to see all the work we did.

Boy, 11

This chapter considers how geography relates to human rights and citizenship education and touches on other areas such as values education and looking to the future.

The chapter is based on the following key ideas:

- Children's agency, participation and action are possible through many aspects of geography learning.
- Children's learning in sustainability, citizenship and human rights education may be explicitly or subtly geographical.
- Children have a meaningful contribution to make in their schools and communities.

This chapter outlines:

- how to encourage children to ask questions about their locality and the wider world;
- rights-based approaches to incorporate children's participation in geography lessons;
- opportunities for children to learn essential aptitudes and skills in local and global communities.

This chapter complements the others in this book, especially Chapters 2 and 3 on literacies and enquiry and Chapters 5 and 6 on school grounds and localities, as well as Chapter 8 on places.

Geography for children

Geography provides many opportunities to develop children's questions, ideas and actions in relation to sustainability, citizenship and human rights education. This can happen in many ways, but often locally, as Eleanor Roosevelt so famously said (1953):

> Where, after all do universal human rights begin? In small places, close to home, so close and so small that they cannot be seen on any map of the world.

As Catling and Willy note, these are key geographical concepts, as 'the quality and nature of the Earth's and human's present and future depends on understanding the interactions in and between the human and physical environments' (2008, p. 49).

Apple, inspired by the work of critical theorists such as Freire, has argued that the structures of society must be challenged and that, he argues, promotes the idea that counter-hegemonic educational work is accomplished 'locally and regionally', and it may be that projects which attempt to make an immediate material and visible difference in their places are most appealing to today's young people (2005). Drawing on such critical pedagogies, Catling argues that children are marginalised in their local neighbourhood and school environments. He states we must reconceptualise how children are viewed in our societies, and that geography has a part to play in this process. He suggests that primary geography must be integrated with a geography of reality that politicises the geographical enquiries that can be undertaken (2005, p. 336) 'not in a partisan sense, but by moving such geographical investigations into active pupil engagement and into following through the findings of such studies by proposing community action.' As can be seen in Figure 9.1, we can provide children the freedom and tools to have experiences with few restrictions so they become empowered as citizens. There is a wealth of research evidence to show that this is possible for children of primary school age (Waldron and Ruane, 2010; Ruane *et al.*, 2010; Pike, 2011b; Oberman *et al.*, 2013). This chapter brings together some of these thoughts, using examples of how these important aspects of children's lives can be explored and acted upon in geography and citizenship lessons through a rights-based perspective.

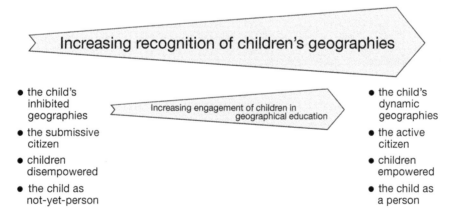

Figure 9.1 Reconceptualising children's geographies (Catling, 2003, p. 172)

CASE STUDY 9.1 Children and their local environment: various senior classes, Ireland

This project involved over 150 children in 8 different schools across Ireland (Pike, 2011b) and was broadly based upon Catling's model in Figure 9.1. It explored the children's experiences of their local environments, including their use of and attitudes to spaces and places, and the interaction of such experiences and their learning.

Children used a range of methods to record their thoughts, including photographs, interviews and drawings. The children described how they experienced affordances of spaces, places and people in a range of ways; for example, by cycling, playing sports and 'hanging out' with friends. The children also revealed varied and dynamic attitudes to their localities. In expressing such opinions, they liked spaces and places where they could take part in activities with friends, especially green areas, shops and youth clubs. Children had varied attitudes to changes in their local environments, but were broadly positive about changes in their localities. The children also described how experiences in their local environment contributed to the different areas of their development, especially their learning. For most children, such experiences emanated from outside the school, with learning in geography in school more likely to be about places further from home.

The findings from this project suggested children's personal geographies, in their local environments, could be used as a basis of primary geography through content and activities such as those outlined in the curriculum. The children's views also suggest the contributions of all children could be used in decison-making beyond schools and that this would enhance their lives.

Geography, citizenship and human rights education

The Council of Europe provides useful definitions for citizenship and human rights education (Council of Europe, 2015):

Education for Democratic Citizenship (EDC) is:

> . . . education, training, dissemination, information, practices and activities which aim, by equipping learners with knowledge, skills and understanding and moulding their attitudes and behaviour, to empower them to exercise and defend their democratic rights and responsibilities in society, to value diversity and to play an active part in democratic life, with a view to the promotion and protection of democracy and the rule of law.

Human Rights Education (HRE) is:

> . . . education, training, dissemination, information, practices and activities which aim, by equipping learners with knowledge, skills and understanding and moulding their attitudes and behaviour, to empower them to contribute to the building and

CASE STUDY 9.2 Human Rights School: Balbriggan Educate Together National School

Balbriggan ETNS is a relatively new school, founded in 2004, but has quickly expanded into a school of over 500 children. The whole school is run as a rights-based community documented by their principal through his blog and writing (McCutcheon, 2010). Children all have a role in the running of the school and in the activities they take part in. Many decisions about what will happen in classrooms are taken by the teacher and children, with the children leading many learning activities and events. The school's role in Human Rights Education goes up a gear each October for Human Rights month. Some of the activities that took place recently were:

- **School referendum**. Children (and later parents) were asked the question: 'As a school, could we be better at preventing unfairness or discrimination against any one of these groups?' The child is asked to vote for one group from the following list where we as a school could do better work than what we are doing currently: Gender, Civil Status, Family Status and Structure, Age, Race/Ethnicity, Religion, Sexual Orientation and Sexuality, Disability, Membership of the Traveller Community. These are the nine grounds on which discrimination must not occur in Irish Law.

- **Self-expression day**. Children spoke to a camera to express: who I am proud to be?

- **The Human Rights factor**. Children performed songs with a Human Rights and Children's Rights theme at a peer concert.

- **School film day**. With popcorn and a cinema atmosphere, the children watched an age-appropriate film that had an Equality or Human Rights theme and discussed it in class afterwards.

- **Visit to a travellers' site**. Children visited a local site for a workshop on Travellers' Rights.

- **Visit to the Islamic Cultural Centre**. Children visited the mosque and centre for an insight into the life and religion of the Muslim families in the school community.

- **Photography exhibition**. Children held an exhibition on Roma culture for the whole school community.

Finally, children elected their class representatives to the Junior and Senior Councils which meet and contribute meaningfully to decisions made in the school.

http://balbrigganetns.scoilnet.ie/blog

Figure 9.2 Human Rights and Citizenship Education and associated action occur through geography (a) displaying the school community's rights and responsibilities, (b) global justice displays and activity, (c) green school committees and curriculum activity and (d) spaces for children

defence of a universal culture of human rights in society, with a view to the promotion and protection of human rights and fundamental freedoms.

Traditionally, the role of citizenship education was to enable members of society to be assimilated into the mainstream culture, whatever their background or culture was (Banks, 2010). However, these ideas changed during the ethnic rights protests movements in the 1960s and 70s, when many previously held ideas about individuals and society were challenged. Today, the role of citizenship is wide ranging and includes local, national and global dimensions, as Banks (2004, pp. 292–3) states:

Citizens in this century need the knowledge, attitudes, and skills to function in their cultural communities and beyond their cultural borders. They should also be able and willing to participate in the construction of a national civic culture that is a moral and just community. The national community should embody democratic ideals and values such as those articulated in the Universal Declaration of Human Rights, the Declaration of Independence, the Constitution, and the Bill of Rights. Students also need to acquire the knowledge and skills required to become effective citizens in the global community.

Citizenship education is not simply about knowing how to be a citizen, it is also about enabling people to make their own decisions and to take responsibility for their own lives and their communities (Citizenship Foundation, 2014). The United Nations Convention on the Rights of the Child (UNCRC), research and programmes, including child-centred policies in education, promote the idea that children are not 'future citizens' (Percy-Smith, 2010), but present citizens, making contributions to their communities and the wider world (Hart, 1997; Adams and Ingham, 1998). Therefore children's citizenship is developed in a large number of ways (DES/NCCA, 1999a; NCCA, 2012), and for children, their everyday interactions locally or ethno-geographies (Martin, 2005; 2008) contribute to this process. As teachers of geography, we can take this idea into the curriculum, by encouraging and harnessing children's thinking so that not only do they learn but they can also take action about things they would like to change.

Both citizenship and human rights education are geographical in nature as the first relates to democratic rights and responsibilities, as well as active participation of people in local, national and global spheres. Where geography is presented as an enquiry led subject, children's questions often relate to issues of rights and citizenship. Furthermore, two articles of the UNCRC can be specifically integrated into geography lessons and help to improve young people's participation in society:

> Article 12: Parties shall assure to the child who is capable of forming his or her own views the right to express those views freely in all matters affecting the child, the views of the child being given due weight in accordance with the age and maturity of the child.

> Article 13: The child shall have the right to freedom of expression; this right shall include freedom to seek, receive and impart information and ideas of all kinds, regardless of frontiers, either orally, in writing or in print, in the form of art, or through any other media of the child's choice.

Initiatives such as Every Child Matters (UK) and the National Children's Strategy (Republic of Ireland) give children a voice on local issues. In the UK, the National Children's Bureau and the Children's Society are promoting children's participation. Across Europe, children's councils and forums are becoming more common and are being covered by local and national media. So not only is teaching geography through issues important in geography, it is beginning to be used at a local and national level in decison-making.

Geography helps children navigate complex and perhaps unsettling issues. However, teaching through geographical issues means that teachers have to suspend their views and allow differing views to emerge. This can be something that is particularly difficult for teachers when they are local and are teaching local issues! Teachers can often feel their role is to be on the side of the environmental agenda. However, geographers' and environmentalists' views are complex and varied, so assuming they agree reduces the opportunities to examine issues in classrooms (Butt 2002; Lambert and Balderstone 2009). Lidstone and Gerber (1998) also suggest there is a need to challenge 'conventional wisdom that the main purpose of geography education is to promote the environmental ethic' (p. 87). Children can be given the opportunity to use and value creative, innovative thinking in the exploration and/or resolution of geographical issues, without having ideas imposed upon them.

Table 9.1 The 'ladder' of participation, with examples

Level of participation – rung of the ladder	Description
1. Manipulation	Children have no understanding of the issues and hence do not understand their actions, e.g. children being made to attend demonstrations that they have no understanding of.
2. Decoration	Children are entertained through performances, or simply providing evidence of their involvement, e.g. photographs of children at events.
3. Tokenism	Children appear to have a voice; they are invited to sit as representatives of children but provided no opportunity to formulate their ideas, e.g. children being asked to represent school at youth council where there are no structures in place to ensure participation.
4. Assigned-but-informed	Children understand the intentions of the project; they know who made the decision concerning their involvement and why; they have a meaningful role, e.g. school council that makes few decisions.
5. Consulted-and-informed	Projects are designed and run by adults but youth understand the project and their opinions are treated seriously, e.g. local planning projects for playgrounds, youth clubs, etc.
6. Adult-initiated, shared decisions with youth	Although adults initiated the project, decison-making is shared with children, e.g. democratically run school councils.
7. Youth-initiated and directed	Children initiate and direct their own projects and adults to leave them alone to design their own projects, e.g. youth club committees that are run by young people.
8. Youth-initiated, shared decisions with adults	Children incorporate adults into projects they have designed and managed, e.g. fair trade campaigns started by children in schools.

Source: Arnstein 1969; Hart, 1997.

When working to promote participation in geography lessons, care must be taken to avoid tokenism when designing learning, including associated action. Using the analogy of a ladder, Hart (1997) outlined differing types of children's participation, based on Arnstein's (1969) model for participation. As can be seen in Table 9.1, activity on the bottom three rungs is simple tokenism, where children are not part of the participation process. Moving up the ladder, children have more of a role in decisions.

To help make the ladder of participation make sense, it is useful to think about some scenarios.

School A: Children decided they wanted to do something to help the environment. They set up an environmental committee and decided to do a transport survey. In their geography lesson, their teacher helped them to map how many children were being driven to school and where they were coming from. They held a meeting and designed posters to encourage parents and children to walk to school. After a few weeks, the number of children walking to school had increased significantly.

School B: Children in the school entered a colouring competition sponsored by a local supermarket. They were photographed for the local paper and the winner received a voucher from the supermarket.

School C: Children in the school learned about the unfairness of trade in their geography lessons. They also learnt about fair trade. They decided they wanted to see what their community could do to help people in less economically developed countries. With their teacher's help, they set up a Fair Trade Committee in school, then a Steering Committee with local politicians and others.

School D: This school needed to set up a school council, as it was required by law. The teachers decided on which children would sit on the council. It met once a month.

Of the scenarios above, schools D and B were certainly tokenism, with the colouring competition so far down the ladder it was on the ground! The environmental club scenario in school A is the highest level of participation as the children worked independently. Overall, the most effective example of children's participation in all dimensions of learning and action was school C. In fact, the scenario here was based on the school in Case Study 9.5.

CASE STUDY 9.3 How amazing are our school grounds? Canal Way Educate Together National School

The children in Junior Infants (4–5 years old) spent time taking part in different activities in the grounds of the school. The school's outdoor space consisted of a large concrete yard and a garden. Before they went out in the school grounds, they talked about what they might find. The children were asked to try and find anything 'amazing to you'. The garden was in the process of being developed, as the school was new to the premises. In fact, the relative wildness of the garden provided far more opportunities to find 'amazing' features! On entering the green part of the school grounds, the first item for discussion was the stinging nettles, and were shown how dock leaves can help a sting (although this is debated)! Next, the children used bags and frames to see and/or collect anything they liked. Throughout the activity, the children talked in a wide variety of ways: using descriptive and imaginative language, and explaining why features were amazing. The amazing features the children found were:

- *Galium aparine* or cleavers, also known as catchweed, stickyweed, robin-run-the-hedge, sticky willow, velcro weed and grip grass to make crowns.
- Various trees, including a horsechestnut tree, from which leaves and branches were admired.
- Holes in the grass, and the mystery of who made them.
- A dead tree that had been carved into interesting shapes and many ants.

The children were very positive about their experience, and they loved the walk in the sunshine and taking their time over the work. The art work they produced had elements of mapping, imagination and story, as can be seen on the school's website (see below).

www.canalwayeducatetogetherns.ie

Figure 9.3 Geography provides opportunities for children to engage with environments by (b, c) observing and collecting data and (a, d) recording and sharing findings

Primary geography and active participation

As outlined in Chapters 4, 5 and 6, children's interactions locally are important to them and provide much material for citizenship, human rights and geography. My own research, working with over 150 children in 8 different schools in Ireland showed the importance of these interactions, as described in Case Study 9.1. Other studies have investigated children's use of virtual on-line spaces (2002, p. 316) and time in local communities, including streets and shopping malls for identity formation (Matthews *et al.*, 2000, p. 281). They have views about the past, present and future of their localities and the wider world (Chawla, 2002; Pike, 2011b; Oberman *et al.*, 2013).

Again, the role of the teachers is essential here, as we can draw on children's experiences to facilitate children's realisation of their democratic values (collaboration, respect, etc.) and roles (participants, social actors, etc.) (Dewey,1897/1998). The variety of activity that takes place in Balbriggan ETNS, in Case Study 9.2, shows that much of the children's learning in human rights education involves interactions and participation with local people, and places, with strong links to places beyond their community, enabled by their teachers.

In classrooms, teaching through issues helps children connect with local and global communities in their geography lessons. In examining the issue of the lane

Table 9.2 Some aspects of citizenship in geography education

Enquiry questions	Possible activities
What jobs do people do in our area?	• Interviewing people • Finding different jobs on local maps, aerial photographs and newspapers • Visit to local workplaces
What harms and helps our area?	• Environmental survey of land, air and/or water • Interviewing local people • Examining stories in local papers
What resources do we use?	• Brainstorms of products (see Chapter 4) • Audit of purchases • Shopping surveys and interviews
What are the conflicts in our area?	• Investigating stories in local newspapers • Interviewing school community – adults and children • Fieldwork in locality
Which organisations help us?	• Survey of local organisations • Homework on investigating the work of an organisation • Guest speakers from organisations
How are we connected to other places?	• Connection circles activity (see Chapter 8) • Supermarket surveys • Contact with other schools via posting letters, Mystery Skypes etc.

Source: Adapted from Catling and Willy, 2008.

(see Chapter 7), children in St James' National School came into contact with many people, some they knew, others they did not. In school and using the locality they:

- decided on a key enquiry question for their work;
- questioned and interviewed people about their views on the lane;
- collated a large amount of data – pictures, questionnaires and written accounts of children, parents and residents;
- represented their findings back to each other and the school community.

CASE STUDY 9.4 Our locality: how might our locality change in the future? 10–12 year olds, Scoil Fhursa

As described in Case Study 6.4, the boys in fifth and sixth classes carried out an enquiry based on the following questions:

- What do people think?
- Which places should change?
- What is the area like?

- What do we think of the area?
- Why was Coolock built? How did it change?

The ideas for activities in geography from the boys included: talking to people, doing surveys and walking around their area, and looking on the Internet. So the next week, the boys carried out a survey on the area around the shopping centre, within groups they focused on different aspects of their enquiry:

- talking to local residents
- taking photographs of features in the locality
- recording their own thoughts on different places in the locality.

This information was used back in the classroom, where groups of boys took on particular questions to answer as shown in Figure 9.4. It was suggested to the boys that we should share their work and ideas with a wider audience. Grandparents Day was coming up in the school, so the boys wrote letters to invite various local representatives and community leaders to hear their presentations, these included:

- all their grandparents and many parents
- local councillors
- nationally elected representatives
- others (e.g. children, teachers and adults in the school).

The children presented their work and were invited to present it further at council meetings. They were also told there were plans to close the underpass and that the plans had already been put forward locally. On reflection, the children were delighted with the work they carried out. Comments included:

It's great we did something with our work, we always do projects, but this time we used it for something. It was really scary presenting our work but I'm really glad we did it.

The work was the boys' own work, but their teacher had facilitated and shaped their learning, as one boy noted:

I learned that there were not as many houses in Coolock as much as there are now, the families in Kilmore were big because lots had many sons and daughters and some people had weird jobs. We interviewed people in the area, we also took photos of bad things and good things of the area. I loved speaking about the project as we learned how to speak in public . . . All of it paid off because the tunnel will shut down and their might be built a new skate park in Kilmore in the future.

The boys' work has led to attention on social media, presentations at TeachMeet meetings and was referred to at the Dublin City Council.

www.scoilfhursa.ie

Figure 9.4 Action through primary geography: how might our area change in the future? (a) waiting to present our findings, (b, c) geographical enquiry and (d) presenting to local residents and decison-makers

In this way, the children were acting as citizens in their local community at a high level as they were influencing decisions made by others. Aspects of citizenship, and just a handful of opportunities, are outlined in Table 9.1; there is considerable synergy between this table and Table 9.2, showing the links between all aspects in this chapter.

Sustainability and primary geography

Sustainability is about leading a life that '. . . meets the needs of the present without compromising the ability of future generations to meet their own needs' (UN, 1987). Education for Sustainability (EfS) (or Education for Sustainable Development (ESD)) is defined as:

> Education for Sustainable Development (ESD) is a learning process (or approach to teaching) based on the ideals and principles that underlie sustainability and is concerned with all levels and types of learning to provide quality education and foster sustainable human development – learning to know, learning to be, learning to live together, learning to do and learning to transform oneself and society.
>
> (UNESCO, 2015)

Table 9.3 Key concepts and possible learning in ESD

Concept	Learning through knowledge, understanding, skills and values	Possible enquiry questions
Inter-dependence	Understand the connections and inter-relationships between people, places and environments at local and global issues, and that decisions taken in one place have an impact elsewhere.	• Where does my food come from? • Where else is our school linked to?
Citizenship and stewardship	Realise our rights and responsibilities to participate in making decisions that affect people, places and environments, and that everyone is entitled to a say in what happens in the future.	• When will we get a skatepark? • Why are the shops closing? • How can we make our school greener?
Diversity	Understand and value the importance of diversity culturally, socially, economically and biologically.	• What foods do our class eat at home? • Why do people move to our area? • What languages are spoken in our school?
Quality of life, equity and justice	Recognise that for any development to be sustainable it must provide equitable benefits to people, improving their lives and well-being.	• How will the renovated hall help our community? • Will the development at our GAA club help all residents?
Sustainable change	Appreciate there are limits to the ways the world can develop, and understand the consequences of unsustainable growth, such as poverty and environmental degradation.	• What is palm oil? • Where does it come from? • Is air travel good?
Uncertainty and precaution	Realise, through learning geography, to be cautious as actions have unintended consequences for people and places.	• What is the impact of buying throwaway items, e.g. plastic bottles? • Should we fly to France on holiday? • Should I eat biscuits with palm oil in?
Needs and rights of future generations	Recognise and act responsibly towards future inhabitants of our world.	• How can we make sure our area is safe for younger children? • How will our area change as climate changes? • How can we spread the world's wealth in a fairer way?

Source: Adapted from Catling and Willy, 2010; Martin and Owens, 2008.

The National Strategy on Education for Sustainable Development aims to ensure that education contributes to sustainable development by equipping learners with the relevant knowledge (the 'what'), the key dispositions and skills (the 'how') and the values (the 'why') that will motivate and empower them throughout their lives to become informed active citizens who take action for a more sustainable future.

(DES, 2014)

ESD (or EfS) helps children learn important concepts (as outlined in Table 9.1) but also enables children to become reflective and critical thinkers in geography. This results in children able to question 'vested- and self-interest in order to develop their own thinking about the type of society they would like to be part of' (Smith, 2012).

Table 9.3 draws on geography educators' ideas about how the subject can contribute to ESD, and provide possible enquiry questions for the classroom. Teachers can encourage children to ask such questions, by thinking carefully about the material they provide for children when generating their ideas for enquiry questions, as outlined in the case study from Knockmahon NS. There may also be occasions where activity, not based on geography lessons, occurs that contribute highly to sustainability (see Case Study 9.5).

CASE STUDY 9.5 Planting a native hedgerow: all classes, St James' National School

During the time the children were carrying out their enquiry about the school grounds (see Chapter 5), a number of developments were taking place in the school grounds. The school had a yard and large field, the grounds were respected and cared for by the part-time caretaker and the children in the school. From the school, there were beautiful views of the surrounding countryside, mountains and the sea. The principal had wished to develop a native hedgerow in the school grounds for a number of years.

Over a number of weeks, a hedgerow was planted, organised by the Parents' Association. One parent organised the purchase of the hedgerow plants, funded from Stradbally Tidy Towns Committee. First, over a number of days, children and parents helped prepare the ground for the hedgerow. A trench was dug and thousands of stones were removed. The children loved finding different stones and bugs among the soil, although they were completely fed up with removing the stones eventually! A permeable membrane was put along the trench and then the plants were ordered; they were bare root plants, and they needed to be planted immediately. One Friday, all the children in the school and some parents helped plant the hedgerow.

Every child chose a tree as 'theirs' and put a decorated label on it. Parents continued to put down mulch and watered the hedgerow over the weeks, and within six weeks the hedgerow was in bud. Children's views on the growing of the hedgerow were very positive, and even when the labels blew off in storms, they were all still able to point out their own part of the hedgerow.

CASE STUDY 9.6 Becoming a Fair Trade Town: Clonburris National School

Children in the sixth class found out about fair trade in their geography lessons and, following this they decided to start a campaign to make Clondalkin, their suburb of Dublin, a fair trade town. The process involved the children working within the school and the wider local community in many ways, including the setting up a steering committee and campaigning online and face-to-face over two years.

In 2013, their hard work paid off and Clondalkin became Ireland's 51st fair trade town. Their children's success was recognised locally and nationally, including by a local councillor (Timmonds, 2015):

> I am very proud to congratulate Paula Kenny and the students of Clonburris school that have successfully made Clondalkin a Fairtrade town. I am delighted to have worked with them to ensure success. What the children have learned and achieved will stay with them through their lives. It's great they have learned so much about social justice.

The fair trade campaign was just one of the many innovative and engaging activities that take place in the school. The school website details the school's focus on the importance of maintaining and enhancing the lives of all those involved in the school.

www.clonburrisns.ie

(a)

(b)

(c)

(d)

Figure 9.5 Geographical learning and connection with place and process, St James' National School (a, b) preparing the ground for a native hedgerow, (c) learning about minibeasts and other life in the ground and (d) learning about planting and hedgerow species.

Acting for the future in primary geography

Geography and citizenship education provides children with opportunities to look to the future, as Walford (1984) notes:

> The sustained study of a number of possible geographies of the short-term and middle-term future will encourage the student to consider those aspects of the future which are desirable and those which are not. Hopefully such geography teaching can vitalise school students into an interest in their own futures . . . In urging that we teach a geography of the future, I do not mean to say that we should give up teaching a geography of the past: but we should make that past the servant of the future. If the future is unavoidable let us at least not walk backward into it.

Hicks has provided some very useful frames for children to shape their idea about the future. He encourages us to get children looking at varied views of the future in order to:

- develop a more future-orientated perspective on their own lives and events in the wider world;
- exercise critical thinking skills and the creative imagination more effectively;
- identify and envision alternative futures which are more just and sustainable;
- engage in active and responsible citizenship in the local, national and global community, on behalf of both present and future generations (2006).

Hicks (2006) asks us to encourage children to think about different futures:

1 *Possible futures* are everything between the best (utopian) and the worst (dystopian) that can be imagined. Possible futures incorporate two other types of futures.
2 *Probable futures* are all those futures that seem most likely to come about, for example in our own lives or as a result of forecasting. People often seem pessimistic about the probable future, especially at a global level, although less so at personal or local levels.
3 *Preferable futures* are all those futures that one most desires to come about because of one's most deeply held values and beliefs. They are the visions of a better world which need to be identified in order to clarify action for positive change in the present.

The considering of possible futures by children provides an ideal opportunity to present their work to other people, as outlined in Chapter 3. These may be local decison-makers, teachers, children, parents. The children in Clonburris National School needed to do all of this in their project focused on making their town a fair trade town.

Figure 9.6 Early years geography enhances HRCE and starts children on the route to active citizenship (a) playing in the school grounds, (b) wayfinding and mark making, (c) working together outside and (d) planting and nurturing

Conclusions

The projects outlined above involved children and adults working together for the good of schools and communities. The geographical aspect to all these projects is clear, as they involve the past, present and future of people and places. Where schools are involved in such community projects, the benefits may outweigh the benefits of other high profile/ high cost programmes, as Boulding stated over 25 years ago (1979).

We may be unnecessarily sabotaging our present, and our children's future, by being blind to the inconsistencies and irrationalities of adult–child interaction in family and community in this century. Mass media programmes about the right to a happy and secure childhood and to a happy and secure retirement cannot substitute for the actual experience of frank and honest confrontation between generations when perceptions, needs and interests differ, in a context of mutual acceptance of responsibility for each other. Neither can special feeding, health and education programmes undertaken for children substitute joint community projects carried out by adults and children together, in which capacities of the young to contribute to the welfare of all receives full recognition.

The opportunities to develop children's learning in geography with citizenship and sustainability are endless. Every opportunity to do so must be taken. Such activity has a value that is way beyond any amount of sitting in a classroom reading from a textbook. However, teachers need to be wary, as there can be so much to do, and so focusing on the interests of the children, while considering the key principles of participation outlined in this chapter, is essential. Children will learn far more through carrying out an enquiry about an issue that is important to them, and acting on it to facilitate change, than they will from trying to solve all the issues in the world!

Reflection and action

- How could your school develop learning through Human Rights, Citizenship and Participation over the next year?
- In a recent activity in geography education, were there opportunities for the children to share their learning with a wider audience? Could they have shared their ideas and questions with decison-makers in their locality?
- When children take part in events and activity in your school, what is their role? Where are they on the ladder of participation? What could your school do to enable higher levels of active participation from the children?

Further resources

Reading

Hart, R. (1979) *Children's Participation: From Tokenism to Citizenship*. Earthscan.
  Also a summary of the ideas in Hart's book available at www.unicef-irc.org/ publications/pdf/childrens_participation.pdf.
Howe, R.B. and Covell, K. (2005) *Empowering Children: Children's Rights Education as a Pathway to Citizenship*. Toronto: University of Toronto Press.
Waldron, F. and Ruane, B. (eds) (2010) *Human Rights Education: Reflections on Theory And Practice*. Dublin: Liffey Press.

Centre for Human Rights and Citizenship, St Patrick's College has produced various resources for schools all thoroughly researched and piloted by teachers with children in schools, including:

  Eco-Detectives – a resource on climate change for all class levels, available in English and Gaeilge (with Department of the Environment).
  Farid's Rickshaw Ride – a children's storybook set in Bangladesh, which explores global connections (with Trocaire).
  Just Children 2 – a teaching resource for integrating Critical Literacy and Global Citizenship Education across the curriculum (with Trocaire): www.spd.dcu.ie/ chrce.

Children's Environments Research Centre, City University, New York links research with the development of policies, environments and programs to fulfil children's rights and improve the quality of their lives. The group aims for a just and inclusive world, where children and youth, in partnership with their families, neighbours and communities, have the opportunity to participate in the creation of environments that support their right to live, learn and play: www.cergnyc.org.

Child Friendly Places is an approach for integrating children's rights into local development initiatives and educational programs through a participatory, intergenerational and child friendly assessment and planning methodology that empowers communities to improve their local conditions and environments with children, adolescents, families, educators, service providers and decison-makers: www.childfriendlyplaces.org.

Clondalkin Fair Trade Town was initiated by the children in Clonburris NS. Online information includes the school website: www.clonburrisns.ie/development-education. html and informative Twitter account (@clondalkinft). The children created an interview (in Gaeilge and English), which is also available online at: www.youtube.com/watch?v =vumXHeQU6zk.

Innovation Happens is a paper by the NCCA outlining innovative thinking across the curriculum: www.ncca.ie/en/Consultations/Innovation_in_schools.

Chapter 10

Making geography work – planning for learning in geography

> Enquiry is powerful . . . it can help children to construct their own investigations which may lead to more focused, personal and relevant outcomes leading to a more positive viewpoint of the subject.
>
> Student teacher

As the quote above from a student teacher illustrates, geography is interesting, relevant and challenging for children and for teachers. The nature of geography means that deciding on what and how to teach it can be rather overwhelming. This chapter aims to outline the many influences on teacher planning and provide guidance for teachers on how to plan engaging geography lessons for children. This chapter outlines:

- planning geography with children at the centre of the process;
- approaching geography planning in a progressive and collegial way;
- planning less, but more effectively;
- offering value for money in resourcing geography;
- planning for all children through creative approaches to differentiation.

Theories and ideas about planning primary geography

There are so many influences on how teachers plan; key thoughts from thinkers in education can help focus our minds on what is important:

- Teachers are essential in supporting children's learning, Lev Vygotsky.
- Experience should be the basis of children's learning, John Dewey.
- Learning is a social experience, Jerome Bruner.

As well as those who have researched classrooms, teachers and teacher education:

- Children should have enriching experiences in geography, Simon Catling (2003; 2005).
- Children come to school as geographers, Stephen Scoffham (1998).
- Everyday geographies inform and enrich geography, Fran Martin (2008; 2010).
- Learners 'need to know' is the basis for planning geography, Margaret Roberts (2003; 2009; 2010; 2013a; 2013b).

This chapter has been written with these ideas, as well as those from teachers and children, in mind.

Traditionally, in geography, elements of the subject were taught separately. Many will recall being taught geography 'skills', 'physical' geography and 'human' geography. Drawing on 2004 school leavers entering initial teacher education (ITE), the all-Ireland study by the Irish Association for Social, Scientific and Environmental Education (IASSEE) (Waldron *et al.*, 2009) found the most common experiences of learning geography in primary school for new teachers were generally content driven and included rote learning. Such experiences are significant, as teachers' previous experiences as learners of subjects influence how they teach. For those with limited experiences, it is important to provide them with the tools to 'break the mould' and become more creative in their planning (Waldron *et al.*, 2009). Teachers can develop their practice in primary geography, through:

- reading, or 'dipping into', books on teaching and learning in primary geography;
- using websites such as the Geographical Association, for personal CPD and to find out about events in your area;
- meeting up with other teachers online or face-to-face through professional networking sites such as Geography Champions or through social media such as Twitter;
- organising CPD within your school, using any of the above resources.

Whatever teachers' experiences of geography, it is important for them to begin thinking about how geography could be conceptualised in schools. Professional development time for all teachers to consider what is important for children and teachers to experience in schools should be provided; this need not be tedious, as can be seen in Figure 10.1. In this time, both the content, pedagogies and resourcing for geography need to be considered.

Planning in primary geography

When planning primary geography, we need to think about the balance of what children learn and how they learn it. Teachers can ensure children have a positive and enriching experience of geography in schools. Children's learning and well-being should always be the focus. As Catling states, the 'essence of building a motivating and effective primary geography curriculum' is one that works with children 'not on behalf of them, or to them, nor ignoring them' (2005, p. 340). We know that children develop new knowledge and understanding in geography, but teachers need to think carefully about what knowledge children are learning (Young, 2008). Therefore, in planning for geography, teachers need to think about what is learned and how it is learned.

- *Children's capabilities in geography.* Bearing in mind children are often capable of higher level thinking and understanding than teachers think (Catling, 2003; Leat, 1998).
- *Supporting children's learning.* Many children need to be supported in their thinking through scaffolding by teachers working with them or providing resources to help children (Vygotsky, 1962).

Figure 10.1 CPD and collaborative planning for primary geography can be very rewarding and inspiring (a, b) taking part in learning and auditing places and (c, d) planning collaboratively

- *Everyday geographies.* Taking care to consider the interactions between every day or ethno-geography (Martin, 2005; 2008) and other types of geographical knowledge (Standish, 2003). Children's interest in geography is often sparked by what is known and what is not known. In my experience, it is always these elements of geography that most interest children!

Schools work within the political, social, economic environments. I found there are many influences on teachers' planning in classrooms (Pike, 2005). This is especially true for recently qualified and student teachers. Influences include:

- *The teacher*: teachers' philosophy, experiences, confidence, attitudes and motivation all influence what and how they teach.
- *The classroom*: the children and their needs and abilities as well as the classroom environment itself, access to resources, including the outdoors, all influence how a teacher plans and teaches.
- *The school*: with its ethos and routines can influence what teachers do. Teachers may feel free or restricted to teach in particular ways because of the real or perceived wishes of others in the school, such as principals, teachers and parents.

Table 10.1 Broad categories for types of planners

Cautious planners	Balanced planners	Adventurous planners	Radical planners
Stay in the structure and well-established ways of working	Assume some of existing planning will stay	Make complete reviews of the content and approaches within schemes	Undertake a radical overhaul starting with a clean slate
Wish to provide a base of knowledge and skills in geography	Consider new curriculum content and approaches alongside existing planning	Draw on many new ideas and resources	Take inspiration from academic geography and/or students' experiences and questions
Only make changes when there are curriculum changes	Ensure new planning is a mixture of new and old	Keep some existing topics and approaches, but tailor them to new structures	Go for new and innovative topics and materials, including some untried

- *The broader context*: teachers are influenced by a large range of other factors, such as the community of the school, decison-makers in education and the wider political context.

Teachers are also influenced by the curriculum and the expectations of those judging education such as school inspectors. It is very important to consider how teachers in turn have an impact on how all of these factors operate. Teachers have an influence on the ethos of a school and the learning that takes place in that school over time. The type of planner a teacher becomes does depend on many factors: philosophies of teaching, ideas about subjects, initial and continuing teacher education experiences and also the many influences from others in education. Other teachers, children and parents all have a role in shaping what is believed to be good learning and so in turn good planning in geography. Table 10.1, outlines a continuum of different categories of planner, ranging from cautious to radical planners. While this is a useful model for teachers to compare themselves to, in reality teachers could probably 'see' themselves in descriptions from across the continuum.

There is evidence that even the newest of teachers have well-formed ideas about teaching (Waldron *et al.*, 2009), and that over time these become both more personal and complex. Figure 10.2 outlines just some of the many influences on teachers and their practices in classrooms. They are influenced by a large range of factors, from other teachers' practices to the availability of resources. The most important influences on how we teach should be the children in our classes, informed by the thinking and research about children's capabilities. This is especially so in relation to children's roles in deciding what and how they learn.

The process of planning for geography is a messy business! Generally, teachers plan using the curriculum, teach lessons and review the learning that takes place, as outlined in Figure 10.1. However the process is far more complex than this, as outlined throughout this chapter.

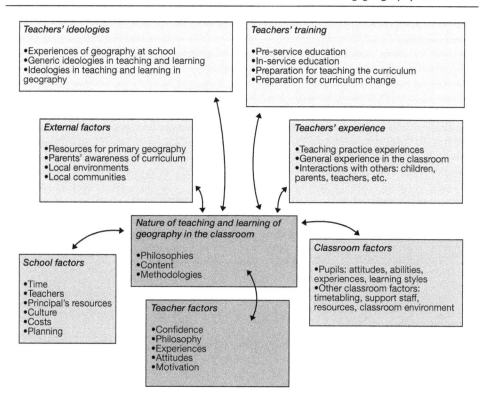

Figure 10.2 The influences on teaching and learning in classrooms

CASE STUDY 10.1 **Primary geography and professional networking**

Geography education is supported well on social media, and there are a number of sites listed at the end of this chapter that will help you plan geography lessons in primary school. The Geography Champions networking site is a collaborative learning community. It has over 2,000 members and is a great place to share ideas, resources and news about primary geography and the primary curriculum. Teachers, including student teachers, are invited to browse the library of Blog Posts, all with keyword links, and add their own posts, links and images. They are also asked to take the time to comment on queries and thoughts submitted by others. There are pages for various places in England, and Ireland has its own group page too.

http://geographychampions.ning.com

Table 10.2 The costs of resources for primary geography

	Cheap or free	*Expensive*
Multi-use	Maps of county, country and world	Aerial photographs of the locality
	Mascots	Maps of the locality
	Seeds, soil, pots	Atlases and globes
	Second hand construction toys	Resource packs on general topics
	Clipboards	Big books
	Applications on devices	Cameras
		DL/ICT devices
Limited use	Newspapers	Textbooks
	Flyers on local events	Resource packs on specific topics
	Information on new developments	Physical geography equipment
		Weather recording equipment

Resourcing primary geography

Resourcing all subjects in primary schools is a challenge, in sourcing, selecting and financing. The resources selected and used in primary geography have an enormous impact on how geography is taught. There are many resources that can be used for teaching, some expensive, others not. The key thought is 'what value for money does this product offer?', as outlined in Table 10.2. A high-quality aerial photograph may cost a substantial amount of money. However, aerial photographs actually provide the good value for money, per use, as they can be used for decades. Conversely, a resource pack or game may be cheap, but may only be used once or twice a year.

While student teachers creatively 'make do' on their placements in schools, teachers and principals in schools can make strategic decisions about what to buy with the funds they have. A major issue in schools is who purchases resources. In the UK, schools purchase resources, but in Ireland and other European countries, schools select then parents supply resources for primary geography. In most Irish schools, parents are asked for a contribution to the teaching of geography, often through the purchase or rental of textbooks. However, many schools are realising that there are many more creative ways to resource primary geography, namely that parents contribute to the purchase of a range of resources. The table in Appendix 11, is very informative in opening up the possibilities for resourcing primary geography. In a typical eight-teacher school with approximately 240 children, a vast amount of money can be spent on primary geography, assuming that each child has a textbook and that the older children will have atlases too; this can amount to about €3,600 per year. In some schools these costs are higher as children have workbooks and textbooks! This represents an enormous investment in 30 of the same resource for each child in a class. Appendix 11 shows the varied and interesting resources this money could be spent on. The table assumes children will experience just five or six geography topics per year, those outlined in Table 10.6. This is relatively straightforward to plan for and allows time for learning (and the linking of learning) to take place. Children get to experience doing geography, using a range of resources, in

CASE STUDY 10.2 Primary geography and social networking

Learning in primary geography is being shared by teachers and children online. For example, the Primary Geography Ireland Facebook page currently has over 3,000 members, sharing and commenting on geographical news and advice for teaching.

Another source for sharing learning in primary geography is sites such as Twitter. Teachers register their classes and share what and how they have been learning in geography and other subjects. Where children are involved in the decisions about what is shared, they are also learning about the issues in online activity. For teachers, such activity online helps them to develop their practice as they consider pedagogies beyond their own experiences.

A suggested list of classes to follow on Twitter is included at the end of this chapter.

www.twitter.com; www.facebook.com

the locality and beyond. The savings for schools and parents are astounding; the eight-teacher school of around 240 children could spend €7,000 less in just three years, and have an amazing array of resources to use.

Children's entitlement to geography

Writing down children's entitlement in geography across the school quickly becomes a geography policy. A policy can help teachers create classrooms that are geography friendly in all aspects. A policy should include:

- a statement of the purpose and nature of geography in the school;
- outlines of what children will experience at different ages;
- information on integration, timing and balance on geography lessons;
- list of resources – and their location;
- examples of children's work; and
- assessment statements: rubrics for different class levels or activities, level statements and so on.

Good policies will also exemplify what can be done in geography, suggesting local opportunities (people and places), as well as outlining the availability of resources in the school for children, Appendix 12. The statement from Balbriggan gives teachers the opportunity to teach geography in their preferred ways. The statement quite clearly articulates what teachers should do. It also clarifies that teaching should follow the good practice laid out in both the curriculum and in Scoffham's edited *Handbook of Primary Geography* (Scoffham, 2010). Underlying these suggestions is a clear move away from the use of textbooks in geography lessons.

Differentiation of children's learning in primary geography

Throughout this book, activities have been featured that are inclusive; all children can take part in them and achieve and enjoy. Differentiation is the adjustment of the teaching process according to the learning needs of the children. There are five points at which differentiation can occur. Behind most theories of differentiation lies the differentiation of strategies according to Bloom's Taxonomy (where the simplest thinking skill is at the bottom).

It is useful for teachers to think of differentiation that:

*   is proactive, as teachers assume children are different types of learners;
*   is to do with the nature of tasks, not the quantity;
*   relies upon multiple approaches to content, process and products within lessons; and
*   focuses upon students – blends whole-class, group and individual learning and teaching.

There are so many ways teachers can differentiate in classrooms. Teachers can develop a culture of difference in the classroom, so that children appreciate that in geography, as well as in all other aspects of what they do in schools, there is difference in:

*   how easy or hard children find particular tasks;
*   how children tackle particular tasks;
*   how well children will do different tasks (in quality, amount, presentations, etc.); and
*   how much children will like doing different tasks.

However, in classrooms, there may be an excess of differentiation, with children constantly being grouped or organised according to ability. Flexible expectations and

Table 10.3 Bloom's taxonomy and geographical questioning

Thinking	Key terms	Examples of questions
Evaluation	Assess, judge, evaluate, compare and contrast	What is the best way to care for Griffith Park? How should space be managed in our school yard?
Synthesis	Reflect, predict, speculate, design, create, combine, hypothesise	What are the best ways to manage the Burren? What can you say about Tramore beach from what you have learnt?
Analysis	Explain, infer, draw conclusions, prioritise	Why did Oxfam make the decisions they did? What is the purpose of Ballymun Regeneration Limited?
Application	Use, interpret, use in a new context, relate	Why does it rain so much in the rainforest? How is the pattern of land uses around Dublin like our town?
Comprehension	Explain, summarise, describe, compare	How do rivers shape the land? Why do people live on flat land?
Knowledge	Define, recall, describe	What is the capital of France? What is the name of a bend in a river?

Source: Bloom *et al.*,1956.

Table 10.4 Differentiation examples in primary geography

Differentiation by...	Examples
Types of tasks set	• Children are given different amounts of written work to do • Children are expected to do different amounts of diagrams
Outcome of activities	• Children are grouped and given different tasks to do • Children are given different activities within groups
Support of other children and adults	• The teacher/support staff target particular children at the first stages of a task • A support teacher works with a child • Certain children are given a writing frame to carry out a task
Scaffolding and sequencing of learning	• Children are provided with an odd one out activity • Children are helped and/or challenged by another adult • Children use a writing frame to shape their ideas
Recording	• Children draw (and label) instead of writing their answers • Children do not record their ideas at all – they simply talk at their own level

Source: After Halocha, 1998.

grouping of children will demonstrate that it is possible for all children to achieve the best they can in geography. Using Bloom's taxonomy to frame differentiation does not work for children if some children are confined to the skills outlined in the lower levels, as those considered 'least able' are also able to think at the higher levels and should be provided with ongoing opportunities to do so. However, the taxonomy is very useful in providing a framework for teachers to encourage children to think broadly and widely. Throughout this book, children's personal learning has been emphasised; this ensures that work is matched to children's needs and wishes. Where geography is taught through enquiry, this is always the case. However, it is useful to consider the types of differentiation that are possible in classrooms, as outlined in Table 10.4

There are many ways to group children in the classroom. For these activities, grouping the children along friendship lines would have worked well. However, in a multigrade class, grouping the children vertically, with groups of mixed ages, works very well. In this way, the older children help younger children. During the fieldwork and follow-up work, this was evident. For example, many older children helped the younger children with tying knots! The teachers helped the children at all stages; however, their input was most evident in helping the children get started on their maps, encouraging them and helping them to plan out their maps, where needed.

CASE STUDY 10.3 Views of teachers: various colleges and schools

During the collation of material for this book, the attitudes of teachers were fascinating. Some liked teaching geography, some did not. At the same time as writing the book, I was also working with student teachers in years one, two and three of their ITE courses.

Some of the comments these student teachers made have been included in the chapters. Patterns in the comments by the teachers were evident, and tended to refer to:

- giving children agency over their learning;
- the importance of the school and locality as a source for learning;
- the integration of cross-curricula themes, such as sustainability, well-being and digital literacies with geography;
- the positive impact engaging geography lessons have on children's learning in literacy and numeracy; and
- the positive attitudes of children towards engaging geography lessons, especially the importance of enquiry.

Comments included:

I believe that it is paramount for children to achieve a sense of appreciation for the environment in which they live and the world around them. (Student teacher)

In geography, we learn more about the local world around and the global world. Children can see the value of their locality as well as more diverse environments. Through investigations, they can actively begin to formulate solutions or future actions to the issues and themes that affect us all, rather than feel powerless. (Teacher)

I plan activities and themes that encourage students to explore their personal geographies and to use these experiences as a starting point to understanding the complexities of the world around them. Helping children draw these clear connections highlights interdependence and the interconnected nature of the world. (Teacher)

The teachers' ideas of what constitutes good learning reflect the findings of different reports on learning (e.g. Plowden Report, Cambridge Review, etc.) as well as guidance contained in the curriculum (e.g. Primary School Curriculum (Ireland), Australian Curriculum, etc.).

Progression in primary geography

Most curricula are spiral in nature, with children being provided with opportunities to deepen all aspects of their learning. It is also important that children move on in all aspects of their geographical learning.

Progression in geography is essential; all too often children in different classes are not challenged sufficiently. In younger classes, children need to be challenged to think geographically. In older classes, the repetition of content needs to be avoided at all costs. These issues occur in all schools, with smaller or larger classes having their own issues. Such progression charts can be used in CPD sessions to clarify what is covered in different class levels. Teachers can also use them to judge when children are achieving above the level expected for their age group. As discussed below, enquiry-based learning with the

Table 10.5 Progression in geography – general progression

Aspect	Younger classes (4-8 years)	Older classes (8-12 years)
Enquiry skills	Asking questions, talking answers, e.g. what, where, why?	Initiating questions, independent enquiry, e.g. what, where, why, how?
Fieldwork skills	Simple/basic field techniques, e.g. identify which way a river flows	More precise measurement, e.g. river measurement – width, depth, speed
Secondary sources	Simple/basic skills, e.g. observation of features on a photograph	Complex skills, drawing on subject knowledge and ideas, e.g. explanation of feature formation
Digital learning	Simple/basic skills; teacher directed, e.g. using representational symbols	Precise, complex skills; greater independence, e.g. spreadsheets for weather data
Location and scale of study	Greater emphasis on small-scale/local, e.g. school grounds	More emphasis on the larger scale; contrasting and distant places, e.g. localities in own country and overseas
Breadth and depth of focus	Narrow focus, e.g. local stream or shopping area	Wider focus, e.g. major river system
Complexity of ideas	Simple links, features, e.g. local journeys	More abstract, e.g. transport systems
Precision of subject language	Basic terms, e.g. stream, hill	Precise, subject specific terms, e.g. tributary
Progression of map skills	Simple, basic, e.g. coordinates	Wider range, precise, e.g. four or six figure references
Development of values and attitudes	Personal views, e.g. likes and dislikes	Critical evaluation, conflicts and solutions, e.g. response to local issues

integration of subjects can make progression harder to work out, as skills emerge from the varied activities children take part in. Again, the use of progression charts can help teachers remember to keep a geographical focus, even where the topic being covered includes different disciplines. Many of these are featured on the Geography Champions website, Ireland group.

Long-, medium- and short-term planning in primary geography

Planning by teachers and children can be split into three broad categories, relating to time. These are long-, medium- and short-term planning.

Long-term planning

Long-term planning refers to the organisation of geography content and approaches, and the integration of geography with other subjects across the school. Table 10.6 shows an

Table 10.6 Whole school long-term plan for geography

Class	Age	Autumn	Spring	Summer
JI	5 years	Our new school Living in our locality	Places we go Spring has sprung!	Capital D Our earth in Space
SI	6 years	Dungarvan – my home town Fabulous France!	Our favourite places Placing our picnic	Blame it on the weatherman
I	7 years	Woods, forests and our tree	St Lucia My home, their home	Our beach Out local environment
2	8 years	Weather (ongoing) Tourism in our area	Sustainable transport	Microclimates in our school
3	9 years	Space – the final frontier England	India and Ireland	Working in our area: The farm/shopping centre
4	10 years	Eire, USA Changing places (jobs in Ireland)	Come to Dungarvan – people in our area	Water Blackwater River
5	11 years	Planning our area Italy	Volcanoes People and Work	Belfast – a contrasting place
6	12 years	Development Brazil – Rio 2016	Ecosystems in our locality Rainforests	The new N25 – which route

example of a long-term plan, or curriculum map, for geography. This simple chart shows the topics that children will investigate across the school. The map shows a balance of place and theme-based topics, across a range of scales. In some terms children do two topics, in others the nature of the topics means they run for longer. Ideally there will be other longer term, incidental geography occurring in the school too, such as 'Places in the News' or 'The Weather in our School'.

Ongoing skills within the above schemes (detailed in schemes) are enquiry, graphical skills (including locations of places), thinking skills, literacy and numeracy. As Krause and Millward (2010, p. 335) argue, 'geography lends itself to cross-curricular work and provides a context for exploring many other subject areas.' The nature of geography as a creative subject (Catling and Willy, 2008, p. 11) provides opportunities for children to carry out many types of collaborative activities, with or without a specifically geographical focus. There are many different combinations of ways to teach by discipline or in integrated ways. Integration can occur on a number of levels:

- integration of philosophies of learning, for example particular approaches to learning;
- integration of content, for example a topic;
- integration of approaches or pedagogies.

Greenwood's work provides a framework for levels of integration of geography in primary schools, in the context of change in the Northern Ireland curriculum from a subject based to more integrated provision, he found that most teachers had a balanced view of integration, and that the focus of different subjects was not lost among excessive integration (Greenwood, 2007). Across the chapters of this book, integration has been considered, especially in the case studies in each chapter.

Timing of lessons, whether one lesson or a series of lessons, can be problematic in teaching. There really are never enough hours in the day, week or year! Teachers plan geography in different ways including:

- discrete geography time once a week
- medium block of geography twice a week, for half a term
- large blocks of geography, possibly integrated with other subjects, through thematic days
- incidental geography, such as recording the weather, 'places in the news time' and 'mascot time'.

Medium-term planning for geography

Medium-term plans, often called 'schemes of work', also are essential tools for teachers planning geography (see Appendices 6, 7, 8.). Medium-term planning is the most common planning teachers take part in. Teachers are constantly thinking in the medium term, as they consider what they plan to do in the coming lessons. There are many different ways to plan in the medium term, but commonly teachers use a template to plan a number of lessons in a particular subject or subjects. Views vary on the best type of scheme, some teachers prefer detailed schemes and lighter daily planning, and others prefer lighter schemes and plan in more detail on a weekly or daily basis. However, teachers generally find their own way to plan that suits them best, although as stated above, planning together is very effective. A useful way to start to think of some aspects of geography planning is as a cube, with sides of themes, places and skills, as show in Figure 1.4. This is particularly useful for planning as, planning involves thinking about different aspects of the subject. In geography, more than one theme or strand is often selected at once, so children may be learning about people's work in Kenya, or characteristics of climate in Brazil. However, we tend to have a main focus when planning geography, such as 'India', 'Our locality' and so on; in any medium-term plan there will be elements of themes, places and skills in geography. Teachers can select a particular theme and then consider how the children will learn, being mindful of the different aspects of geography.

- *Stage 1: The big piece of paper stage!* Before getting to the stage of completing a template, it is a good idea to literally throw ideas down on paper. These could include key questions, resources and ideas for lessons. Planning together in this way, teachers can find that planning is a positive experience as ideas flow!
- *Stage 2: Using a template.* Once the ideas have flowed, it is a good idea to use a template to plan. There are many types available. Some teachers prefer to plan loosely and then think about each lesson; others prefer to have detailed medium-term planning. To teach through enquiry, it is important not to over-plan in the medium term. Detailed medium-term plans can give little scope for adapting planning to children's questions, ideas and needs.

There are some very straightforward but important points to remember when carrying out long-term planning in geography:

- *Focus must be on the children.* If children are to have a role in curriculum making, through enquiry approaches, then teachers do not need to plan every last activity children perform. Long-term planning should be loose enough for opportunities for children and teachers to decide the content and approaches that should be taken. There should be chances to wind up topics or to extend them according to the needs and wishes of the learners. Teachers will always have the curriculum or guidelines they are following at the fore of their minds, but few of these are overly prescriptive in geography.
- *Children's learning should be the main focus of planning.* By simply writing 'the children will . . .' in plans ensures that focus is kept. This is especially useful for new teachers who understandably tend to think lesson planning is all about them!
- *Review and change if necessary.* Teachers should remember to reflect upon and if necessary, change their medium-term planning. For example, for student teachers, it is important to include older versions of medium-term plans in folders during School Placement as evidence of reflection in planning.

Overall, there are advantages and disadvantages to each of these ways of timing geography, however a combination of the above would ensure children have varied and flexible geographical experiences.

Short-term planning for geography/lesson planning

Short-term planning refers to the daily process of planning (see also Appendices 9 and 10). As a first-year student teacher, it is likely this is the main type of planning you do. But fear not, you will only use these for your first year or so of college! For example, in my own college, under-graduate students only do short-term planning in their first

Table 10.7 Different timing for geography lessons

	Blocked	Weekly	Incidental
Advantages	• Teachers can collect thoughts on teaching modules together • Teachers can pool resources • Children can take time to think through work they are doing • Integration can be planned or arise from the work children do	• Geography can have a reasonable amount of time	
Disadvantages		• Teacher priorities may mean geography only takes place late in the school day	• Children may not have time to think through

year, after spending a significant amount of time working alongside teachers and children, without writing any plans! Short-term planning, like all other levels of planning, should be focused on the needs and interests of the children, with the curriculum in mind, along with the many factors outlined above! Lesson plans for new teachers are time consuming, however with experience these are often outlined very briefly, with medium-term plans being used much more, therefore a short-term plan should include:

- the class, year, title, timing and so on of the learning
- an enquiry question as the basis for the whole plan
- learning outcomes or objectives (knowledge, understanding, skills, attitudes and values)
- curriculum references (content and approaches)
- activities the children will take part in (including how they will be organised), including introductory and concluding activity
- lists and locations of resources to support teaching and learning
- differentiation notes – including support and extension for particular children.

All planning should be flexible, especially at the beginning of a series of lessons. However, all lessons may take a different direction from the teachers' plan. On School Placement, student teachers are unlikely to amend lessons significantly once teaching them, but established teachers do this frequently.

In planning lessons, teachers should consider very carefully what learning children will gain from the lesson; they should ask themselves these types of questions:

- What do I want children to get from this lesson?
- What will one child's experience of this lesson be (think of your most able, most quiet, most boisterous, etc.)?
- What will a child be doing 5, 10 and 15 minutes into this lesson – will they be engaged at all times?
- Will children have a role in what happens in the lesson?

Making extra time for geography

In many contexts, time for geography education is tight. Teachers who are passionate about instilling in children a love of geography can always find ways to enhance children's experiences. These would include:

- teaching geography within a topic or theme for a day or series of days, perhaps through an event being organized at the school – such events can include other members of the local community;
- introducing geographical elements into another topic, for example through a literacy project based on children's favourite stories, where there is scope for children to investigate real and imagined places;
- in assemblies or whole school events, choose geographical themes or places. For example, a celebration day could include games from around the world;
- displays of 'Places in the News', 'Our connections' or 'Green Schools Noticeboard' are all geographical and informative;

- for homework, encourage children to interact with people, places, events and issues at a local, national and international level: children are delighted to look out for news articles or watch the news as homework; and younger children can ask adults they know about an aspect of their lives (e.g. work, hobbies, childhood memories, etc.).

Geography is such an everyday subject that many aspects of children's loves are geographical. This book has aimed to provide quality learning activities for children in primary schools, from conceptualising the subject, to frameworks and ideas, through to planning for learning. Geography is a wonderful subject to help children make sense of the world, from their street and school to vast continents they may never visit. When geography is learned in engaging and challenging ways, it enhances many aspects of children's lives, and I hope this book has enabled readers to see these opportunities.

Reflection and action

- Imagine someone came into the room that had never heard of geography. What six key words would you use to tell them what geography is?
- Group the words from above and decide what are the most important 'big ideas' within your context for children. Use these as your own school's big ideas. Share them with the children – or better still do the activity with children first then teachers!
- Use CPD or personal time to consider the question: 'what type of teacher of geography would I like to be'?

Further resources

Geography Champions networking site is a collaborative learning community. It has over 2,000 members and is a place to share ideas, resources and news about primary geography and the primary curriculum. There are group pages run around the UK and Ireland: http://geographychampions.ning.com.

The Geographical Association is an independent charity with a core objective to further geographical knowledge and understanding through education. They promote and support geography teaching by producing resources for teachers, running CPD events and influencing policy makers: www.geography.org.uk.

Seomra Ranga is a website to share practical resources for the primary school classroom on the web: www.seomraranga.com.

Appendices

Appendix 1: Progression in learning through enquiry in primary geography

Class	Infants classes		1st/2nd		3rd/4th		5th/6th	
	Activity	Examples	Activity	Examples	Activity	Examples	Activity	Examples
Questioning	Ask questions about natural and human features in the immediate environment	Who lives in this place? What is this place like?	Ask questions about natural and human features in the immediate environment	What animals and plants live here? What has changed since I was last here?	Ask questions about natural and human features and processes in the environment and their interrelationships	What makes this place different from other places? How does the farmer use this land?	Ask questions about natural and human features and processes in the Environment and their interrelationships	How have humans changed this place and why? Why should a factory locate in this place?
Observing	Observe, compare and discuss natural and human features in the local environment	What happens when it rains?	Observe, compare and discuss natural and human features in the local environment	Colours and textures in the built environment; Different plants and animals in contrasting environments	Observe, discuss and describe natural and human features and processes in the environment and their interrelationships	Shapes and sizes of natural features; Colours and textures of buildings and streetscapes	Observe natural and human elements and processes in the environment and their interrelationships	Colours and textures of natural materials; Farm and settlement patterns in rural landscapes
Predicting	Guess and suggest what will happen next in a situation	Suggest whether a new bridge will be built in the locality	Suggest outcomes of an investigation, based on observations	Suggest when water in a river will be muddy	Offer suggestions (hypotheses) based on observations about the likely results of an investigation	Suggest why rivers may flood; Suggest why a new school may be needed	Offer suggestions (hypotheses) based on a number of observations; Make inferences based on suggestions and observations; Propose ideas or simple theories which may be tested by experimentation	Suggest why earthquakes occur; Suggest why locals may oppose a new motorway
Investigating and experimenting	Carry out simple investigations set by the teacher, make observations and collect data	Measure puddles after rainfall	Carry out simple investigations and collect information from a variety of sources	Direct observations in the environment; Classroom investigations; Books, ICT, other media	Carry out simple investigations and collect information from a variety of sources; Observations and experiments in the environment and classroom	Use improvised rain gauge; Use a trundle wheel; Use a compass	Carry out simple investigations and collect information from a variety of sources	Use an anemometer; Use the CSO website to collect population data; Use a compass
Estimating and measuring	Estimate and compare distances in an informal way	From home to school is longer than the journey from home to the park	Begin to use simple methods to estimate, measure and compare distances	Use non-standard units of length to measure distances; Use balance to compare weights	Use appropriate simple instruments and equipment to collect data; Use appropriate standard units of measurement	Rainfall in mm; Distances in metres and kms	Use appropriate simple instruments and techniques to collect data; Use appropriate standard units of measurement	Rainfall in mm; Distances in metres and kms; Wind speed using Beaufort scale
Analysing	Sort and group objects according to observable features	Rocks, pebbles, mud in soil sample	Sort and group people, features, events and natural phenomena; Begin to look for and recognise patterns and relationships in the environment; Draw conclusions from simple investigations	The people who work in shops, offices or factories; Living things on the seashore, on the farm or in the park; Connection between dark clouds and rainfall	Sort, group and/or classify data on people, features, events and natural phenomena using a range of appropriate criteria; Look for and recognise patterns and relationships in the environment; Interpret information and offer explanations; Draw conclusions from suitable aspects of the evidence collected	Types of plants in an environment; Types of shops or buildings in an urban area; Seasonal patterns in weather observations; Water and land masses on maps	Sort, group and/or classify data on people, events and natural phenomena; Using a range of appropriate criteria; Look for and recognise patterns and relationships in the environment; Interpret information and offer explanations; Draw conclusions from suitable aspects of the evidence collected	Group buildings according to use in an urban area; Group fields according to crops grown on a farm; Daily patterns in traffic flow on a road; Links between wind direction, temperature and rainfall
Recording and communicating	Describe and discuss his/her observations orally using an expanding vocabulary; Represent findings	Pictures; Weather charts; Using ICT	Describe and discuss observations orally using an expanding vocabulary; Represent findings	Friezes; Pictograms; ICT	Record and present findings and conclusions using a variety of methods	Spoken/oral form; Pictorial form; Photographic form; Diagrammatic form; Graphical forms; Using ICT	Record and present findings and conclusions using a variety of methods	Spoken/oral form; Pictorial form; Photographic/Diagrammatic form; Graphical form; Using ICT

Appendix 2: Progression in mapping through enquiry in primary geography

Class	Infants 4–6 years	1st/2nd 6–8 years	3rd/4th 8–10 years	5th/6th 10–12 years
Representations of places: globes, maps, pictures, etc. **Make/draw maps, pictures, etc.**	Refer to or use simple drawings of areas: • home and immediate surroundings • classroom, school and playground • other places and imagined places Make model buildings with bricks, Lego and other play materials	Record areas in the immediate environment and places in stories using simple picture maps, models and other methods: • *my room, my home, its surroundings* • *my way to school and shops* • *imagined areas in stories or from children themselves*	Make simple maps of home, classroom, school and immediate environment: • *symbols (e.g. for objects and walls, for land and water)* • *key, index and simple grid-style reference* Develop an understanding of and use some common map features and conventions	Construct some simple maps and models of natural and human features in the local environment: • *make sand models of local beach*

Class	Infants 4–6 years	1st/2nd 6–8 years	3rd/4th 8–10 years	5th/6th 10–12 years
Use maps, pictures, etc.	Become aware of globes as models of the Earth: use and play with standard globes, soft globes, toy globes, etc *Become aware of globes on television, etc.*	Explore the outlines and plans of small everyday items: • *small objects such as pencil case or box* • *model buildings from toy farm or train set* Develop some awareness of maps and if possible aerial photographs of limited areas in the locality Explore directions in the classroom using simple signpost maps Identify land and sea on maps and globes Use maps of Ireland and the globe to develop an awareness of other places	Develop some familiarity with, and engage in practical use of, maps and photographs of different scales and purposes: • *plans of a room or building, maps from models and toy houses, maps and aerial photographs of familiar areas, maps of locality, Ireland, EU and the world, maps from internet, etc.* Develop an understanding of and use some common map features and conventions: • *a sense of aerial perspective* • *symbols (e.g. for objects and walls, for land and water)* • *key, index and simple grid-style reference* • *align (or set) a map of a limited area* Identify major geographical features and find places on the globe	Develop familiarity with, and engage in practical use of, maps and photographs of a variety of scales and purposes: • *maps of locality, Ireland, Europe and the world* • *bus, train and other route maps, aerial photographs* • *maps on CD-ROMs and other electronic sources* Develop an understanding of and use common map features and conventions: • *symbols (e.g. contour shading for mountains and lowland)* • *key, index and simple grid-style references* • *align (or set) a map of locality or region scale* Compare maps, globes, aerial photographs, satellite photographs and other remotely sensed images. Recognise key lines of latitude and longitude on the globe: • *Equator, Tropics of Cancer and Capricorn, Arctic and Antarctic Circles, Greenwich Meridian, International Date Line latitude and longitude of Ireland* Develop some awareness of problems of map construction and the effect of various map projections on relative size of countries Importance of perspective and bias in map construction

(Adapted from DES/NCCA, 1999a)

Appendix 3: Auditing the locality for primary geography

What geography can be studied locally?

Obvious	Not so obvious	Unexpected/magical
What places are obvious for geography: rivers, beaches, shopping centres, woodlands, etc.	*What places are not so obvious for geography:* *streets of homes* *playgrounds* *children's places: youth centres, streets, etc.*	*What places could be used for some unexpected geography: streets for looking at patterns and processes, hidden places, etc.*

What other elements of children's learning can also be developed?

Developing understanding of geographical features and processes
Developing a sense of place
Developing geographical skills
Cross-curricular activity and content

What equipment/resources do we have/do we need for geographical fieldwork?

Have	Need immediately	Need to acquire
Schools generally have: *clipboards, pencils, etc.*	*For fieldwork you need to have:* *cameras, applications for computers/tablets*	*It is very useful to have:* *frames, etc. for focusing attention data logging equipment, such as weather equipment, dataloggers, etc.*

How could we use other adults in our community?
Do ensure all those helping on fieldwork or talking to the children are aware of how you are intending for them to learn! Also remember that those working with children will need clearance form school/state, e.g. police checks, garda clearance, etc.

Parents, carers and relatives	Retired people connected to the school	People who volunteer/work in other capacities
There are many people who can assist in fieldwork, especially parents of the children	*The older community of a locality is a valuable wealth of information for geography lessons*	*Parents and others who already work with children are fantastic to draw on for geography lessons*

What do we need to get to complete a fieldwork emergency kit?

Have	Need immediately	Need by start of next year

Medical equipment – ask a local pharmacy to supply/sponsor
Spare clothes – ask parents for contributions

When will we do a safety audit of the locality?

Appendix 4: Checklists for fieldwork in primary geography

Item	Check before trip	Check on day
List of children – names, carers'/parents' numbers, medical information		
List of all staff and helpers – names, next of kin numbers, medical information		
Parental consent forms for each pupil		
Mobile telephone, with numbers of school, principal, bus driver, local doctors, hospitals, police, rescue services. Keep these in two phones		
Camera/phone – camera pictures will be better quality		
First aid kit – see below		
Detailed programme/organisation of activities		
Equipment (e.g. trundle wheels, compasses, etc.)		
Spare pencils, sharpeners and erasers		
Sacks for recyclable and non-recyclable waste		

For longer trips in areas of water/hills/mountains you should also consider:

Throw bags – for water rescue		
Survival equipment – blanket, foil, etc.		

Children will always need:

Rucksack		
Clipboard with pencil		
Maps		
Activity sheets		
Warm waterproof clothing, including coat		
Strong footwear		
Lunch and drink		

Appendix 5: Conducting a safety audit for fieldwork in primary geography

Location: Drumcondra Road, area near shops
Time of day: 9am–11am
Number of staff/children: 3 (teacher, SNA, secretary)/30 (fourth class)

	1	2	3	4	5
How severe?	Very minor injury requiring no treatment	Minor injury requiring only first aid treatment	Minor injury but requiring hospital treatment	Injury requiring urgent hospital treatment	Very severe life-threatening event
How likely?	1	2	3	4	5
	Highly unlikely	Unlikely	Possible	Likely	Very likely

Hazard	Severity /10 (1 to 10)	Initial likelihood /10 (1 to 10)	Initial risk score/100 (Severity X Likelihood)	Management What will teachers and adults will do to reduce risk?	New likelihood (1 to 10)	Final risk score/100 (Severity X New likelihood)
Children getting wet	4	2	8	Bring a coat. Change day if very wet.	1	4
Children falling over on path	3	2	6	Teachers to walk route first. Teacher at front and one at back. Keeping each group together. Buddy system.	1	3
Children getting hit by a car	10	2	20	As above. Also use crossing. Teachers to stand in road until all have crossed.	0.1	1
Children getting seperated from the group	10	3	10	Keeping each group together. Adult with each group.	0.1	1
Children getting taken by a stranger	10	1	10	Keeping each group together. Adult with each group.	0.1	1
Children having a medical incident	5	2	10	Checking all children have medication. Adult with any child that has a medical issue.	1	5
Totals	The chance of these risks occurring approximately is 64/600		64/600	The chance of these risks occurring is approximately 15/600	–	15/600

Appendix 6: Medium term/2 week integrated plan: Loving our Landscape

Key questions

Devised by children, to include:

- What is Drumcondra like?
- How do people represent places in art, poetry and music?
- How can we represent Drumcondra?
- How is Drumcondra changing?
- Why do places change?
- How might Drumcondra be in the future?

Geography

Curriculum: Investigation/Enquiry, Sense of place, Sense of place, Using and making maps, Local natural and human environment, Environmental awareness and care

- Fieldwork in school grounds: Recording in words and pictures features of the locality (paired)
- Looking at plans of the school – present and future (groups)
- Drawing maps, with keys, of the school (paired)
- Taking part in fieldwork in the locality (paired) to investigate changes

English/Irish

Curriculum: Describing

- Enquiry: Talking about the school, devising enquiry questions about the school – past, present, future (small groups)
- Fieldwork in school grounds: Recording in words and pictures features of the locality (groups)
- Poetry: Looking at poems describing landscape e.g. Heaney – Digging
- Writing: Writing personal poems about the landscape of the school grounds (individual)

Mathematics

Curriculum: Spatial awareness

- Mapping: Making a scale map of the school buildings and grounds
- Competition: Map can be entered into the OSI Map my School Competition
- Scale: Using maps of the locality to recognise changes in the locality

What do I want children to get out of this?

- To appreciate further their local environment
- To learn about how places area described/drawn by others (poetry, art, etc.)
- To make representations of the locality: maps, images, collages, photographs, etc.
- To begin to appreciate the forces that change places

History

Curriculum: Local studies, primary sources, Life in 1900

- Past/sources: Investigating Drumcondra in the past: Looking at photographs and other sources of Drumcondra
- Fieldwork: Taking part in fieldwork to examing changes in the locality – using photographs, observation and completing writing/drawing frames

SPHE

Curriculum: Developing self-confidence, Relating to others, Developing citizenship, Living in the local community

- Interacting with others from the locality

Art

Curriculum:

- Drawing: Drawing maps, with keys, of the school (groups)
- Responding to art: Personal response ot art of landscapes (individual – class)
- Drawing and making: Drawing the landscape of the school for inclusion into a school collage

Title:

Our landscape

Key enquiry question:

What is Drumcondra like?

Classes: 1st – 3rd

Date: Spring

Integration by theme/skills

Resources

- Local aerial photographs and maps
- Drumcondra – streets, parks, new developments, etc.
- Frames/clipboards
- Poems
- Large paper
- Local people
- Range of paintings of landscapes (Irish and English)
- Poems about landscape (Heaney: Digging)

Appendix 7: Medium-term plan: What jobs do people do in our area? People and work

Pedagogies: Geography	Content: Geography – Strands and strand units
Main focus	**Main focus**
• Developing and answering enquiry questions.	• People living and working in the locality.
• Geographical investigation skills.	**Secondary focus**
• Using maps and photographs.	• People living and working in a contrasting locality.
• Fieldwork in the locality.	• Features of the locality.
• Use of ICTs: Microsoft Excel and Microsoft PowerPoint.	

Curriculum references = Other subjects (content and pedagogies)

SPHE Myself: Self-identity, Developing self-confidence; Myself and others: Relating to others, expressing and respecting opinions, local communities

English/Literacy Oral language development (discussion, sharing information, devising questions); Writing

Mathematics/Numeracy Data: Categorising information, Collecting data, Sorting data

Objectives/Outcomes In completing these activities the children will be able to:

Knowledge	Skills
• Define primary, secondary and tertiary jobs	• Devising questions for enquiry
• Define inputs, outputs and processes	• Working through enquiry
• Know some of the jobs carried out in the locality	• Interviewing adults and children
Understanding	• Taking part in a visit to company: Fieldwork
• Describe the process of making some products	• Using Presentation packages (PowerPoint)
• Describe the changing nature of work in the locality	• Using Spreadsheets (Excel)
Attitudes and values	• Presenting their work to others (children, parents)
• Appreciating the work others do	
• Realising the impact of their purchases	

Resources

From children: Favourite items, Newspapers with job adverts

From school: Marker pens, scrap paper, PCs, card for display, photographs, interviews, OSI maps, clipboards

Key question Key words Key concepts	Activities Teacher/children Including organisational strategies
A. What's our favourite objects? People, Processes, Resources	1. Children talk about their items. 2. Children draw or place their item in the centre of a piece of paper. They then brainstorm all the people, processes, resources that went into it. 3. Pairs or individual. Talking as much as possible! At this stage the teacher helps by prompting the children. Not using the terms. Ideas put down.

Generating ideas

B. What jobs do people we know do?	1.	Children talk about people they know and their work as well as jobs they would like to do when they get older.
	2.	Children write jobs onto sheets of paper. Children sort jobs into different categories.
	3.	Children are later encouraged to sort jobs into making/proving a service.
Primary, Secondary, Tertiary	4.	Teacher pulls out primary jobs (farming, forestry, etc.) and asks 'What is different about these?'. Children should note that these are about taking things from the earth.
Public, Private		Teacher tells children the terms primary, secondary, tertiary. Teacher asks 'What do you notice?'. Children should notice that PST is a 'chain' or 'string' of things that happen to an item – a 'process'.

Generating enquiry questions

C. What do we want to find out?	1.	Children look at photographs of different industries.
	2.	Teacher puts key words on the board – aided by the children.
	3.	Children write down questions they have about people, work and industries – local and non-local.
Enquiry	4.	Children sort the questions into categories. Children decide on main question in each category.

Finding out answers to enquiry questions

	1.	Children interview other children in school about jobs parents do.
	2.	Children collate figures into categories (5th/6th) or simply into PST (3rd–6th).
D. What jobs do people do in our area? (1)	3.	Children use Microsoft Excel or data handling package to make graphs.
	4.	Children select most appropriate graph for their data. Pie-chart or bar graph show data best – but allow children time to talk about why they think each is best.
		Extension: Children paste graphs into Microsoft Word and write a. What they found out b. Why they chose the graph they did. Other children will have done this verbally only.
	1.	Children devise interview questions to ask someone they know about their job.
E. What jobs do people do in our area? (2)	2.	Teacher or children devise an interview schedule as a writing frame – one A4 sheet. Children interview a person about their current or previous job, family or not – but local.
	3.	Children share what they have found out in class.
	4.	Children design poster using PowerPoint or Publisher on the job they have found out about.
		Extension: Children add words to their poster using the notes facility on PowerPoint.
	1.	Children watch videos of making products. Children list all that happens.
F. What happens in local factories?	2.	Children categories activity – they should figure out that there are 'inputs', 'processes' and 'outputs' (IPOs). Teacher encourages children to put their lists into these categories.
	3.	Children research company and prepare questions to ask at a local factory.
	4.	Fieldwork: Children visit local factory. Children complete IPO sheet for factory. Children write up what they have found out – poster, etc.

Appendix 8: Medium-term plan: Incredible India

Incredible India

Subject: Geography, with Global Citizenship and English

Timing: 5 hours

Class level / age: 1st and 2nd (6–8 year olds)

Key skills (content and skills)

A sense of place: Develop an awareness of people and places in other areas

A sense of space: Develop some awareness of spaces in distant places

Enquiry and Investigation – ALL ASPECTS

Maps, globes and graphical skills/

Picturing places: Identify land & sea on maps and globes, use maps and globes to develop an awareness of other places

Content (strands)

My family and community: Become aware of and learn to value the diversity of people who live in the local community and the contribution they make

Homes and Shelters: Recognise that people live in a variety of homes

People and places in other areas: Become familiar with some aspects of the lives of people and especially of children in other areas, appreciate ways in which people in different areas depend on one another and on people living in other parts of the world

Planet Earth in space: develop familiarity with the spherical nature of the Earth

Integration, through geography activity

- English: Developing imaginative talk/writing, oral development
- SPHE: Citizenship
- Global citizenship
- SESE: Enquiry skills

Extra activities, through other subjects

- Drama – life in India
- Art – designs and patterns
- Religion/global citizenship– Festivals: Diwali, etc.

Aims

Know: some physical features of India, Some features of life in India, Some aspects of Indian culture, Some changes in India

Understand: Some ways that India is different and similar to Ireland

Skills: Use maps of India (atlas, online and paper), describe places in India using images and video

Attitudes and Values: Develop an appreciation if the diversity of life in India

Progressional Sequence:

- Children complete a 'Starting out sheet' on India
- They talk about their connections with India (pair – whole class)
- Children look at photographs of India (free pairs)
- Children talk in pairs about the photographs (free pairs)
- Children devise questions they would like to know about India (group)
- Teacher writes these down on a flipchart (whole class)
- Finding India on maps and globes (pairs)
- Describing where India is, talking about how large India is (pairs)
- Children match captions to photographs (pairs)
- Children discuss what surprised them (paired talk -> class discussion)
- Children watch sections of the Chembakolli to Bangalore DVD and discuss who produced the resource
- Children discuss similarities and differences – to do with each other – then about life in India and life in Ireland (pairs)
- Children plan a trip to India: list where they would go, what they would bring, etc

Assessment strategies:

Children's pictures and writing will be used to assess their understanding of life in India

Children will be recorded talking about India

Resources:

Photo pack on India/DVD on India

Atlas/globe

Map of India

Indian articles: food, clothes – these will include traditional and modern items

Differentiation:

Children will complete work to their own level

Some children will develop a deeper understanding of life in India than others

Appendix 9: Medium-term plan: What is my locality like?

What do I want children to get out of this?

To know features in their locality, to describe places in their locality, to make and use maps of their locality

To know why key features of the locality are located as they are

Extension (1st and 2nd – after JI/SI go home): To explore ideas about the locality in the future

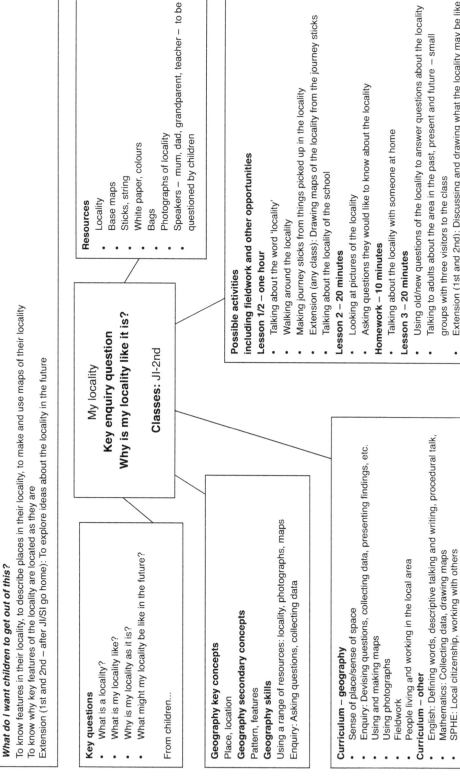

My locality

Key enquiry question

Why is my locality like it is?

Classes: JI–2nd

Resources

- Locality
- Base maps
- Sticks, string
- White paper, colours
- Bags
- Photographs of locality
- Speakers – mum, dad, grandparent, teacher – to be questioned by children

---

Key questions

- What is a locality?
- What is my locality like?
- Why is my locality as it is?
- What might my locality be like in the future?

From children...

Geography key concepts

Place, location

Geography secondary concepts

Pattern, features

Geography skills

Using a range of resources: locality, photographs, maps

Enquiry: Asking questions, collecting data

Curriculum – geography

- Sense of place/sense of space
- Enquiry: Devising questions, collecting data, presenting findings, etc.
- Using and making maps
- Using photographs
- Fieldwork
- People living and working in the local area

Curriculum – other

- English: Defining words, descriptive talking and writing, procedural talk,
- Mathematics: Collecting data, drawing maps
- SPHE: Local citizenship, working with others

Possible activities

including fieldwork and other opportunities

Lesson 1/2 – one hour

- Talking about the word 'locality'
- Walking around the locality
- Making journey sticks from things picked up in the locality
- Extension (any class): Drawing maps of the locality from the journey sticks
- Talking about the locality of the school

Lesson 2 – 20 minutes

- Looking at pictures of the locality
- Asking questions they would like to know about the locality

Homework – 10 minutes

- Talking about the locality with someone at home

Lesson 3 – 20 minutes

- Using old/new questions of the locality to answer questions about the locality
- Talking to adults about the area in the past, present and future – small groups with three visitors to the class
- Extension (1st and 2nd): Discussing and drawing what the locality may be like in the future

Appendix 10: Short-term plan/lesson plan: What features are in our locality?

Key enquiry question: What features are in our local area? **Overall aim:** To observe features in the local area – school and immediate area	

Curriculum references = Pedagogies: Geography – skills and concepts development

- **A sense of place** become aware of, explore and discuss some of the distinctive human and natural features of the locality
- **A sense of space** use locational terms, discuss and record in journeys to and from places in the immediate environment
- **Maps, globes and graphical skills/Picturing places** refer to or use simple drawings of areas
- **Geographical investigation skills** Questioning, observing, investigating and experimenting, analysing, recording and communicating

Curriculum references = Content: Geography

Human environments: School describe areas within the school, make simple drawings of school, immediate surroundings and journeys to and from school

Human environments: The local natural environment become aware of, explore and discuss some aspects of natural environments in the immediate locality of the school, observe, collect and investigate a variety of natural materials in the local environment, record and communicate experiences and observations using oral language and pictures

Environmental awareness and care: Caring for my locality observe, discuss and appreciate the attributes of the local environment, appreciate that people share the environment with plant and animal life

Curriculum references = Other subjects (content and pedagogies)

- **English:** Asking enquiry questions, describing places – verbally and in pictures/models/journey sticks
- **Gaelige:** Children are told and use some words in Gaelige – incidentally through out the lesson
- **SPHE:** Living in the local community: recognise and appreciate people or groups who serve the local community and how their contribution enhances the quality of life of others

Resources Frames (optional), clipboards (optional), cameras (optional), string, sticks, crayons, paper, etc.

Previous learning

- Enquiry: Children have asked questions in geography before – relating to games we play
- Knowledge: Children know what 'similar' and 'different' mean – through work on families in history/literacy
- Fieldwork: Children have carried out a walk in the school before – signs of autumn – in science/geography/literacy

Objectives/outcomes In completing these activities children will be able to:

Knowledge	Skills
- Features of the natural environment - Features of the human environment - (Interactions between people and their environments)	- Observing the locality - Talking as a geographer about place - Drawing/making the locality
Understanding - People make features in the school and locality - Most features are made or changed by people – even natural ones	**Attitudes and values** - Valuing the locality/school - Attachment to places - Working together/enjoying and being a geographers!

Timing	Teacher activity	Children's activity
Introduction **20 minutes**	Teacher puts photograph of natural and human feature on board – tree from school grounds and school building Teacher explains the work 'feature'	**What is the difference between these two items?** Children, in pairs, sort photographs into human and natural Children pushed to explain WHY they put pictures where they did – metacognition
Development **one hour**	Teacher, SNA and others take children on walk – all know focus of lesson: human, natural, both features	**What features are in our area?** Children take a walk in the school grounds. They talk about natural and human features. They take photographs of different features.
	Teacher helps children with tasks! *NB There will be constant talk about what the children are and what type of feature they were!*	**Three options** (children or teacher choice!) Make journey sticks/Make maps – could all pick a feature and then make a 'class map'/Make models – could all pick a feature and then make a 'class model'
Closure **five minutes**	Teacher asks children what features they saw today.	Talk in pairs, then class **What features did we see? Were they human or natural?**

Appendix 11: Resourcing for primary geography: costings

Option A

Item	Infants	1st and 2nd Class	3rd and 4th Class	5th and 6th Class
Workbooks (60X€10)	€600.00	€600.00	€600.00	€600.00
Photocopying	€50.00	€50.00	€50.00	€50.00
Bus hire	€100.00	€100.00	€100.00	€100.00
	€750.00	**€750.00**	**€750.00**	**€750.00**

Option B

Infants

Photocopying/paper	€50.00
Bus hire	€150.00
Plans of school	€20.00
Local aerial image	€20.00
Digital camera (1)	€40.00
Weather equipment	€10.00
Laminating	€20.00
Clipboards (5)	€8.50
Bench	€100.00
Lego	€20.00
Mascot bear	€15.00
Big books (2)	€35.00
Early years' globe	€30.00
Space resources	€20.00
Water resource pack	€20.00
Miscellaneous	€20.00
	€578.50

1st and 2nd Class

Photocopying/paper	€50.00
Bus hire	€150.00
Maps of locality	€20.00
Local aerial image	€20.00
Digital camera (1)	€40.00
Weather equipment	€10.00
Laminating	€20.00
Clipboards (5)	€8.50
Bare root trees	€100.00
Lego	€20.00
Mascot bear	€15.00
Big books (2)	€35.00
Tourism resources	€30.00
Globe	€20.00
Coasts resource pack	€20.00
Miscellaneous	€20.00
	€488.50

3rd and 4th Class

Photocopying/paper	€50.00
Bus hire	€150.00
Maps of locality	€20.00
Local aerial image	€20.00
Digital camera (1)	€40.00
Weather equipment	€10.00
Laminating	€20.00
Transport photographs	€8.50
Bangalore resource	€20.00
Resources on England	€20.00
Rivers resources	€15.00
Food resources	€35.00
Farm resources	€10.00
Miscellaneous	€20.00
	€428.50

5th and 6th Class

Photocopying/paper	€50.00
Bus hire	€150.00
Maps of locality	€20.00
Local aerial image	€20.00
Digital camera (1)	€40.00
Weather equipment	€10.00
Laminating	€20.00
Volcanoes resources	€8.50
Rainforest resources	€30.00
Resources from council	€20.00
Resources on Italy	€20.00
Fair trade products	€10.00
Brazil resources	€10.00
Miscellaneous	€60.00
	€410.00

Geography Statement

Geography is part of the cluster of SESE subjects as set out in the Revised Curriculum. It is acknowledged in this school that Geography will be taught in two conceptual ways:

(a) SESE Thematic approach where themes will be explored in the context of History, Geography and Science, and to a lesser extent Learn Together and SPHE. Guidelines for the development and pedagogy of this themed approach are covered in document SESE Overview in this school plan.

(b) As Geography, a discrete subject where specifically Geographical themes will be studied according to the rigours and best practice of Geography education.

The remainder of this document deals with guidelines for the teaching of Geography in this manner. Guidelines for the teaching of Geography:

- When planning and teaching Geography must ensure to plan according to both the "Skills and Concepts Development" and the "Strands and sub-strands" as set out on pages 16/17 (Infants), 28/29 (1st/2nd), 44/45 (3rd/4th) and 62/63 (5 th /6th) of the Geography Curriculum book.
- Teaching pedagogy and teaching themes should be according to that set out in the text 'Primary Geography Handbook' by Stephen Scoffham, multiple texts of which are available in the staff workshop.
- Textbooks for the teaching of Geography should be used minimally, and when/if used should only form a fraction of the resources used for the teaching of the subject. The teacher may select any text from the bank of Geography texts that have been built up over the years. Sometimes exercises in the texts may make for good teacher-based assessment of children's geographical knowledge.
- Fieldwork is seen as an imperative pedagogy for the teaching of geography of all classes. Over the duration of their geographical education in their 8 years in this school, the children should have been taken on study trips to the following local areas of geographical significance:

  1 The newly planned and built housing estates of the immediate geographical locality of the school.
  2 The rocky seashore of Blackrock, at the end of Bath Road
  3 The fishing harbour
  4 The Railway Station
  5 The Viaduct
  6 The beach shore (town-beach)

7   St George's Square
8   Placenames of Balbriggan
9   The Stephenstown Industrial estate
10   The retail square (Dunne's Stores) next to the school.

Geography Statement 2

All ICT available to the teachers (Desktop computer suite in the classroom, mobile trolley of laptops and Interactive Whiteboard) should be used in the teaching of geography. Particular use should be made of the class's own digital camera in their local studies and for the examination and display of geographical work.

The notion of 'Active Citizenship' as promoted in the Caring for the Environment strand of the Geography Curriculum is prioritized in this school as it is in keeping with our mission statement, Educate Together ethos, understanding of multiculturalism and association with Children's Rights. It is encouraged especially in our commitment to Green Schools campaign and projects (see 3.056 Green Schools in this school plan)

References

Adams, E. and Ingham, S. (1998) *Changing Places: Children's Participation in Environmental Planning*. London: The Children's Society

Advisory Group On Citizenship (1998) *Advisory Group on the Teaching of Citizenship and Democracy in Schools*. London: QCA. Accessed from: www.teachingcitizenship.org.uk/resource/advisory-group-citizenship-report-crick-report, 17 March 2015.

Aitken, S.C. (2001) *Geographies of Young People: The Morally Contested Spaces of Identity*. London and New York: Routledge.

Alexander, R. (2000) *Culture & Pedagogy: International Comparisons in Primary Education*. Oxford: Blackwell.

Alexander, R., Armstrong, M., Flutter, J., Hargreaves, L., Harrison, D., Harlen, W., Hartley-Brewer, E., Kershner, R., MacBeath, J., Mayall, B., Northen, S., Pugh, G., Richards, C. and Utting, D. (2010) *Children, Their World, Their Education: Final Report and Recommendations of the Cambridge Primary Review*. London: Routledge.

Apple, M. (2005. Doing Things the 'Right' Way: Legitimating Educational Inequalities in Conservative Times. *Educational Review*, 57(3): 271–93.

Arnstein, S.R. (1969) A Ladder of Citizen Participation. *Journal of the American Planning Association*, 35(4): 216–24.

Australian Curriculum, Assessment and Reporting Authority (ACARA) (2011) *Australian Curriculum*. Accessed from www.australiancurriculum.edu.au 17 March 2015.

Bacon, K. and Matthews, P. (2014) Inquiry-Based Learning With Young Learners: A Peirce-Based Model Employed to Critique a Unit of Inquiry on Maps and Mapping. *Irish Educational Studies*, 33(3): 351–65.

Balbriggan Educate Together National School (BETNS) (2012) *Balbriggan Educate Together National School Website*. Accessed from: http://balbrigganetns.scoilnet.ie/blog, 17 March 2015.

Ball, D., Gill, T. and Spiegal, B. (2013) *Managing Risk in Play Provision: Implementation Guide*. London: Play England.

Ballantyne, R. and Packer, J. (2002) Nature-Based Excursions: School Students' Perceptions of Learning in Natural Environments. *International Research in Geographical and Environmental Education*, 11(3): 218–36.

Banks, J.A. (ed.) (2004) *Diversity and Citizenship Education: Global Perspectives*. San Francisco: Jossey-Bass.

Banks, J.A. (2010) Human Rights, Diversity and Citizenship Education, in F. Waldron and B. Ruane (eds), *Human Rights Education: Reflections on Theory and Practice*. Dublin: Liffey Press, pp. 15–42.

Barnes, D. and Todd, F. (1995) *Communication and Learning Revisited*. Portsmouth, NH: Heinemann.

Beck, I.L., McKeown, M.G., and Kucan, L. (2002) *Bringing Words to Life*. New York: Guilford Press.

Bednarz, S.W., Heffron, S. and Huynh, N.T. (eds) (2013) *A Road Map for 21st Century Geography Education: Geography Education Research*. (A Report from the Geography Education Research Committee of the Road Map for 21st Century Geography Education Project.) Washington, DC: Association of American Geographers.

Biddulph, M.A. and Adey, K. (2004) Pupil Perceptions of Effective Teaching and Subject Relevance in History and Geography Key Stage 3. *Research in Education*, 71(1): 1–8.

Blades, M. and Spencer, C. (eds) (2006) *Children and Their Environments: Learning, Using and Designing Spaces*. Cambridge: Cambridge University Press.

Blades, M., Blaut, J.M., Darvizeh, Z., Elguea, S., Sowden, S., Soni, D., Spencer, S., Stea, D., Surajpaul, R. and Uttal, D. (1998) A Cross-Cultural Study of Young Children's Mapping Abilities. *Transactions of the Institute of British Geographers*, 23(2): 269–77.

Blaut, J.M. (1991) Natural Mapping. *Transactions, Institute of British Geographers*, 16(1): 55–74.

Blaut J.M. and Stea, D. (1971) Studies of Geographic Learning. *Annals of the Association of American Geographers*, 61(2): 387–93.

Blaut, J.M., Stea, D., Spencer, C. and Blades, M. (2003) Mapping as a Cultural and Cognitive Universal. *Annals of the Association of American Geographers*, 93(1): 165–8.

Bloom, B.S., Engelhart, M.D., Furst, E.J., Hill, W.H. and Krathwohl, D.R. (1956) *Taxonomy of Educational Objectives: The Classification of Educational Goals. Handbook I: Cognitive Domain*. New York: David McKay.

Botelho, M.J. and Rudman, M.K. (2009) *Critical Multicultural Analysis of Children's Literature: Mirrors, Windows, and Doors*. London: Routledge.

Boulding, E. (1979) *Children's Rights and the Wheel of Life*. Edison, NJ: Transaction Publishers.

Bruner, J.S. (1957) *Going Beyond the Information Given*. New York: Norton.

Bruner, J.S. (1966) *Toward a Theory of Instruction*. Cambridge, MA: Belkapp Press.

Bruner, J.S. (1977) *The Process of Education*. Cambridge, MA: Harvard University Press.

Butt, G. (2002) *Reflective Teaching of Geography 11–18*. London: Continuum.

Casey, T. (2003) School Grounds Literature Review: Phase One of the Scottish School Grounds Research Project 2002/3. Stirling: Grounds for Learning, Sports Scotland and Play Scotland.

Catling, S. (1998) Values in English Primary Geography Series, in M. Naish (ed.), *Values in Geography Education*. London: University of London.

Catling, S. (2003) Curriculum Contested: Primary Geography and Social Justice. *Geography*, 88(3): 164–210.

Catling, S. (2005) Children's Personal Geographies and the English Primary School Geography Curriculum. *Children's Geographies*, 3(3): 325–44.

Catling, S. and Willy, T. (2011) *Achieving QTS Teaching Primary Geography*. Exeter: Learning Matters.

Catling, S., Greenwood, R., Martin, F. and Owens, P. (2010) Formative Experiences of Primary Geography Educators. *International Research in Geographical and Environmental Education*, 19(4): 341–50.

Central Advisory Council for Education (1967) *Children and their Primary Schools (The Plowden Report)*. London: HMSO.

Centre for Excellence in Enquiry-Based Learning (CEEBL) (2015) *What Is Enquiry Based Learning?* Accessed from www.ceebl.manchester.ac.uk/ebl, 17 March 2015.

Chawla, L. (ed.) (2002) *Growing Up in an Urbanising World*. London: UNESCO/Earthscan.

Christensen, P. and O'Brien, M. (eds) (2003) *Children in the City*. London: RoutledgeFalmer.

Citizenship Foundation (2014) *What Is Citizenship Education?* Accessed from www.citizenship foundation.org.uk/main/page, 17 March 2015.

Clark C. and Uzzell D. (2006) The Socio-Environmental Affordances of Adolescents' Environments, in C. Spencer and M. Blades (eds), *Children and their Environments: Learning, Using, and Designing Spaces*. Cambridge: Cambridge University Press.

Cochran-Smith, M. (2003) The Unforgiving Complexity of Teaching: Avoiding Simplicity in the Age of Accountability. *Journal of Teacher Education*, 54(1): 3–5.

Comishan, K., Dyment, J.E., Potter, T. and Russell, C.L. (2004) The Development and Implementation of Outdoor-Based Secondary School integrated Programs. *Applied Environmental Education and Communication*, 3(1): 47–54.

Cotton, D. (2006) Teaching Controversial Environmental Issues: Neutrality and Balance in the Reality of the Classroom. *Educational Research*, 48(2): 223–41.

Cummins, M. (2010) Eleven Years On: A Case Study of Geography Practices and Perspectives Within an Irish Primary School. Unpublished M.Ed thesis, St Patrick's College.

D'Arcy, P. (1989) *Making Sense, Shaping Meaning*. London: Heinemann.

Darling-Hammond, L. (2006) Constructing 21st-Century Teacher Education. *Journal of Teacher Education*, 57(3): 300–14.

Darling-Hammond, L. (2010) Teacher Education and the American Future. *Journal of Teacher Education*, 61(1–2): 35–47.

De Róiste, A., and Dinneen, J. (2005) *Young People's Views about Opportunities, Barriers and Supports to Recreation and Leisure*. Dublin: The National Children's Office. Accessed from www.dcya.gov.ie/documents/policy/young_peoples_views_about_opportunities.pdf, 17 March 2015.

Department for Education (2014) *National Curriculum in England: Geography Programmes of Study*. Accessed from www.gov.uk/government/publications/national-curriculum-in-england-geography-programmes-of-study, 17 March 2015.

Department of Education (Ireland) (1971) *Primary School Curriculum: Teachers' Handbook (Part 1)*. Dublin: Department of Education.

Department of Education and Science/National Council for Curriculum and Assessment (DES/NCCA) (1999a) *Primary School Curriculum: Introduction*. Dublin: Stationery Office.

Department of Education and Science/National Council for Curriculum and Assessment (DES/NCCA) (Ireland) (1999b) *Primary School Curriculum: Geography*. Dublin: Government Publications Office.

Department of Education and Science/National Council for Curriculum and Assessment (DES/NCCA) (Ireland) (1999c) *Primary School Curriculum: Geography – Teachers Guidelines*. Dublin: Government Publications Office.

Department of Education and Skills (2014) *Education for Sustainability: The National Strategy on Education for Sustainable Development in Ireland, 2014–20*. Accessed from www.education.ie/en/publications/education-reports/national-strategy-on-education-for-sustainable-development-in-ireland-2014–0.pdf, 17 March 2015.

Department of Education and Skills (2015) *DEIS: Delivering Equality of Opportunity in Schools*. Accessed from www.education.ie/en/schools-colleges/services/deis-delivering-equality-of-opportunity-in-schools-/, 17 March 2015.

Devine, D. (2003) *Children, Power and Schooling*. Stoke-on-Trent: Trentham Books.

Dewey, J. (1897/1998). My pedagogic creed. In L.A. Hickman and T.M. Alexander (eds), *The Essential Dewey: Pragmatism, Education, Democracy*. Bloomington, IN: Indiana University Press. pp. 229–35.

Dewey, J. (1900/1902/1990) The *School and Society/The Child and the Curriculum*. Chicago, IL: University of Chicago Press.

Dewey, J. (1900/1976). The School and Society. In J.A. Boydston (ed.), *John Dewey: The Middle Works, 1899–1924* (Vol. 1, pp. 1–112). Carbondale, IL: Southern Illinois University Press.

Dewey, J. (1938/2007) *Experience and Education*. New York: Collier Books.

Dolan, A.M., Waldron, F., Pike, S. and Greenwood, R. (2014) Student Teachers' Reflections on Prior Experiences of Learning Geography. *International Research in Geographical and Environmental Education*, 23(4): 314–30.

Dooley, T., Dunphy, T. and Shiel, G. (2014) *Mathematics in Early Childhood and Primary Education (3–8 Years): Teaching and Learning*. NCCA Research Report No. 18. Dublin: NCCA. Accessed from www.ncca.ie/en/Publications/Reports/NCCA_Research_Report_18.pdf, 17 March 2015.

Downs, R.M. and Stea, D. (1977) *Maps in Minds. Reflections on Cognitive Mapping*. New York: Harper and Row.

Downs, R.M., Liben, L. and Daggs, D. (1988) On Education and Geographers: The Role of Cognitive Developmental Theory in Geographic Education. *Annals of the Association of American Geographers* 78(4): 680–700.

Firth, R. (2007) *Geography Teachers, Teaching and the Issue of Knowledge*. Nottingham: Centre for Applied Research in Teacher Education, Curriculum and Pedagogy.

Firth, R. (2011) What Constitutes Knowledge in Geography? In D. Lambert and M. Jones (eds), *Debates in Geography Education*. Abingdon: Routledge.

Fjørtoft, I. and Sageie, J. (2000) The Natural Environment as a Playground for Children. Landscape Description and Analyses of a Natural Playscape. *Landscape and Urban Planning*, 48(1): 83–97.

Flynn, M. (1998) A Study of Gender Differentiation in Primary School Playgrounds. *Irish Educational Studies*, 17(1): 148–60.

Flynn, M. and Lodge, A. (2001) Gender Identity in the Primary School Playground. In A. Cleary, M. Nic Ghiolla Phadraigh and S. Quin (eds), *Understanding Children, State, Education and Economy*. Cork: Oak Tree Press.

Freire, P. (1970) *Pedagogy of the Oppressed*. New York: Continuum.

Freire P (1994) *Pedagogy of Hope: Reliving Pedagogy of the Oppressed*. New York: Continuum.

Freire, P. (2004) *Pedagogy of Indignation*. Boulder, CO: Paradigm.

Gash, H. (1985) Irish Educational Studies. *Foundations and Practice of the New Curriculum*, 5(1): 86–101.

Geographical Association (2015) *The GA's Primary Position Statement*. Accessed from www.geography. org.uk/cpdevents/curriculum/positionstatement 17 March 2015.

Geographical Association (GA) (2009) *Geographical Association – Manifesto for Geography*. Sheffield: Geographical Association. Accessed from www.geography.org.uk/resources/adifferentview, 17 March 2015.

Geographical Association (GA) (2011) *The Action Plan for Geography 2006–11: The Final Report and Evaluation*. Sheffield: Geographical Association. Accessed from www.geography.org.uk/download/ ga_apgfinalreport.pdf, 17 March 2015.

Geography Advisors and Inspectors Network (2002) *Thinking About the Future*. Unpublished Handout.

Gerber, R.V. (2001) Attitudes to Geography in Australia. *Australian Geographer*, 32(2): 221–39.

Gibson, J.J. (1979) *The Ecological Approach to Visual Perception*. Hillsdale, NJ: Lawrence Erlbaum.

Green, J., Shaw-Hamilton, A., Walsh, M., Pike, S. and O'Mahony, O. (2013) On Our Own, With A Bit of Help: Geographical Enquiry in Our School, *Primary Geography*, 80(1): 28–29.

Greene, S.M., and Hogan, D.M. (eds) (2005) *Researching Children's Experiences*. London: Sage.

Greenwood, R (2007) Geography Teaching in Northern Ireland Primary Schools – A Survey of Content and Cross-Curricularity. *International Research in Geographical and Environmental Education*, 16(4): 380–98.

Guthrie, J.T. (2001, March). Contexts for engagement and motivation in reading. *Reading Online*, 4(8). Accessed from: www.readingonline.org/articles/art_index.asp?HREF=/articles/handbook/guthrie/ index.html, 17 March 2015.

Halocha, J. (1998) *Coordinating Geography Across the Primary School*. London: Routledge.

Ham, S. and Sewing, D. (1988) Barriers to Environmental Education. *The Journal of Environmental Education*, 19(2): 17–24.

Hanson, S. (2004) Who Are 'We'? An Important Question for Geography's Future. *Annals of the Association of American Geographers*, 94(4): 715–22.

Hart, P. and Nolan, K. (1999) A Critical Analysis of Research in Environmental Education. *Studies in Science Education*, 34(1): 1–69.

Hart, R. (1979) *Children's Experience of Place: A Development Study*. New York: Irvington Press.

Hart, R. (1992) *Children's Participation: From Tokenism to Citizenship*. Florence: UNICEF International Child Development Centre. Accessed from www.unicef-irc.org/publications/pdf/childrens_ participation.pdf, 17 March 2015.

Hart, R. (1997) *Children's Participation: The Theory and Practice of involving Young Citizens in Community Development and Environmental Care*. London: Earthscan.

Harwood, D. and Rawlings, K. (2001) Assessing Young Children's Freehand Sketch Maps of the World. *International Research in Geographical and Environmental Education*, 10(1): 20–4.

Harwood, D. and McShane, J. (1996) Young Children's Understanding of Nested Hierarchies of Place Relationships. *International Research in Geographical and Environmental Education*, 5(1): 3–29.

Haycock, K., and Crawford, C. (2008) Closing the Teacher Quality Gap. *Educational Leadership*, 65(7): 14–19.

Heffron, S.G. and Downs, R.M. (eds) (2012) *Geography for Life: National Geography Standards* (2nd edn) Washington, DC: National Council for Geographic Education.

Heft, H. (1979) The Role of Environmental Features in Route Learning: Two Exploratory Studies of Wayfinding. *Environmental Psychology and Non-Verbal Behavior*, 3(3): 172–85.

Heft, H. and Wohlwill, J.F. (1987) Environmental Cognition in Children. In D. Stokols and I. Altman (eds), *Handbook of Environmental Psychology*. New York: John Wiley.

Helburn, N. (1998) The High School Geography Project: A Retrospective View, *Social Studies*, 89(5): 212–18.

Hicks, D. (2006) *Lessons for the Future: The Missing Dimension in Education*. Victoria BC: Trafford Publishing.

Hinde, E., Osborn Popp, S.E., Dorn, R.I., Ekiss, G.O., Mater, M., Smith, C.B. and Libbee, M. (2007) The Integration of Literacy and Geography: The Arizona Geoliteracy Program's Effect on Reading Comprehension. *Theory and Research in Social Education*, 35(3), 343–65.

Holloway, S., Rice, S. and Valentine, G. (eds) (2003) *Key Concepts in Geography*, London: Sage.

Hopwood, N. (2011) Young People's Conceptions of Geography and Education. In G. Butt (ed.), *Geography, Education and the Future*. London: Continuum, pp. 30–43.

Irish National Teachers Organisation (INTO) (1995) *The Primary School Curriculum: An Evolutionary Process*. Dublin: INTO.

Jackson, P. (2006) Thinking geographically. *Geography*, 91(3): 199–204.

Karkdijk, K.J., Van Der Schee, J. and Admiraal, W. (2013) Effects of Teaching with Mysteries on Students' Geographical Thinking Skills, *International Research in Geographical and Environmental Education*, 22(3): 183–90

Kidd, D. (2014) *#Nurture 2014/15 with a Little #Teacher5aday*. Accessed from https://debrakidd.wordpress.com/2014/12, 17 March 2015.

Kilkelly, U. (2007) *Barriers to the Realisation of Children's Rights in Ireland*. Dublin: Ombudsman for Children.

Kirchberg, G. (2000) Changes in Youth: No Changes in Teaching Geography? Aspects of a Neglected Problem in the Didactics of Geography. *International Research in Geographical and Environmental Education*, 9(1): 5–18.

Kitchen, R. (2013) Student Perceptions of Geographical Knowledge and the Role of the Teacher. *Geography*, 98(3): 112–21.

Krause, J. and Millward, J. (2010) The Subject Leader, in S. Scoffham (2010) *The Handbook of Primary Geography*. Sheffield: The Geographical Association.

Kuhlthau, C.C., Maniotes, L.K., and Caspari, A.K. (2012) *Guided Inquiry Design: A Framework for Inquiry in Your School*. Santa Barbara, CA: Libraries Unlimited.

Kyttä, M. (2006) Environmental Child-Friendliness in the Light of the Bullerby Model. In C. Spencer and M. Blades (eds), *Children and their Environments: Learning, Using and Designing Spaces*. Cambridge: Cambridge University Press.

Lambert, D. (2004) *The Power of Geography*. Sheffield: The Geographical Association. Accessed from www.geography.org.uk/download/npogpower, 17 March 2015.

Lambert, D. and Balderstone, D. (2009) *Learning to Teach Geography in the Secondary School: A Companion to School Experience* (2nd edn), London: Routledge.

Leat, D. (1998) *Thinking through geography*. Cambridge, Chris Kington Publishing.

Liben, L. and Downs, R. (1977) On Education and Geographers: The Role of Cognitive Developmental theory in Geographic Education. *Annals of the Association of American Geographers*, 87(1): 159–67

Lidstone, J. and Gerber, R. (1998) Theoretical Underpinnings of Geographical and Environmental Education Research: Hiding Our Light Under Various Bushels. *International Research in Geographical and Environmental Education*, 7(2), 87–9.

Louv, R. (2005) *Last Child in the Woods: Saving Our Children from Nature Deficit Disorder*. London: Atlantic Books.

Malone, K. and Tranter, P.J. (2003) *Children's Environments: A Study of Children's Environmental Learning in Relation to their Schoolground Experiences*. Melbourne, Victoria: RMIT University.

Mannion, G., Mattu, L. and Wilson, M. (2015) Teaching, Learning, and Play in the Outdoors: A Survey of School and Pre-school Provision in Scotland. Scottish Natural Heritage Commissioned Report No. 779. Accessed from www.snh.gov.uk/publications-data-and-research/publications/search-the-catalogue/publication-detail/?id=2225, 17 March 2015.

Martin, F. (2005) Ethnogeography: A Future for Primary Geography and Primary Geography Research? *International Research in Geographical and Environmental Education*, 14(4): 364–71.

Martin, F. (2006) *Teaching Geography in Primary Schools: Learning to Live in the World*. Cambridge: Chris Kington Publishing.

Martin, F. (2008) Ethnogeography: towards liberatory geography education. *Children's Geographies*, 6(4): 437–50.

Martin, F. (2012a) The Geographies of Difference. *Geography*, 97(3).

Martin, F. (2012b) Thinking Differently about Difference. The Development Education Association. Accessed from http://clients.squareeye.net/uploads/dea/documents/thinkpiece_FranMartin.pdf, 17 March 2015.

Martin, F. (2013) Same Old Story: The Problem of Object-based Thinking as a Basis for Teaching Distant Places. *Education 3–13*, 41(4): 410–24.

Martin, F. and Owens, P. (2008) *Caring for Our World: A Practical Guide to ESD for Ages 4–8*. Sheffield: Geographical Association.

Matthews, H. (1987) Gender, Home Range and Environmental Cognition, *Transactions of the Institute of British Geographers, New Series*, 12(43): 46–56.

Matthews, H. (1992) *Making Sense of Place: Children's Understanding of Large-Scale Environments*. Hemel Hempstead: Harvester Wheatsheaf.

Matthews, H. and Limb, M. (1999) Defining An Agenda for the Geography of Children. *Progress in Human Geography*, 23(1): 59–88.

Matthews, H., Limb, M. and Taylor, M. (2000) The Street as Thirdspace: Class, Gender and Public Space. In S. Holloway and G. Valentine (eds), *Children's Geographies: Living, Playing, Learning*. London: Routledge.

McCutcheon, F. (2010). In F. Waldron and B. Ruane (eds), *Human Rights Education: Reflections on Theory and Practice* Dublin: Liffey Press, pp. 15–42.

McNally, J. (2012) Going Places: The Successful Implementation of the Primary School Curriculum – Geography. Unpublished M.Ed thesis, St Patrick's College, Dublin.

Moore, R. (1986) *Childhood's Domain*. London: Croom Helm.

Moore, R. and Wong, H. (1997) *Natural Learning: The Life History of an Environmental Schoolyard*. Berkeley, CA: MIG Communications.

Moore, R.C., Goltsman, S.M. and Iacofano, D.S. (eds) (1992) *Play for All Guidelines: Planning, Design and Management of Outdoor Play Settings for All Children* (2nd edn). Berkeley, CA: MIG Communications.

Murray, D. and Millar, N. (2005) *Our Children. . . . Their Future. . . . Why Weight? Part 3: Physical Activity in Primary Schools – Facilities and Practices*, Dublin: Health Service Executive, pp. 27–36.

Naish, M., Rawling, E. and Hart, C. (1987) *Geography 16–19: The Contribution of a Curriculum Development Project to 16–19 Education*. London: Longman for School Curriculum Development Committee.

National Children's Office (NCO) (2000) *National Children's Strategy*. Dublin: Government Publications Office.

National Geographic (2015) Geography and Literacy Connection. Accessed from http://education.nationalgeographic.com/media/reference/assets/geography-and-literacy-connection-1.pdf, 2 November 2015.

National Governors Association Center for Best Practices/Council of Chief State School Officers (NGACB/CCSSO) (2014) *Common Core State Standards: English Language Arts.* Washington D.C.: NGACBP/CCSSO. Accessed from www.corestandards.org, 17 March 2015.

National Research Council (US) (2006) Learning to Think Spatially: GIS as a Support System in the K-12 Curriculum. Washington DC: National Academies Press. Accessed from esrik-12gis.emich.edu/k12/pdf/learning%20to%20think%20spatially.pdf, 12 February 2015.

NCCA (2012) Aistear: A Framework for Early Childhood Education. Accessed from www.ncca.biz/aistear/pdfs/principlesthemes_eng/idandbelonging_eng.pdf

NCCA (2012) *Aistear: The Early Childhood Curriculum Framework.* Accessed from www.ncca.biz/aistear, 17 March 2015.

Nichols, A. and Kinninment, D. (eds) (2001) *More Thinking Through Geography.* Cambridge: Chris Kington Publishing.

Norman, M. and Harrison, L. (2004) Year 9 Students' Perceptions of School Geography, *Teaching Geography*, 29(1): 11–5.

Noronha, Y. (2012) *Children's Views of Climate Change.* Unpublished M.Ed thesis, St Patrick's College, Dublin.

Nundy, S. (1999) The Fieldwork Effect: The Role and Impact of Fieldwork in the Upper Primary School, *International Research in Geographical and Environmental Education*, 8(2): 190–98.

O'Neill, C. (2010) Young Children's Spatial Abilities and the Development of Their Spatial Cognition. Unpublished M.Ed thesis, St Patrick's College.

O'Keeffe and O'Beirne (2015) *Children's Independent on the Island of Ireland Study.* Limerick: Mary Immaculate College.

Oberman, R., O'Shea, F., Hickey, B. and Joyce, C. (2014) Children's Global Thinking: Research Investigating the Engagement of Seven-to-Nine-Year-Old Children with Critical Literacy and Global Citizenship Education. Dublin: CHRCE. Accessed from www.spd.dcu.ie/site/chrce/documents/GlobalThinkingResearchreportbyRowanOberman.pdf, 17 March 2015.

Olwig, K.F. and Gulløv, E. (eds) (2004) *Children's Places.* London: Routledge.

Oulton, C., Day, V., Dillon, J. and Grace, M. (2004) Controversial Issues – Teachers' Attitudes and Practices in the Context of Citizenship Education. *Oxford Review of Education*, 30(4): 489–507.

Owens, P. (2015) Mapping: Getting on Track. *Primary Geographer*, 75(1): 6–7.

Oxfam (1997) *A Global Curriculum for All.* Oxford: Oxfam.

Oxfam (2015) GO Bananas Resources. Accessed from www.oxfam.org.uk/education/resources/go-bananas, 17 March 2015.

Payne, P.G. and Wattchow, B. (2009) Phenomenological Deconstruction, Slow Pedagogy, and the Corporeal Turn in Wild Environmental/Outdoor Education. *Canadian Journal of Environmental Education*, 14(1) pp. 15–32.

Percy-Smith, B. (2010) Councils, Consultation and Community: Rethinking the Spaces for Children and Young People's Participation. *Children's Geographies*, 8(2): 107–22.

Piaget, J. and inhelder, B. (1956) *The Child's Conception of Space.* New York: Norton.

Pike, S. (2006) Irish primary school children's definitions of 'geography'. *Irish Educational Studies*, 25(1): 75–92.

Pike, S. (2010) 'For Once, Just Listen to a Kid': Children's Rights and Local Communities. In F. Waldron and B. Ruane (eds), *Human Rights Education: Reflections on Theory and Practice.* Dublin: Liffey.

Pike, S. (2011a) *Eco-Detectives Teachers' Resource Pack: Environmental and Climate Change Investigations for Primary Schools.* Dublin: Department of Environment, Heritage, Local Government and Centre for Human Rights and Citizenship Education.

Pike, S. (2011b) If You Went out It Would Stick': Irish Children's Learning in Their Local Environments. *International Research in Geographical and Environmental Education*, 20(2): 139–59.

Pike, S. (2012) 'It's About the Things We Don't Notice Every Day': 10 Years of Children's Definitions of Geography. Paper presented at the Charney Manor Geography Conference, Oxford.

Pike, S. (2013a) 100 Years of Enquiry Learning: The Influence of John Dewey, *Primary Geography*, 82(3): 26–8.

Pike, S. (2013b) 'It's About the Things We Don't Notice Every Day': 10 Years of Children's Definitions of Geography. Presented at Charney Manor Geography Conference, Oxford.

Pike, S. and Ryan, M. (2012) Using Big Ideas for Big Places: Australia. *Primary Geography*, 79(1): 30.

Punch, S. (2000) Children's Strategies for Creating Playspaces: Negotiating independence in Rural Bolivia. In S. Holloway and G. Valentine (2000a) *Children's Geographies: Playing, Learning, Living*. Oxford: Routledge.

Rickinson, M., Dillon, J., Teamey, K., Morris, M., Choi, M.Y., Sanders, D. *et al.* (2004) *A Review of Research on Outdoor Learning*. Slough: National Foundation for Educational Research and King's College London.

Roberts, M. (2003) Learning Through Enquiry: Making Sense of Geography in the Key Stage 3 Classroom. Sheffield: Geographical Association.

Roberts, M. (2009) Investigating Geography. *Geography*, 94(3): 181–88.

Roberts, M. (2010) Geographical Enquiry. *Teaching Geography*, 34(1): 6–9.

Roberts, M. (2013a) *Geography Through Enquiry: Approaches to Teaching and Learning in the Secondary School*. Sheffield: Geographical Association.

Roberts, M. (2013b) The Challenge of Enquiry-based Learning. *Teaching Geography*, 37(2): 50–2.

Robinson, N.M. and Koshy, V. (2004) Creative Mathematics. In R. Fisher and M. Williams (eds), *Unlocking Creativity: Teaching Across the Curriculum*. London: David Fulton.

Roosevelt, E. (1953) *In Our Hands*. Speech Delivered on the Tenth Anniversary of the Universal Declaration of Human Rights. Accessed from www.un.org/en/globalissues/briefingpapers/humanrights/quotes.shtml, 17 March 2015.

Rosling, H. (2015) Gapminder Website. Accessed from www.gapminder.com, 17 March 2015.

RTE (2005) *Hanafin Bemoans School 'No Running Policies'*. Accessed from www.rte.ie/news/2005/0522/hanafinm, 17 March 2015.

Ruane, B., Kavanagh, A.M., Waldron, F., Dillon, S., Maunsell, C. and Prunty, A. (2010) *Young Pupils' Engagement With Issues of Global Justice*. Dublin: Centre for Human Rights and Citizenship Education, SPD and Trócaire. Accessed from www.spd.dcu.ie/site/chrce/documents/TrocaireCHCREreport.pdf, 17 March 2015.

Sarah Thomson (2007): Do's and Don'ts: Children's Experiences of the Primary School Playground. *Environmental Education Research*, 13(4): 487–500

Scoffham, S. (1998) *Primary Sources: Research Findings in Primary Geography*. Sheffield: Geographical Association.

Scoffham, S. (2010) *Handbook of Primary Geography*. Sheffield: Geographical Association.

Scoffham, S. (2013) *Teaching Geography Creatively*. London: Routledge.

Seomra Ranga (2014) *Signs of Spring Project 2014*. Accessed from http://chirpstory.com/Li/193379, 17 March 2015.

Simmons, D. (1998) Using Natural Settings for Environmental Education: Perceived Benefits and Barriers. *The Journal of Environmental Education*, 29(1): 31–3.

Smyth, E. (2010) An Investigation into Parents' and Children's Attitudes to Geography and a Locality Based Geography Experience. Unpublished M.Ed thesis, St Patrick's College.

Spencer, C. and Blades, M. (eds) (2006) *Children and their Environments: Learning, Using, and Designing Spaces*. Cambridge: Cambridge University Press.

Standish, A. (2003) Constructing a Value Map. *Geography*, 88(2): 149–51.

Stenhouse, L. (1975) *Introduction to Curriculum Development*, London: Heinemann.

Storey, C. (2005) Teaching Place: Developing Early Understanding of 'Nested Hierarchies'. *International Research in Geographical and Environmental Education*, 14(4): 310–12.

Thomson, S. (2007) Do's and Don'ts: Children's Experiences of the Primary School Playground. *Environmental Education Research*, 13(4): 487–500.

Tide (2015) The Development Compass Road. Birmingham: Tide. Accessed from www.tideglobal learning.net, 17 March 2015.

Timmonds, F. (2015) *Clondalkin Becomes a Fairtrade town*. Accessed from: www.francistimmons.com/clondalkin-becomes-a-fairtrade-town, 17 March 2015.

Titman, W. (1994) *Special Places; Special People – the Hidden Curriculum of the School Grounds*. Godalming, UK: WWF.

UNESCO (2015) Teaching and Learning for a Sustainable Future. Accessed from www.unesco.org/education/tlsf/mods/theme_d/mod23, 17 March 2015.

Valentine, G. (1996) Angels and Devils: Moral Landscapes of Childhood. *Environment and Planning D: Society and Space*, 14(5): 58.

Valentine, G. (2000) Exploring Children and Young People's Narratives of Identity. *Geoforum*, 31(2): 257–67.

Valentine, G., Holloway, S.L. and Bingham, N. (2002) The Digital Generation? Children, ICT and the Everyday Nature of Social Exclusion. *Antipode*, 34: 296–315.

Vygotsky, L. (1962/1986) *Thought and Language*. Cambridge, MA: The Massachusetts Institute of Technology Press.

Waldron, F. (2003) Irish Primary Children's Definitions of History. *Irish Educational Studies*, 22(2): 63–90.

Waldron, F. (2004) Making the Irish: Identity and Citizenship in the Primary Curriculum. In C. Sugrue (ed.), *Ideology and Curriculum: Irish Experiences, International Perspectives*. Dublin: Liffey Press, pp. 122–40.

Waldron, F. and Ruane, B. (eds) (2010) *Human Rights Education: Reflections on Theory and Practice*. Dublin: Liffey Press.

Waldron, F., Pike, S., Greenwood, R., Murphy, C., O'Connor, G., Dolan, A. and Kerr, K. (2009) *Becoming a Teacher: Primary Student Teachers as Learners and Teachers of History, Geography and Science: An All-Ireland Study* (A Report for the Standing Conference on Teacher Education North and South (SCoTENS)). Armagh: Centre for Cross Border Studies.

Walford, R. (1984) Geography and the Future, *Geography*, 69(3): 193–208.

Walsh, T. (2012) *Primary Education in Ireland, 1897–1990*. Bern: Peter Lang.

Walsh, L. (2006) The Ability of Early Years Children to Engage with Graphicacy Processes in Geography. Unpublished M.Ed thesis. Dublin: St Patrick's College.

Webster, A., Beveridge, M. and Reed, M. (1996) *Managing the Literacy Curriculum*. London: Routledge.

Weldon, M. (2010) The Wider World, Chapter 15 in S. Scoffham (ed.), *Handbook of Primary Geography*. Sheffield: Geographical Association.

Whittle, J. (2006) Journey Sticks and Affective Mapping, *Primary Geography*, 59(3): 11–13.

Wiegand, P. (1995) Young Children's Freehand Sketch Maps of the World. *International Research in Environmental and Geographical Education*, 4 (1): 19–28.

Wiegand, P. (2006) *Learning and Teaching with Maps*. Abingdon and New York: Routledge.

Wikipedia (2015) Enquiry Based Learning Accessed from en.wikipedia.org/wiki/inquiry-based_learning, 17 March 2015.

Wood, P. (2006) Developing Enquiry Through Questioning. *Teaching Geography*, 31(2): 76–8.

Young, M.F.D. (2008) *Bringing Knowledge back in: From Social Constructivism to Social Realism in the Sociology of Education*. London and New York: Routledge.

Zelenski, J.M., Dopko, R.L. and Capaldi, C.A. (2015) Cooperation is in Our Nature: Nature Exposure May Promote Cooperative and Environmentally Sustainable Behavior. *Journal of Environmental Psychology*, 42(1): 24–31.

Index